The
Data Warehouse
Mentor

About the Author

Robert (Bob) Laberge is the founder of several Internet ventures and a principal consultant for the IBM Industry Models and Assets Lab, which has a focus on data warehousing and business intelligence solutions.

Bob began his career back in the late 70s, when Bill Gates was a mere millionaire, and has since worked as a developer, database administrator, data modeler, project manager, data architect, enterprise information architect, DW/BI auditor, and strategist in addition to being an innovative entrepreneur. Since then Bob has travelled the globe extensively, mentoring, training, and demonstrating data warehouse and business intelligence practicalities and solutions through design, optimizations, best practices, and common sense at the conceptual, logical, and physical levels. Bob has successfully helped over 50 large organizations spanning the retail, insurance, healthcare, railways, telecommunications, government, e-business, and banking sectors.

Bob holds a Masters of Business Administration from the University of Durham in the UK. He can be reached at datawarehousementor@gmail.com.

About the Technical Editors

David Marcotte is Kantar Retail's SVP of Retail Insights Americas with expertise in International Retail, Merchandising, Retail Operations, Supply Chain, and Business Intelligence. He is a professional speaker on a wide range of topics and also a trainer for in-depth seminars, having worked with numerous Fortune 500 companies across the globe. Recently he was the lead researcher and writer of the 2010 Retailing Emergent Markets study for the Coca-Cola Retailer Research Council, which summarized findings in China, Peru, Turkey, Poland, South Africa, and Brazil. Prior to joining Kantar Retail, he was a lead in the Global Business Intelligence group within IBM. In that capacity, he was part of development teams for a range of solutions in retail including loss prevention, pricing, category management processes, merchandising planning, supply chain, merchandising, and sales forces optimization. He was also the business and project lead for IBM's Retail Data Warehouse Solution, during which he first worked with the author, Bob Laberge. He has worked with a range of retailers and manufacturers for their solution needs including Sony, Sobeys, D&S, Falabella, Shoppers Drug Mart, and Kroger. David has served on a number of industry boards and panels, including the IRI Product Advisory Board and the Efficient Consumer Response (ECR) group. He can be reached at David.Marcotte@KantarRetail.com.

Ken Yu has been working in the Information Management and Data Architecture space for over 25 years. He has been an enterprise information architect, project manager, data modeler, database administrator, and developer in various industries and applications. In 1995, Ken joined IBM to support large database clients and provide operational leadership. As an information management consultant, he has provided mentoring and training throughout the enterprise in the topics of data governance, master data and metadata management, and the value of data modeling and reference models. He has been prime for design, development, technical architecture, and operational processes for numerous mission-critical applications, business intelligence and data warehouse solutions. Today, Ken is the Principal Consultant for Cypselurus Inc., based in Toronto, Ontario, Canada.

The
Data Warehouse
Mentor
Practical Data Warehouse and Business Intelligence Insights

Robert (Bob) Laberge

New York   Chicago   San Francisco
Lisbon   London   Madrid   Mexico City
Milan   New Delhi   San Juan
Seoul   Singapore   Sydney   Toronto

The McGraw·Hill Companies

Cataloging-in-Publication Data is on file with the Library of Congress

McGraw-Hill books are available at special quantity discounts to use as premiums and sales promotions, or for use in corporate training programs. To contact a representative, please e-mail us at bulksales@mcgraw-hill.com.

The Data Warehouse Mentor: Practical Data Warehouse and Business Intelligence Insights

1234567890   QFR QFR   10987654321

ISBN   978-0-07-174532-1
MHID   0-07-174532-7

Associate Acquisitions Editor Meghan Riley	**Technical Editors** David Marcotte Ken Yu	**Production Supervisor** Jean Bodeaux
Editorial Supervisor Patty Mon	**Copy Editor** Margaret Berson	**Composition** Glyph International
Project Manager Tania Andrabi, Glyph International	**Proofreader** Paul Tyler	**Illustration** Glyph International
Acquisitions Coordinator Stephanie Evans	**Indexer** Karin Arrigoni	**Art Director, Cover** Jeff Weeks
		Cover Designer Jeff Weeks

This book project is dedicated to my beautiful and gifted wife and precious son. You two are my life and I thank God every day for our journey together—no matter the page or word count!

Contents at a Glance

Contents

Acknowledgments

Special thanks to my technical editors, David Marcotte and Ken Yu, for your help in reviewing my notes and in relaying your perspectives and comments. Your valuable feedback guided efforts towards this successful final deliverable. Many, many thanks!!

David Marcotte is a global retail business and analytics guru with far too much knowledge for one person in this industry.

Ken Yu is a technical expert in data design and data flow who has worked in a number of sectors and has a practical and common-sense approach to data modeling and data architecture.

And a special thanks to my wife Rakhee Laberge (MBA, B.E) for all your reviewing, comments, and insights.

Introduction

This book consists of a collection of discussions on different topics within the data warehouse world. The book is organized to represent the building of a data warehouse system from both business and technical perspectives with an emphasis on building a tangible solution in plain and simple terms. These insights are from three decades of personal experience from over 50 organizations in over 20 countries where I worked as an independent consultant, an employee, and in partnership with the IBM Industry Models and Assets Lab.

This book explains the components and different alternatives in building a data warehouse along with a mixture of pros and cons for choosing one path over another. Building a data warehouse is unique for each organization but can be guided by the knowledge obtained from the many differing data warehouse and business intelligence environments from organizations around the globe. The book presents data warehousing topics first from a high-level overview to ensure that the terminology and context is understood, and then goes into detail to clarify the topic at hand. These topics all pertain to data warehousing, business intelligence, and performance management.

There are no rules in building a data warehouse, but many guidelines. The main fundamental point of this book is to build to suit your specific organization's needs based on specific and understood business requirements while creating an open and flexible architecture for future endeavors. Many organizations squander large budgets for an initial centralized data warehouse with business intelligence reporting, only to find that the solution is too specific for one or two uses and fails to satisfy future requirements. Of course, we cannot predict the future, but we can anticipate future data requirements and usage to a level where we can ensure that the design and build environment is flexible and open to change without having to redesign and rebuild from scratch each time.

Many organizations' leaders are realizing that corporate data is a fundamental asset to the company and must be organized, structured, and maintained to ensure that their business information is shared throughout the enterprise with quality, governance, and ownership. Businesses cannot operate without information systems, and information systems cannot exist without business purpose. Working together to support each other and working together with full consciousness of the information architecture and usage allows the business to become a smarter organization.

About This Book

Part I: Preparation

Part I presents basic concepts and insights into business intelligence and data warehousing. The idea for this section is to introduce the basics for management consideration.

Chapter 1: Data Warehouse and Business Intelligence Overview   Chapter 1 gives overviews of business intelligence and data warehouses and ends with frequently asked high-level questions relating to implementing a data warehouse system.

Chapter 2: Data in the Organization   Chapter 2 discusses data as a corporate asset and gives insights into organizing the data.

Chapter 3: Reasons for Building   Chapter 3 discusses the reasons for and against building a data warehouse system. The reasons "for" are typical scenarios for building a data warehouse, and the reasons "against" are based on the ability to move forward with a development project within the organization given its culture and limitations.

Chapter 4: Data Warehouse and Business Intelligence Strategy   Chapter 4 gives insights into a plan of action with discussions on where and how to start a project, depending on whether the effort is geared toward a business reporting solution or a data organization and structuring effort.

Chapter 5: Project Resources: Roles and Insights   Chapter 5 discusses key roles for data warehouse project efforts and team structures with best practices.

Chapter 6: Write-It-Up Overview   Chapter 6 gives a brief overview of the content of typical project charter, project scope, and statement of work documents.

Part II: Components

Part II presents the basic components of a data warehouse system. The idea for this section is to become more familiar with the technical aspects of a database warehouse and business intelligence system. This section discusses the ingredients of a data warehouse system to support the corporate asset and business intelligence efforts.

Chapter 7: Business Intelligence: Data Marts and Usage   Chapter 7 discusses the details of data marts and usage from data models to performance considerations.

Chapter 8: Enterprise Data Models   Chapter 8 discusses enterprise data modeling along with examples of how-to and general issues.

Chapter 9: Data Warehouse Architecture: Components   Chapter 9 discusses the different types of data warehouse architectures from a modeling and data flow perspective.

Chapter 10: ETL and Data Quality   Chapter 10 discusses the generalities of the data acquisition and distribution layers in a data warehouse system along with data quality insights.

Chapter 11: Project Planning and Methodology   Chapter 11 discusses data warehouse and business intelligence project planning methodology.

Part III: Let's Build

Part III presents a practical hands-on perspective on building a data warehouse system. The idea for this section is to look at typical build scenarios and efforts along with data governance and post-efforts review.

Chapter 12: Working Scenarios   Chapter 12 discusses building a data warehouse and business intelligence system using top-down, bottom-up, and hybrid methodologies and discusses several other topics, including a brief look at enterprise information architecture.

Chapter 13: Data Governance   Chapter 13 discusses enterprise data governance including organization structure, data quality, ownership, and change management.

Chapter 14: Post-Project Review   Chapter 14 discusses the aspects of the data warehouse and business intelligence project after development efforts.

I put this book together to be used as an overall guide in building a data warehouse system. Its goal is to relay an understanding of the many issues seen today in data warehousing and to introduce insights from multiple viewpoints. My hope is that this book will help you in your data warehousing endeavors.

Enjoy!

Robert (Bob) Laberge
Contact: datawarehousementor@gmail.com

PART

I

Preparation

A management overview discussion on
data warehouse and business intelligence systems.

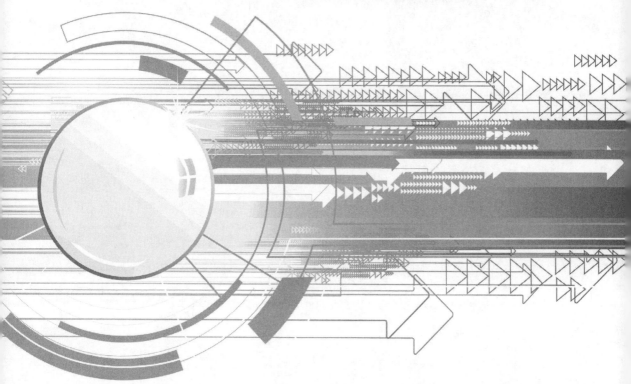

Data Warehouse and Business Intelligence Overview

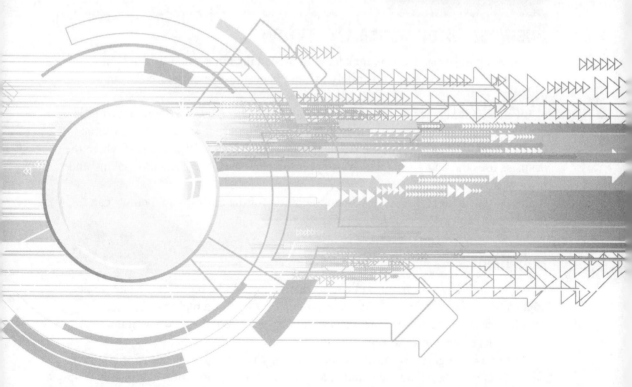

Many organizations are contemplating, developing, planning, or currently using a data warehouse system. This type of system is becoming more popular as organizations are strategically deciding to treat their corporate data as an asset. Companies are funding projects to structure, organize, cleanse, document, and centralize their data. The depth of understanding derived from these complex systems provides companies with a discernible competitive advantage in the marketplace.

Business and information technology are interwoven. In today's organizations, one cannot function without the other; therefore, they use best practices to guide development efforts for all projects. For a moment, consider the complexities facing IT and the direction and requirement of the business. For most businesses, IT can magnify the business efficiencies if done right, or it can devastate the business resources if done wrong.

This book will define and explain the many facets of a data warehouse system from practical business and technical perspectives. In short, this book gives insights into data warehouse and business intelligence systems with a focus on best practices and a goal of success for the business and IT alike.

Business Intelligence Overview

Empowering business decision makers with trusted data in a value-driven context that is usable and delivered in a timely manner is business intelligence (BI) in a nutshell.

Business intelligence is a wide topic. Many books have been written on business intelligence detailing purpose, value, and very specific usage scenarios. This topic is fundamental to a data warehouse from a usage point of view. BI is the part where the business uses the underlying data to support informed business decision making and processes.

Let us start with BI first to get an appreciation for the basics, and then we can move into a larger data warehouse perspective.

Definition

Business intelligence is an umbrella term referring to skills, processes, technologies, applications, and practices used to support business decision making. Business intelligence deals with used data, or past data, in a desired context to help make business decisions for tomorrow.

Business intelligence is mostly focused on internal information about operational issues as they pertain to tactical and strategic planning. Information is typically structured in one fashion or another and is focused and/or gathered from current business processes. The output of the underlying data is mostly used for internal analysis but can also be used in conjunction with external analysis such as with SWOT and PEST competitive analysis efforts.

SWOT analysis provides information helpful in matching a firm's resources and capabilities to the competitive environment in which it operates. A scan of the internal and external environment is an important part of the strategic planning process. Environmental factors internal to the firm usually can be classified as strengths (S) or weaknesses (W), and those external to the firm can be classified as opportunities (O) or threats (T). Such an analysis of the strategic environment is referred to as a SWOT analysis; see QuickMBA: http://www.quickmba.com/strategy/swot/. PEST (Political, Economic, Social, and Technological), is a scan of the external macro-environment in which the firm operates; see QuickMBA: http://www.quickmba.com/strategy/pest/.

Business intelligence is based on initial key performance indicators (KPIs) in the quest for determining business goals. These KPIs can be broken down into measures, aka facts, fundamentally sourced from within the organizations' operational systems or aggregated from these fundamental operational measures. Facts are normally numeric and quantifiable, thus being additive. Typically, analysis in a BI environment is performed at an aggregated level rather than at an instance level; for example, an organization wants to know how many customers exist, live, and/or purchase in a specific region as opposed to where an individual person lives and how much he or she purchased. The later scenario can be taken or derived from an existing operational system, but, that said, there is no reason why this information cannot be extracted from a business intelligence system as long as the system holds data at the appropriate granularity. I have witnessed situations in several organizations where the fundamental data of how much an individual customer has purchased is not always available in the operational systems, and therefore the BI environment is used as a central merging area of events and fundamental data. Some may create an operational data store (ODS) for current granular information, but an ODS tends to have limited history, which is why a BI environment is most often used.

A good business intelligence system has been described as being accurate, timely, of high value, and actionable: *accurate* in the sense that data is trusted; *timely* meaning that data is available on a regular schedule; *of high value* meaning useful to the business user; and *actionable* meaning that the information can be used in the business decision process. Concluding that the organization has 12 power-lift trucks is nice, but is it useful to the business decision process? If it is, then there is a purpose to having the underlying data; if not, what is the point of spending the effort and budget on baking the data when it is not useful to the business or actionable by the business?

Value of Business Intelligence

Business intelligence gives the business decision makers the ability to query the data themselves.

Back in the late 1970s when I started in the computer industry, when a business user had a question requiring access to the data, they would send a memo via interoffice mail requesting a report to the IT department. The memo would explain the required specifics and the IT manager would schedule someone to work on the effort. The mini-project involved lots of telephone calls back and forth with the business as both tried to figure out exactly what was required along with the underlying data components. Once the purpose and requirements were more or less understood, IT would write a program to create the necessary report. The process took days and sometimes weeks depending on the complexity of the request. The effort was always hampered due to communications. IT was trying to figure out what the user wanted in data terms records and fields (no tables and column terminology back then), and the business user was trying to figure out how to explain the request using as simple and understandable business terminology as possible. IT typically had no clue as to the data context or what decisions the user was trying to formulate by using the report. Conversely, the business user had no clue as to the records and fields holding the data, which resulted in neither IT nor the business user knowing exactly nor effectively how to guide the other. Eventually, as IT learned more of the business and the user more of the data, together business and IT were able to produce reports in a timely manner of a day or two.

Today business intelligence empowers the business user to query the data directly. This seemingly small advancement has helped reduce the decision-making process from days and possibly weeks down to minutes. BI is to the business decision process as a television remote control is to a couch potato—empowering. Imagine how long it would take (or how long it used to take) to get up and walk to the television set each time you wanted to change channels! Having a remote control massively reduces this time and effort while empowering the viewer to channel-surf at will. The same empowerment concept when applied to the computing industry is called "business intelligence."

Business intelligence massively increases the business users' ability to process information. Just as channel surfing allows the viewer to get an idea as to the actual content of what is available on the many television stations fairly quickly, business intelligence gives the user the ability to query the information directly and as often as desired without the need to involve IT in every step. Of course, having a requirement focus in advance allows IT to fine-tune efforts on designing and building an environment to support this efficiency with only the required data for the business needs at hand, just as a television guide allows the viewer to quickly search for programs on specific days and at specific hours, and using specific themes such as comedy, drama, movies, and so forth.

Due to the quick turnaround between data availability and business usage of the data, feedback of data quality issues has led the proverbial IT construction and repair crew to react much more rapidly to evolving business needs. This has led to data being available in a structured and timely manner with much focus on accuracy and quality, allowing the business to gain more insight and react more quickly to the business environment.

In the ideal, business intelligence is

▶ Empowerment—directly usable

▶ Fast—responsive

▶ Timely—available

▶ Accurate—trusted with quality

▶ Usable—has value

Breakdown of Business and Intelligence

The term business intelligence implies that the business has a person or group of people capable of making business decisions, and that the underlying information upon which the decision is based is trusted.

The people involved in decision making hopefully are in a position whereby they can be expected to have the background, education, and experience to make the required decisions to move the business forward, whether in a functional, tactical, or strategic manner. These people need a stone to stand on when deciding which direction the organization, line of business, department, or resulting action should take. This proverbial stone is information. Without proper or trusted information, the decision process can easily be contaminated, thus rendering the final outcome completely inappropriate.

Information is data in context. For information to be correct, a better word would be *dependable*; the underlying data must be trusted. Therefore, great importance is placed on the quality of the data. If management receives multiple conflicting informational details such as counts of products sold or cost of operating production-line machines, how can a person derive appropriate and proper decisions and therefore correctly know which business direction to take? If you drive to a fork in the road with no signs, how can you tell which route to follow? A sign must be posted pointing the way; this is fundamentally trusted information in a timely manner.

Data is fundamental to information, and this data must be trusted. To be trusted, the data must have a high level of reliability, aka quality, otherwise known as integrity.

Several years back, a project undertaking involved an automobile insurance organization that was trying to formulate a marketing strategy based on the types of automobiles they insured. Unfortunately their data-capturing system for automobile types, makes, and models was completely manual and did not deliver appropriate data integrity. Company clerks, who manually typed the individual insurance policy details into the computer systems, would simply type in whatever the policy stated, with no quality control. Unfortunately, to make matters worse, at times there were many typing errors that went uncorrected. For instance, a FORD automobile was entered as FORD, FRD, ORD, RFOD, Mustang Ford, 98 Food and so forth. Without cleansing this data at the source to ensure that the policy was indeed describing a FORD automobile, every use of this data item down the line within this organization was at risk. Absolutely no decisions based on automobile types, makes, and models would be accurate, and therefore this information was completely lost to the organization. Imagine an automobile insurance company not being able to accurately describe automobile manufacturers for their policies—seems silly, doesn't it? Well, this is a true case that went on for years. I am happy to report that since the organization initiated a business intelligence effort along with a data quality effort, the data is now cleansed, trusted, and used regularly within the business. Now the brokers, underwriters, and adjudicators can all trust the data and make informed decisions upon this aspect of the business data.

Business Intelligence Success Factors

Many of the factors that affect a successful BI implementation are not necessarily the same as those for a data warehouse. A data warehouse system typically expresses itself as BI to the end user, but a data warehouse system can or may focus only on the data aspect without specific regard for business usage; in such a situation, business intelligence becomes a subcomponent of the larger data warehouse system. A data warehouse that is not imminently and directly usable to the business may be part of a master data management effort to centralize on a specific vocabulary or to coordinate a centralized data effort. This effort would clearly be a foundation phase preceding business usage—getting all the ducks in a row, so to speak!

As noted in Wikipedia ("Business Intelligence," 2010), Naveen K. Vodapalli lists the following as the critical success factors for a business intelligence implementation:

▶ Business-driven methodology and project management

▶ Clear vision and planning

▶ Committed management support and sponsorship

▶ Data management and quality issues

- ► Mapping the solutions to the user requirements
- ► Performance considerations of the BI system
- ► Robust and extensible framework

It suffices to say that a BI effort must be business-driven to be successful. The nature of BI is to add value to the business; therefore, there must be a clearly focused business purpose driven by the business itself and championed by executive management so that it does not turn out to be some manager's pet project or hampered by internal politics.

Since the underlying data is fundamental to the success of the effort, there must be a tight collaborative partnership among IT, the developers, and the business unit—the customer. IT must put heavy thought into data management and requires executive management to enforce any source-system data quality corrections if need be (and there is always a need!!). Additionally, IT must perform due diligence in ensuring that whatever is built is flexible enough to be extended with future phases and efforts.

In the end, the business will expect a realistic response time from the BI solution, whether this expectation is verbalized or not. If the proverbial button is pressed and the system takes 30 minutes to respond with a resulting report, there will be issues, the worst being non-use of the system. If the business does not use the newly built solution even though it cost thousands or millions to create, the overall effort and investment are lost. Therefore, ensuring a usable environment is a priority, and such usage is a sign of success for both the business and IT.

Purpose of BI

There are many purposes for and methods of performing business intelligence. In other words, there are many types of business intelligence and business analysis. Understanding each type and therefore being able to plan for the right environment can add much value to the business.

Every organization produces some sort of reporting regarding the ongoing aspects of their business. Management spends much time reading, interpreting, and basing decisions upon these reports. Otherwise, how would individuals know the current status of events within the business? At a rudimentary level, enterprises capture inventory, production progress, sales, and so forth. To track events in such areas requires a report of one sort or another. As the organization grows and events unfold, comparisons to previous metrics and efforts are analyzed to know if progress is above, below, or the same as previous time periods. Viewing the data from different perspectives such as by product types, by geographic regions, or whatever adds more clarity to events. More information gives greater insights, which allows for a clearer picture of the current environment with expectations of what to do next. Business intelligence depends on business data being available and usable by the management to gain business insights to support business decision making.

Years ago I was analyzing the business intelligence requirements of a large European bank. They were all excited about creating a data warehouse system and producing great business intelligence to guide their efforts forward. The number one point on their list was to ensure a business-as-usual environment. This meant that their first priority was to replicate reports currently being used by the business. The idea was to add value to the reporting environment by setting a new foundation platform whereby there would be a one-stop-shopping scenario. All data would come from this one central and trusted environment. This meant that all reports would be based on the same data—no more disparate systems, just one central warehouse holding cleansed data. From this foundation, advancements could be planned, designed, and constructed to move the organization forward. All seemed well thought-out. So we proceeded to get a view of their reporting needs. At that point someone literally wheeled in 120,000 business reports that had been produced from hundreds of source systems. Imagine running a business on that many reports produced from so many different systems. Imagine the confusion, the discrepancies, the redundancy, the data quality issues, and the quarterly reporting craze that must have been going on.

The point is that without analyzing the purpose and type of business intelligence, organizations are bound to create and re-create their reporting environment over and over again, basing their future on the exact same errors as in the past. Determining the type of business intelligence to be done and the output delivery method will greatly enhance the overall usage and effort.

For the bank scenario I described, there was obviously more work to be done in classifying the different lines of business; determining the business processes, areas of analysis, methods and priority of analysis; understanding who was to access what; whether drill-down and drill-up was required; how dynamic the reports were to be, and so forth. Much more analysis needed to be done before any planning or design efforts could begin.

Business intelligence has many purposes, including but not limited to:

- ▶ Benchmarking or baselining
- ▶ Trending or predictive analysis
- ▶ Affinity grouping, aka market basket analysis, or segmentation
- ▶ Performance management
- ▶ Associative analysis, aka data mining
- ▶ Subject area analysis

Each of these serve a specific purpose based on usage. Baselining refers to creating an environment whereby, for instance, monthly store sales can be compared in terms of being more or less than the previous 18-month rolling average store sales, globally, regionally, or locally. Predictive efforts could involve the analysis of expected sales over the next three to five years given the previous several years of monthly sales while also being compared to its associated industry sector sales. Affinity grouping could help marketing in understanding the top 100 selling items as they relate to the top ten secondary selling items, perhaps helping product and store planogram efforts. A specific focus on customer relationship management may look at customer lifetime value or customer lifetime progression analysis, tagging products or services to customers as they age or enter lifecycle changes. Data mining could include the manual effort of discovering associations between data components in the quest to analyze market segments as they pertain to events. Subject area analysis may involve insights into product lines.

The point here is to understand the purpose of the business analysis and to create business intelligence based on this specific purpose. Keeping a distinct business requirement focus while managing the fundamental underlying data is the key to a successful and flexible business intelligence solution.

BI User Presentation

The business intelligence outcome or presentation of the outcome can be in several forms:

- ▶ Reports
- ▶ Queries
- ▶ OLAP
- ▶ Dashboards
- ▶ Scorecards

Everyone is familiar with reports. These are static, typically scheduled pre-run routines that produce specific layouts. You get what you see. Organizations have been using these since the beginning of time.

When a person desires to look into specific correlations or details, there is always the option to write structured queries either manually or with assistance. These are typically SQL-based but can be assisted with the aid of the drag-and-drop features of BI tools. An example of a structured query is: Select Product.Name from Product where Product.Color = "blue".

Online analytical processing (OLAP) is another form of data inquiry mechanism. This method gives dynamic aspects to typically static reporting. As the term denotes, these reports are online as opposed to being created in a batch run or printed for manual delivery.

OLAP empowers the end user with the ability to actively drill down or drill up within a report. A starting point might be sales in a region such as Canada for a specific time period such as 2010. The user may then wish to look at (drill down to) sales per province and then down again to sales by major city. Essentially OLAP is the concentration of many reports all rolled into one.

In the old days, the following reports could have been produced independently:

- ▶ Sales in Canada for 2007: 1 report
- ▶ Sales in Canada per Q1, Q2, Q3, Q4 for 2007: 4 reports
- ▶ Sales in Canada per month for 2007: 12 reports
- ▶ Sales in ten Canadian provinces for 2007: 10 reports
- ▶ Sales in ten Canadian provinces per Q1, Q2, Q3, Q4 for 2007: 40 reports
- ▶ Sales in ten Canadian provinces per month for 2007: 120 reports
- ▶ Sales by ten Canadian provinces per month for 2007 by major city: $10 \times 12 \times 20 = 2400$ reports

Total number of reports calculated the old way would be: $1+4+12+10+40+120+2400 = 2587$ reports. Now add five years of history, and that's an easy 12,935 business reports. Now add 20 products, and that brings the total to 258,700 possible reports.

We could of course produce the final detailed report as seen later in this chapter in Figure 1-5, but in many instances this is the result of multiple request iterations over a number of months; "could one more item be added to the report please?" I remember spending lots of time in the early 1980s rewriting report programs, rescheduling nightly batch jobs, and rediscussing the produced report with "what-if" we added this or that type of scenarios. The more dimensions added, each with its own cardinalities, the more complicated the report became and the longer it took to generate.

The OLAP method requires an underlying structure typically designed in a cube fashion, which allows for the dynamic creation of reports based on the grain of the dimensions. *Granularity* refers to the level of detail; date granularity can be day, week, month, quarter, year, and so forth. These dimensions or varying parameters, for reporting scenarios just described, are

- ▶ Date hierarchy: time, time period, or date: calendar year, calendar quarter, calendar month
- ▶ Geographic hierarchy: geographic area: country, province, major city
- ▶ Products (which may have several hierarchies in its own right)

An example of a typical OLAP cube is Figure 1-1. The little squares are the representation of a measure ("sales" for our example) by specific product,

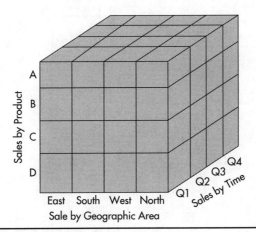

Figure 1-1   *OLAP multidimensional cube*

geographic area, and time (date). Cubes are also known as star schemas, which is a type of data model. The term "data models" refers to how the data is designed, which may be star, snowflake, third normal form, or other style. These data models all present data in various formats: physical-type models consist of tables and columns, while logical-type models consist of entities and attributes. These star schemas are also known as data marts or analysis areas. Note that while many consider data marts to be cubes, in reality they can be other types of designs as well, such as third normal form. More information on data model types will be presented as we progress through the book.

Any combination of simple dimensions can produce thousands of reports at the click of a button. Drill down from country to province, then from calendar year to calendar quarter to calendar month. Further drill-down to major city and days is also possible if the underlying structures allow for the data at such granularities. Drill-up is the same concept as drill-down but going from lowest to high level of granularity (month to quarter, then quarter to year). Figures 1-2 through 1-5 provide an example of drill-down using two of the three dimensions: geographic area and time period.

An important point to mention is that the drill-down or drill-up is typically quite quick. Response time from clicking the button in the BI tool to the presentation of the report should be seconds to minutes. Remember, this is not an operational

Canadian Sales		
		2007
Geographic Area	Totals	
Canada	945	945

Figure 1-2   *High-level geographic area and year report*

Canadian Sales		
		2007
Geographic Area	Totals	
BC	36	36
Alberta	131	131
Saskatchewan	173	173
Manitoba	36	36
Ontario	67	67
Quebec	251	251
New Brunswick	36	36
Nova Scotia	78	78
PEI	86	86
Newfoundland	51	51
Canada	945	945

Figure 1-3   *Drill-down by geographic area showing provinces*

transaction system where response times are subseconds. In the OLAP world, since there can be millions and possibly billions of underlying data rows, response times should be quick but can span a number of minutes. An important aspect of business intelligence is performance. Results must be usable and therefore are expected to not take one to two hours each time a button is clicked.

Dashboards and scorecards, as shown in Figure 1-6, are another special type of reporting focused on visual representation. These typically contain highly aggregated key performance indicators showing how business measures have been doing and how they are currently doing against some predetermined range. A scorecard is the

Canadian Sales					
		2007			
Geographic Area	Totals	Q1	Q2	Q3	Q4
BC	36	12	6	12	6
Alberta	131	15	13	20	83
Saskatchewan	173	90	22	13	48
Manitoba	36	12	6	12	6
Ontario	67	10	16	38	3
Quebec	251	50	102	87	12
New Brunswick	36	12	6	12	6
Nova Scotia	78	38	10	25	5
PEI	86	6	10	46	24
Newfoundland	51	12	24	9	6
Canada	945	257	215	274	199

Figure 1-4   *Drill-down further on date from year to quarters by province*

Canadian Sales												
		2007										
Geographic Area	Totals	Q1			Q2			Q3			Q4		
		Jan	Feb	Mar	Apr	May	Jun	Jul	Aug	Sep	Oct	Nov	Dec
BC	36	3	4	5	1	2	3	4	5	3	2	1	3
Alberta	131	4	5	6	4	3	6	8	9	3	32	45	6
Saskatchewan	173	2	43	45	6	7	9		7	6	4	32	12
Manitoba	36	3	4	5	1	2	3	4	5	3	2	1	3
Ontario	67	2	4	4	5	5	6	4	32	2	1	1	1
Quebec	251	2	43	5	6	87	9	0	0	87	6	1	5
New Brunswick	36	3	4	5	1	2	3	4	5	3	2	1	3
Nova Scotia	78	32	4	2		4	6	3	21	1	3	1	1
PEI	86	2	3	1	4	3	3	5	34	7	8	9	7
Newfoundland	51	3	4	5	1	2	21	1	5	3	2	1	3
Canada	945	257			215			274			199		
		56	118	83	29	117	69	33	123	118	62	93	44

Figure 1-5   *Drill-down further on date from quarter to months, still by province*

same concept as a school report card. The scorecard shows how specific business key performance indicators have been doing in relation to previous levels. The dashboard is similar to an automobile dashboard with visualization of how the enterprise is currently operating. These reports are typically for upper management to get a feel of the organization at a high level. But there's no reason why these types of visual reporting mechanisms cannot be used in the daily operations of the organization, for instance in a call center scenario; perhaps showing number of calls received or average time spent per call compared to average per week and average per month.

BI Tool and Architecture

Remember the first lines from the BI definition section of this chapter: "Business intelligence is an umbrella term referring to skills, processes, technologies, applications, and practices used to support business decision making." Well, when you're looking at BI tools, do not simply look at the user presentation perspective. BI spans the data warehouse system as well as focusing on the retrieval and presentation aspect of data in a specific context.

A major component of BI is how the data is captured, cleansed, and held, and the compatibility of the data with the user presentation tool. The underlying data repository and the BI tool work hand in hand. Both must be designed to function as one, or else there will be a number of disconnects. The idea is that the data must be architected for retention as well as for usage, which means that the BI tool must be able to handle special designs in an efficient and timely manner. If the tool requires the data in one particular design other than what has been supplied, more effort will surely be required along with additional data movement and optimization.

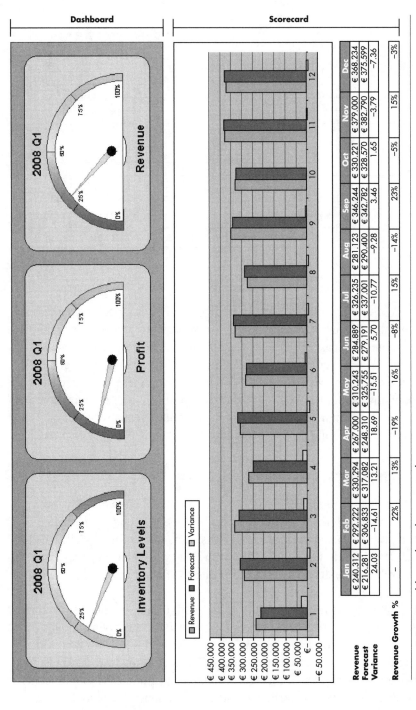

Figure 1-6   *Dashboard and scorecard*

In short, the BI tool is not an independent item. It must be coordinated with the underlying database, architecture, and overall solution. Business intelligence is a solution, not just a tool or cube or specific report. There are many vendors selling tools, each with their own nuances and special usage scenarios. Be sure the tool is compatible with your databases, your platform operating system, browser, and planned technical architecture. Test the tool with your own data to ensure that it functions as advertised. Sales pitches can be quite slick; test all features on your own system before spending thousand of dollars.

Advancements Due to Globalization

Over the past several decades, with technology advancements and modernization leading to information being much more easily accessible on the Web and with experts and consultants travelling the world more frequently, there have been global advancements in BI and data warehousing. The diverse world cultures and different business structures and strategies have ironically helped the development of standardizations. Telecommunications companies in Jakarta, Indonesia; Mumbai, India; or Toronto, Canada can all reap the benefits of globalization due to the use of best practices, line-of-business or industry data models, tools, and development and/or usage methodologies.

Bill Inmon is accredited with developing a standardized architecture methodology for structuring enterprise data to support business intelligence. Ralph Kimball also developed an architecture methodology consisting of guidelines and components for specifically building business intelligence environments based on a data bus structure. Both are keen to focus on business requirements, whether data and/or reporting, to help the business attain a higher level of business decision making. Individually or together in a hybrid fashion, both methodologies form approaches in designing and building an environment to help organizations optimize their performance in managing their business decision-making process, which is called a "data warehouse."

Business intelligence is a component of the data warehouse. Understanding a business intelligence environment requires an appreciation for the overall data warehouse system and for the different approaches to designing and building such an environment.

Data Warehouse Overview

Business intelligence was discussed prior to the data warehouse topic because most data warehouse systems come into existence to create some sort of business value, which is typically business intelligence. Now let us look at the definition of a data warehouse in more detail.

Definition

A data warehouse (DW), aka warehouse, is a system for collecting, organizing, holding, and sharing historical data. It consists of "used" data as the data comes from operational systems that capture and use the data within the context of that system's purpose. Of course, other systems or sources are also possible, but in a DW project the term "operational systems" is widely used. There is usually more than one source system for a data warehouse. Data warehouses are typically thought of as enterprise-wide, but in many instances can be focused on a particular line of business such as finance or marketing.

The term "data warehouse" is often used to refer to a data warehouse system and at times in reference to the data warehouse repository. Throughout this book it will be used to refer to the overall system. The term "data warehouse repository" will be used when referring to the large central database or its design, which are components of the data warehouse system.

A data warehouse is used by the business users for decision support. Decision support in this context is synonymous with business intelligence, which is the usage of the data and the manner in which it is gathered, held, and presented within the data warehouse.

Business users, aka end users, run queries in one manner or another on the data within the data warehouse environment to support their process of making business decisions. The type of inquiries can range from simple queries, trend analysis for data over time, comparative analysis, data mining for associative analysis, extrapolation or predictive analysis for future expectation, and mixtures of these or others depending on the business usage requirements.

Many confuse a data warehouse system with a data warehouse project. Look at it this way: A project, regardless of the line of business or its purpose, has definitive start and end dates. A data warehouse, on the other hand, is a system that has lifecycles, as shown in Figure 1-7. A data warehouse is built or added to via projects.

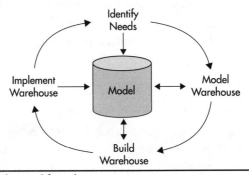

Figure 1-7   *Data warehouse lifecycle*

For instance, to create a data warehouse, a project is undertaken to determine what exactly to build. Another project at a later time may be funded to add or expand the data warehouse environment yet again.

A classic data warehouse lifecycle is to identify the business needs, or requirements, as well as high-level technical requirements. Remember, a data warehouse has both a business and IT symbiotic relationship; one cannot survive without the other. Once it is determined why the data warehouse effort is required and a budget has been approved with the go-ahead to build, the design or modeling phase (or macro phase) begins, which includes technical and data architecture, data modeling, process modeling, and so forth. Then after the planning and designs are done, the actual building can begin. This step involves the micro-tasks of physically building the environment, which includes creating the database, determining indexes, writing extract, transform, and load (ETL) jobs, writing reports, and so forth. Lastly, for the project at hand, the implementation of the warehouse is the setting of all the components into a production status and the deployment to the business user community in order to actively expand the business insights and opportunities. As a disclaimer, these are the high-level steps in a data warehouse project effort, but that is not to say that the underlying tasks must necessarily be in a waterfall development approach.

Data Warehouse System

As with any system, the main components are input, process, output and feedback, as shown in Figure 1-8. For a data warehouse system, the input involves identifying and capturing the data. Data quality at this point is critical because any incorrect data will cause inaccurate output as it trickles down into all underlying processes,

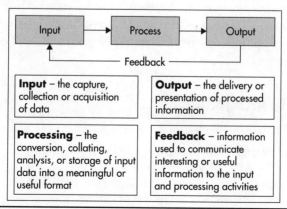

Figure 1-8   *Basic system components*

subsystems, and eventual business analysis and decisions. Transforming and loading the data into a central environment can span the input and process areas.

The central environment is typically one large database but can be a combination of databases possibly on different servers in different locations, but regardless of the setup, they should all be choreographed from one central design. The process aspect of this central area is to transform and hold the data in a structured and organized manner. Structuring the data is done via data architecture and more precisely a data model. A logical data model is used to design and understand the fundamental, descriptive, and associative characteristics of the data and therefore the business. A physical data model is used to optimize the data for usage in a database and related environment.

The outbound portion of the system is to transfer the data to those who need it. The data can be designed in a number of different ways. Typically this is referred to as a combination of data marts, which can span the performance layer and the user presentation area/layer depending on how they are discussed. Data marts are smaller versions of the central environment that conform to the logical and/or physical central data models but are optimized for end user–specific usage. In this context the data marts are referred to as the *performance layer*. This might involve materialized query tables created by the system, specialized access paths, virtual views, and so forth. The user presentation area is the portion of a data warehouse the business people actually use, which is typically done with some sort of reporting tool such as Cognos, Microstrategy, Business Objects, Crystal Reports, and/or SAS. Other tools include Microsoft Access, manual SQL, Excel, or a combination of any of these and others. The user presentation area sits atop the underlying specific data marts.

The feedback portion of the system is based on the output and input portions. When deriving or aggregating data, the result could be required for later use. In this case, it may be practical to keep the aggregation for later usage such as calculations. Therefore this output data is now required to circle back as input into the data warehouse system. This newly derived measure is now sourced from the data warehouse itself and can be used as the foundation of future inquiries. There are certainly methods of optimizing this feedback approach, which all depend on where within the output process it is created.

Data Warehouse Architecture

The architecture of a data warehouse is the design of the data warehouse system. Think of the architecture as the blueprints. One very popular manner of representing the data warehouse architecture is by using a data flow diagram, as shown in Figure 1-9. The reason this is so popular is that it gives a really good overview of the underlying components. A data warehouse is a complicated system. It may seem like an easy undertaking—take source data, centralize into a nicely structured database, and run some reports—but in reality it is quite complicated and time-consuming.

I have seen naïve projects begin without regard for business usage and attempt to build a data warehouse without business purpose, without source system insights, without proper planning, and without executive support. I've also seen projects in which an IT data manager decides to build a data warehouse in hopes that business will jump on its existence once it is built. One particular IT-focused customer had executive support because they talked upper management into the amazing possibilities of having a great understanding of the organization's data. Well, upper management missed one important point—tangible usage. The project seemed to be lasting forever and could no longer be contained solely in the IT data management budget because resources were being consumed that affected other budgeted efforts. A data warehouse architecture data flow diagram was eventually created and it became apparent that efforts were only focused on the data population and organization aspects of the overall solution. If you build a portion of a product simply because it is a good idea, it does not necessarily ensure that someone will purchase it. There are costs to continue development, costs in advertising/promoting, costs in distribution and usage. Ensure that the business requires and will use the product before building it, no matter how great the idea or concept may seem.

Figure 1-9 shows the data flowing from left to right within a data warehouse system. Used alone, this graphic helps in understanding the components of a data warehouse system. Adding organization-specific information to it will help communicate a realistic view of the overall solution and give insight into ongoing efforts.

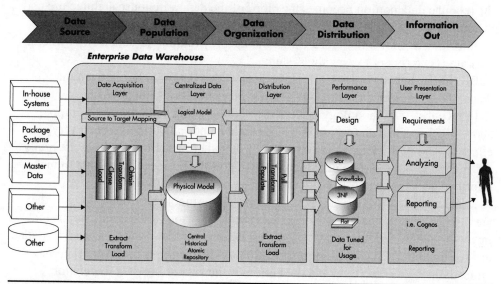

Figure 1-9 *Data warehouse architecture—data flow*

At the left are the input source systems, which are typically operational systems within the organization and can include feedback sources from nearly every one of the other layers. Following are numerous processes to capture, populate, and organize the data. And finally on the right is the distribution of data and the usage or output of the information to the business community.

Each one of these layers should be expanded in the design, build, and implementation phases of the project, but first, requirements must be gathered. The *raison d'être* (French for "reason for being") for a usage must be determined. If a budget is to be spent for the development of a data warehouse and therefore a monetary value placed on the system or product, there should be a real, tangible useful purpose to its existence with an estimated return on investment (ROI), as with any business venture effort.

Some argue that structuring the data is of massive value to the organization in itself, which is true, but without a business-specific usage, how do you know if spending two weeks on one particular data aspect is of later value or not over some other data concept? In general, do not build a pure data foundation in hopes of business becoming interested at some later point; build with business value goal or purpose up front. An organized and structured data foundation should be a by-product of the business value approach and solution.

Data Flow Terminology

Many in the data warehouse world use the terms "top-down" and "bottom-up" when referring to a data warehouse. Most discussions using these terms take them from the data flow architecture. Here's the trick; if you turn Figure 1-9 clockwise 90 degrees, the inbound data portion becomes the "top" of the data warehouse architecture and the output portion, aka the business usage portion, ends up at the "bottom" of the architecture, as shown in Figure 1-10. Another way to think of data flow is whether the data is entering or exiting the system.

Bill Inmon's methodology primarily deals with a data warehouse from the top down, meaning from the data point of view but not to say without business purpose. Ralph Kimball's methodology is from the bottom up, meaning business purpose above all else with data to support it. The author finds a hybrid approach very effective, and it promotes efficiency in project and efforts. Both methods are really driving to the same end point, which is to support the business being able to make informed decisions by structuring and organizing the underlying data.

Many confuse these top-down and bottom-up terminologies, but as long as they are distinguished in the discussion, all is fine. The reason for the confusion is that many misunderstand the context of the discussion. For data flow the top is the data and the bottom is the usage. For information usage, the top is the business usage, typically business reporting, and the bottom is the supporting data foundation, as seen in Figure 1-11. Both views are appropriate as long as the context is

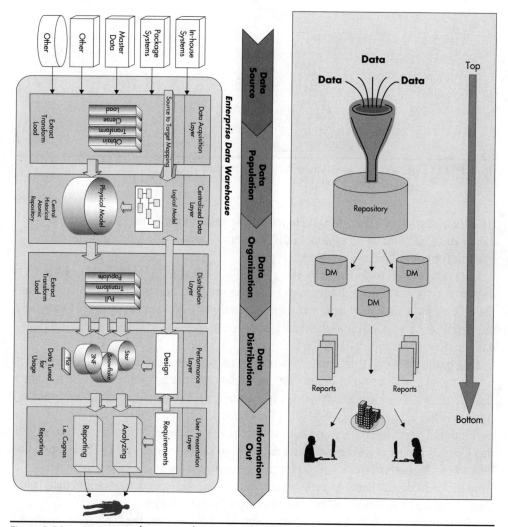

Figure 1-10   *Data warehouse architecture: data flow*

distinguished and maintained throughout the discussion. This book will always refer to the data flow top-down and bottom-up scenario unless otherwise noted.

Data Warehouse Purpose

A data warehouse environment is built to hold historical data integrated from a number of source systems in an organized manner. Operational systems are built for specific functions, such as point-of-sale processing, billing systems, inventory control, and so forth. These systems are not always enterprise-based and are not built

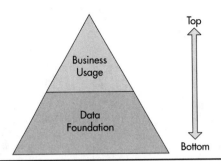

Figure 1-11   *Data warehouse architecture: information usage*

for data analytics or data mining. Hence a new environment must be created to merge the data from these systems into one central area, called a data warehouse system, for overall enterprise usage.

Data quality can be an issue in one system, but when merging disparate systems, data quality is paramount. I have never seen an organization with absolutely perfect data. One customer came close but then they only had one source system. Once they merged a second system into their data warehouse, they were surprised to find that data quality issues rapidly surfaced.

Due to the merging of multiple systems, a data warehouse must pay attention to modeling, aka structuring or organizing, the data to ensure a common vocabulary and flexible design. For instance, system A has a sex code of 0 for Male and 1 for Female. System B has a gender code of M, F, U (unknown). When merging these two systems, a commonality in vocabulary and data values must be created. We might decide to call this Gender Type and define the codes as M, F, and U representing Male, Female, and Unknown. This seems quite simple for this example, but ask several business users from different departments in your organization what the term demographic means to them. I am sure the result will be a number of different answers.

The primary reason for having a data warehouse is to sort out the "spaghetti" mess that every organization has either from disparate systems built over the years, or merging of organizations, purchased systems, or whatever. The mess is in the terminology, or vocabulary, and in data values. Figure 1-12 shows how operational (source) systems can each play a role in enterprise analytics. Without a centralized environment, reporting becomes difficult, inconsistent, incorrect, of high maintenance, and unreliable due to data quality issues, redundant loading routines, impact to source systems, and so on.

A centralized "atomic" data warehouse repository, Figure 1-13, cleans up most of these issues. If you centralize the data for the enterprise, a vocabulary emerges, allowing the users to all speak with the same terminology. And it allows all data to have a high level of quality since each object must be analyzed and profiled for it to be merged into a central data warehouse repository—or at least should be.

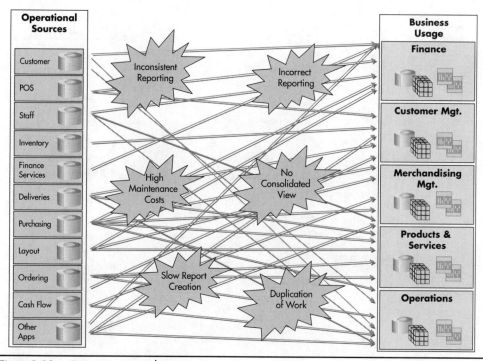

Figure 1-12 *Reporting spaghetti mess*

With reporting from a central environment, data on each report can be accounted for. If there are any issues, the sourcing of each data component can be traced back to its origin simply because the loading of the data warehouse is under the control of the data warehouse group and hence all loading programs can be reviewed.

The term "atomic" in this sense refers to the level and granularity of the data. The business could use a term such as demographics, but IT would decompose this into data items such as person, age, income, address and so forth. This fine level of data is the atomic data level and the granularity is the level of data capture. The spaghetti mess also refers to the disparate granularities of data being captured.

If a transaction happens several times a day, then the granularity is at the level of data capture, which is the transaction level for this example. For instance, a customer purchases an apple from a fruit store in the morning. In the afternoon the same customer purchases another apple from the same store. The lowest level of granularity is each "purchase," or point-of-sale transaction.

The atomic data level is the lowest level of possible data capture and at the finest level of data components possible. The data model design is a normalized form,

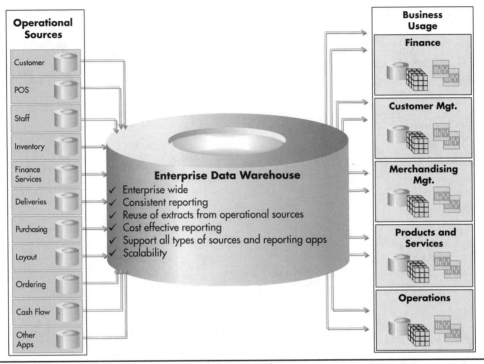

Figure 1-13 *Structured and organized data warehouse repository*

which could be third normal form, bus architecture, or star schema. At this level the idea is to capture the lowest grain of the business events and data pillars (terms that will be described in Chapter 2).

Data Structure Strategy

Data warehouses typically evolve from a need to understand information at the enterprise level and also from a strategic or tactical direction within the organization.

As organizations grow, especially after mergers and acquisitions, management needs to know what information is available and how data from disparate systems mix together, as shown in Figure 1-14. Or the organization may be keenly aware of the competitive environment and needs an edge to ensure its position within the marketplace. Both scenarios require an in-depth knowledge of the organization's data asset. For this a master data management effort is usually undertaken. This entails identifying all data values and setting a common vocabulary and structures along with ownership, change control, and so forth.

Vocabulary means to set a definition and example, if possible, for each data object. *Structures* refers to creating a blueprint for each object from fundamental,

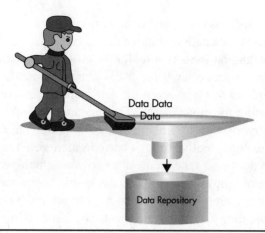

Data Data
Data

Data Repository

Figure 1-14   *Structuring and organization enterprise data*

descriptive, and associative viewpoints. Identifying the actual data is exactly what it says; each value for every object should be identified and documented. If gender type can only refer to Male, Female, and Unknown, then this is the universe of values for this data object. Anything new would be something to look into to ensure that there were no processing or loading errors. You may not want to profile an individual's last name, but you would certainly want to remove pre- and post-titles such as Dr. or PhD, as these are data objects themselves but are only necessary if they have value to the business.

When you're selling your home, buyers are much more impressed if the place is neat and clean; the same idea applies to an organization. Having all your data structured and organized lets a potential investor and/or buyer know that management is on their toes, and it is a requirement for regulatory compliance in certain countries. It also gives organizations insight into the operations, thus allowing management the opportunity to make well-founded business decisions at all planning levels. A structured and organized data environment can give management an insight into the worth and value of the company and the company's placement within the marketplace.

Data Warehouse Business

Personally, I like to think of a data warehouse system including its management and development teams as its own independent company within the larger picture of the organization. In this context the company manages a data warehouse environment and produces customer solutions, which include business intelligence solutions. Customers commission the company to build tangible optimized data environments, typically with business reports specific to the customers' needs.

Customers are the business users, and commissioning is a service-level agreement to ensure timely and accurate data within the data warehouse system along with the creation of data marts and business reports for the customers. Data quality is expected or the customer goes elsewhere, just as in an open market system.

The reason for thinking this way about the data warehouse system is that it is quite a big system within the organization. The fundamental aspect is data, which is a major asset of the organization. Thinking of the whole thing as a business allows the involved people to consistently strive to bring in more revenue, just as in a real business. Individuals no longer take on the attitude of an employee of a large organization, but that of innovative entrepreneurs within an up-and-coming business-solution organization. Individuals do not run off and build quick solutions for specific customers; they discuss requirements and issues with management, who determine the appropriate course of action for the data warehouse organization. Each new project, whether to enhance the current system or expand the system for new customer requirements, is an extension of the organization and of product output.

For these reasons and this perspective, a data warehouse is a true organization-strategic asset and therefore should have executive ownership. This means a management focus on enhancing the asset, structuring the asset to meet the organization's strategic direction and ensuring data quality, not only within the data warehouse system but for the source operational systems for data pertaining to the data warehouse. Centers of Competence or Excellence are good examples of how to run the data warehouse and business intelligence division within an organization.

Frequently Asked Questions

I've been involved in more data warehouse projects than I can count all over the world, and it seems as if the same questions are asked over and over again by the development team, the business users, and executive management alike. It's interesting how globalization has people in the four corners of the earth from different cultures, different languages, and different lines of business all asking the same types of questions, as described in the next few sections.

A data warehouse system can be quite the undertaking, with many intricate processes, designs, requirements, and the coordination among all of these. All these technicalities, all the while trying to manage the organization's internal politics, can be daunting. After spending time deeply involved in the details, it can be quite easy to lose sight of the fundamentals and exactly why the strategy and development have taken the direction they have. Even after organizations have built previous data warehouses, they can still become disenchanted with an enterprise data warehouse effort or business intelligence altogether. For these people, the following few sections are a compilation of classic recurring questions and (hopefully) satisfying replies.

Feel free to send your questions to the Data Warehouse Mentor group on www.linkedin.com. I or another member will gladly respond to the best of our abilities to help you out in the most timely and accurate manner in which we can hopefully give valuable and usable information in your context.

Current Systems Good Enough?

Rather than creating a new data warehouse system, why not just access the source (operational) systems directly?

▶ Typically, operational systems are not interested in keeping history on all the data. Therefore a new data warehouse environment must be created to ensure that all versions of the data are captured over time.

My source system does capture and hold all data over time, so why create a data warehouse?

▶ Data in source systems is optimized for usage. If the source is from a point-of-sale system, a mediation system, or a billing system, for example, these systems are specifically designed for their primary purpose and not for associating one component to another in an analytically desired manner. To do this the data must be pulled, structured, and placed into a data warehouse system so it can be used in whatever manner desired. This is also why capturing the data at its finest level of granularity is rather important.

▶ Also many source systems are closed. Prepurchased packages usually have no documentation about the underlying tables, columns, or how they associate to each other. This makes understanding the context of the data nearly impossible and querying the data very difficult. The software manufacturer normally makes the data available through the software application or via an application program interface (API).

My source system is open, has full documentation, and holds all data over time. Why should I build a data warehouse?

▶ Well, if this is the case, then perhaps you do not require a data warehouse for your current purpose. Check if you have data quality issues; fix if necessary and query your data as is—if you don't mind having large and long-running queries on your operational systems.

▶ Remember, your operational systems run the company business. If you interfere with these by slowing down operational response times or delaying business processes or backups, this can hinder your business productivity. It's best to create a new environment and copy the data from the source system as required.

▶ Typically more than one source system is used in business intelligence, and a data warehouse environment is perfect for merging such disparate systems and aggregating the overall data, allowing queries to run on one common enterprise environment.

▶ Another important point is in setting an enterprise vocabulary for your organization. With multiple source systems and applications, it is very likely that a term in one system is similar to but still different in another system. Or it may be completely different between both systems. Having a central data warehouse environment allows for a master data management effort in terminology and data values as well.

Well, all this sounds great; why not replace our current operational systems with a data warehouse?

The answer goes back to several of the same points mentioned earlier:

▶ Data in operational systems is optimized for usage. Point-of-sale systems, mediation systems, or billing systems, for example, are all specifically designed to capture specific real-time information.

▶ The model and therefore database for a data warehouse is designed specifically for historical data in a manner optimized for holding and reporting. Operational systems are designed for capturing and subsecond response times. Data warehouses can have millions and billions of rows gathered over the years; therefore, response times can be minutes or even longer depending on the requirements.

▶ Remember, your operational systems run the company business. If you interfere with these by slowing down operational response times or delaying business processes or backups, this can hinder your business productivity. It's best to create a new environment and copy the data from the source system as required.

What Is the Value of a Data Warehouse?

Why create a data warehouse effort? Why not just obtain (referring to their own departments) a handful of smart IT folks to create the reports as need be?

Many organizations have business departments with their own IT staff who are maintaining certain aspects of their operational systems and/or are tasked with producing their required reports and/or being the go-to person to produce on-the-spot reports based on specific requirements. These IT folks are constantly trying to get access to one system or another, copying data from one source system to their own environment and replicating that data multiple times as it is sent all over the department. The end result is that different groups have different concepts, vocabulary becomes local rather than enterprise, and reporting becomes misleading.

The point is that the value lies in having a central common enterprise area for all business users to access the same underlying data. The context of that data or information can be in any manner the individual users determine appropriate for their duties and purposes. But the underlying data would be common to everyone. This means the vocabulary is common, the data values are common, and the structures are common to all in the organization. Data becomes an asset to the organization as a whole, not just departmentally. Banks, insurance firms, phone companies, and airlines cannot operate today without computer systems that can handle the underlying mountains of data. If the data is incorrect, the results are incorrect, which leads to inappropriate decision making (for those decisions based on the underlying data, of course). The point is to ensure that the fundamental asset is secure and trustworthy.

Several years ago while I was in discussions at a customer site in Norway, both marketing and finance department representatives were sitting at the same table. I thought, what a great opportunity to demonstrate the business value of a data warehouse. I asked how many products the organization produces. The answer from one department was 450; the other department quickly jumped and literally said, "Are you nuts? We have 14,000 products." The point was made; they each had their own data and interpreted it in their own way. The value of a data warehouse is to ensure that the organization can base their decisions on the same fundamental data, using the same vocabulary/definition throughout the enterprise.

It is all about ensuring that the enterprise data asset is managed appropriately for the business to access and used as need be.

Actual value in monetary terms is different for each organization, but the business goals are typically the same:

▶ Deeper insight into product base including quality assessments

▶ Deeper understanding of current business processes

▶ Deeper insights into customers and customer relationships

▶ In-depth knowledge of current operations

▶ Identification of market opportunities

▶ Improved marketing strategies

▶ Deeper insights into financial areas such as

　▶ Customer accounts and trends

　▶ General ledgers

　▶ Product costs and profits

　▶ Transactional analysis

▶ Comparative insights against the competitive environment

How Much Will It Cost?

This is always a difficult question. Cost is relative and depends on the current environment and what the organization wants to do with a data warehouse. There is no straight answer to this question. To access the cost, consider the following areas:

- ▶ Current technology vs. anticipated technical requirements
  - ▶ Servers or machines
  - ▶ Databases
  - ▶ Disk space
  - ▶ Data models
  - ▶ Tools:
    - ▶ Data capture tools
    - ▶ ETL tools
    - ▶ BI usage tools
  - ▶ User licenses
  - ▶ Maintenance costs
- ▶ Current vs. expected expertise
  - ▶ Is appropriate talent available in-house?
  - ▶ Are resources currently available?
  - ▶ What are the education costs for IT and business users?
  - ▶ What are the external expert resource costs?
- ▶ The scope for the project
  - ▶ Top-down or bottom-up
  - ▶ Finer focus is more effective and cheaper
- ▶ Ongoing system costs
  - ▶ Production maintenance

When all is said and done, cost will be a factor of expected return on investment of the overall data warehouse and business intelligence system.

How Long Will It Take?

This is another good question that keeps most data warehouse managers awake at night. Many projects are given a specific timeline with a drop-dead date to finish all development and produce a final usable result. The problem is that most data warehouse projects succumb to scope creep. More and more seemingly small items are constantly added to the project as it progresses. These may seem small and inconsequential at the time, but cumulatively they do add up to increase the project deliverables and ultimately will extend the deadline. Later, when difficulties arise, management has a funny way of jumping back to the start and stating how everything was supposed to be done in xx months. The little extensions seemed trivial, but somehow all hell broke loose and the project turned into a runaway state.

Best practice is to limit initial scope. Focus on fundamental data before complex derivations (cost and profit for instance). Do not model the entire organization but only the most fundamental data as required by the very clear business purpose or goal. Ensure that the project effort has a very precise documented and approved plan with set goals. A qualitative goal is nice, but it must be quantified so it can be measured and attained.

Best practice is to not start from scratch. A good practice is to purchase as need be. For example, purchasing a prebuilt data model will help greatly with organizing and structuring the enterprise data with naming standards, definitions, and relationships between the components. However, be warned that purchasing an intricate data model must be done with an understanding that the model may need tweaking and should be used as a reference. No purchased data model is exactly what any one organization is looking for, but with expertise it can certainly ramp up efforts on any data warehouse project. Depending on an initial scoping, and given appropriate client subject-matter experts and source-system analyst insights, a purchased model should take between six to nine weeks to map out the organization's fundamental data.

Best practice is also to ensure that the project has a seasoned full-time data warehouse project manager. Just because a person is a good project manager for an operational system project does not imply that this person is a good data warehouse project manager. And ensure that the project is not run by the timekeeper, a person good at driving a project plan but little or no authority or experience in managing the actual project and resources. Ensuring that a task is done does not make a project manager. Knowledge, experience, and authority are key to the project manager role.

Best practice is to ensure that a data warehouse project has a seasoned data warehouse architect. A project manager removes political hurdles and plans the steps of the project, while the data warehouse architect ensures that technical details are correct and data flow is proper and development is headed in the proper direction. For that matter, ensure that the data warehouse has senior experienced data warehouse and business intelligence staff. Do not populate the staff with rookies, as this will greatly slow the project down.

With a fully seasoned staff, a limited data warehouse effort with a kick start (not from scratch) should take six months for the initial stage. So the next question is, what is a limited scope?

With one particular customer, I was tasked to determine how cost was calculated for a specific line of products and how that calculation was used in a particular department. The idea was that cost is an essential concept to the business and needed to be fully understood in that department.

Usually when cost or profit comes into a data warehouse scope, it becomes quite a complicated matter. While an organization is very keen to understand these two areas, especially for analysis, these are very difficult and intense concepts within any organization, with a large trickle-down effect to many other departments and areas within the organization. My suggestion is to not begin a data warehouse initiative to determine cost or profit up front. First, start the data warehouse based on fundamental data; get all your ducks in a row before determining how they fit together and form cost or profit insights. As a rule, business concepts such as cost and profit must be defined by the business as input to the data warehouse system. All terms and calculations must be known to the data warehouse up front; this is a major aspect of determining an enterprise vocabulary.

In trying to determine cost for this one customer, the business analysts were brought in for an understanding of how the business functions in that area. It turned out that they pulled certain types of data from several operational systems and created a special report with underlying derived data. This was then passed over to another person in the department, who imported it into their MS Access database for further massaging. Later the secretary imported the data into Excel and distributed the file to at least ten other individuals, who proceeded to derive what they required in their own special way. The problem was that when one of those users discussed cost with the business analysts, they had their own twist on it, and none of them had a holistic view of the concept.

The point is to be aware of the implications of the project focus before determining the duration of the project effort. This can be quite difficult but an up-front necessity before planning on overall duration.

What Will Make Us Successful?

This is a great question, which every management person should be asking before the project begins and every month thereafter. How can we succeed with this project, with these resources, with this budget, and with this timeline?

Scenario: You win the lottery and end up purchasing an existing company. A vice president approaches you and says we need a data warehouse. Okay, you say, that sounds interesting, let's discuss it. The first thing is to ask the guy for a definition of a data warehouse and how will it help the business. The VP is just beaming with enthusiasm and explains that he heard that all the data in the company should be pulled into one central area, and once this is shown to the business, they will just love it and they will do lots of amazing things with it, which will advance the business by leaps and bounds. What would you say?

Nothing can guarantee that the project will be successful, as there are always risks. To remove or limit the risks, the following best practices have been proven time and time again.

Step 1: Research

Look into what a data warehouse is, what business intelligence is, and how it is used. You do not have to become an expert; you can always hire experts, but become familiar with the topic, key points, and basic vocabulary. One of the reasons this book came into existence is that I was talking with a director of business intelligence who abruptly stopped me in our discussion and with a bit of contempt in her voice said, and I quote, "What's all this talk about data marts, what's a data mart? I want a data warehouse." Needless to say, I was taken aback, wondering how that person obtained the position of BI director. I vowed to one day write a book explaining all the aspects of the topic. So the first step is research; go to the bookstore, buy a book on data warehousing and business intelligence (this book, of course), get a pot of coffee, and begin the education process. Key players such as BI director, DW/BI sponsor, and business leads should all be somewhat familiar with a data warehouse system and business intelligence in general.

Step 2: Strategic Alignment

By now the concepts of data warehouse and business intelligence should be solidifying. You are not an expert, but you should be able to discuss the topic. The next step is to determine whether a data warehouse (and this refers to cost, effort, and value) can be useful to the organization. What is the business strategy for the next five years? How is it to be attained? What are the main business process areas and the plan for these? What/where are the current and expected trouble spots? How can a business intelligence effort help out and fit into the overall strategy of the organization?

Step 3: Focus, or Limited Scope

This is an extremely important point. Do not try to boil the ocean. In other words, do not plan on doing everything at once. Focus on something concrete that is important to the long-term strategy of the organization and which will clearly add value to the business. High visibility is critical to have buy-in from the business. But limit the scope to ensure that the effort is technically possible. Think big but start small. A 90-day effort should show some tangible result with visible value. Pick an area that is straightforward, easily understood, has a clear deliverable, and for which you have the technical skills in-house. Do not build until the plan is solid and details are known.

Step 4: Value

While this may seem sensible, many disregard this aspect of a data warehouse effort. For the first iteration of the project, there may not be much value because a data warehouse requires a foundation to be built, meaning that the startup or learning curve is high in the first round. However, there must be value to the organization. Show how a centralized product vocabulary is created and agreed to, how customers are identified and centralized, or how data quality is in place that was sorely lacking before. Then show that the next phase adds value based on its dependency on the initial effort. The point is to show tangible value and promote it each step of the way to IT, the business, and executive management.

Step 5: Metrics

For business value to be realized, it must be quantifiable. In other words, it must be tangible, accountable, and numeric in some form. We must be able to count something, or compare something. Saying the data is clean is nice but not enough. It must be quantified; for example, 95 percent of all customers now have valid and usable addresses. The quantitative degree of improvement is vital to make a strong impression with the business and upper management.

Step 6: Goals

Success must be seen by all. IT can say their goals of building a foundation of clean data have been reached, but if the business is unhappy with the final result, then goals are not aligned. There must be a coordination of goals and purpose with IT and the business. Do not expect goals to materialize during the project; determine in advance the specific goals and plan on how they can be attained and agreed upon. Decisions about what is realistic, measurable, achievable, within budget and within the timeline can take months to agree on. Do not leave this item open with hopes that all will come to light during development. Keep users in the loop at all times during development, but even before, keep them in the loop during the planning phase.

Step 7: Executive Support

If there is no clear executive sponsor for the project, walk away. If upper management is not willing to put themselves on the line for this enterprise-level project, the probability of a successful conclusion is very low. An enterprise data warehouse is a strategic asset and requires executive oversight and support. The executive must support and champion the project. There must be enthusiasm reinforcing the development team and the business. At one customer's kick-off project meeting, the recently retired CEO showed up to encourage the group. Sounds odd, but this guy had near-celebrity status and sitting with the team discussing how he was back as the executive champion specifically for the data warehouse effort was a super boost to both camps. Throughout the project he would regularly attend quarterly status meetings and really get involved. His support was paramount to the project and really inspired a level of importance. Political roadblocks were removed at the top levels, and the project was able to move forward without hindrance.

Step 8: Business Sponsor

A data warehouse or business intelligence project is specifically for the business to help in the business decision-making process. If the business is not on board with the project or jumps ship midway, the effort is in real jeopardy. A subject matter expert is an absolute must to ensure that IT understands what and where the focus lies. These are the experts who guide the IT people in building what the business requires and ensuring that the deliverable is usable. Think of these people as the owners of the house you are renovating. If they don't like what you are building, they won't use it.

Step 9: Data Management

A real key to creating a data warehouse system with business intelligence is in structuring the data. This one point can make or break a data warehouse or business intelligence effort. Ensuring that the data is organized at an enterprise level, meaning with a vocabulary and structures, is a fundamental aspect of a data warehouse. Purchasing a prebuilt model can greatly help with this effort.

Step 10: Data Quality

Business intelligence is nothing if the underlying data has little or no integrity. What is the point of creating a system if data quality is not a recognized effort? On several projects, overly keen project managers were willing to ignore data quality in hopes that just building the system would be of more value than the data it held. All these efforts ran aground when the system was used by the business. It's kind of similar to opening a gift only to find that you cannot use it because the batteries were not included.

Step 11: Performance Usage

Once all is said and done, when the business presses the proverbial button, if the response time is too long, the solution will not be used. Ensure that the design takes into account the physical aspects such as data volumetrics, database joins, indexing, and so forth. These all form part of the expected performance levels.

Step 12: Flexible Framework

I once bought ten clothes hangers to stow my ten shirts in the closet. I was quite pleased until I bought another shirt! Ensure that the system that is built can accommodate the next phase. The framework must be flexible enough to build upon at a later date. Remember, a data warehouse is a system, meaning that it will probably be added to, and therefore it needs to be flexible to accommodate additions.

Data in the Organization

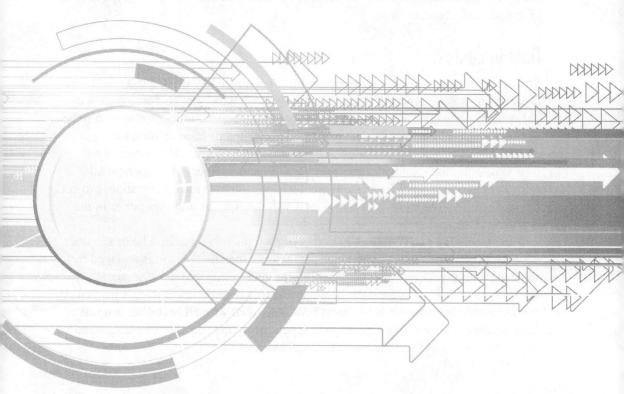

Banks, phone companies, credit card companies, and every other type of business require computers to do business because the amount of data is just too much for us poor humans to manage without a little help. With computing systems we can manage our data, but in order to do so, the data must be organized in some sort of context for the computer programs to interpret and process.

The importance of this corporate data is driving businesses to invest heavily in data warehousing and data management to ensure that the asset is used to its fullest potential with integrity and quality. This chapter discusses aspects of the corporate asset, topics of data organization, and a business perspective of the value in organizing the data.

Corporate Asset

For data to be considered an asset to the corporation, it must be understood and useful to the business. Usable data must be in the context of the business, reliable for use by the business, and defined so that the business can understand its purpose and IT can manage it successfully.

Data in Context

From a business point of view, organizations are managed by individuals who make decisions on how to proceed, which essentially is what to do next. These decisions, depending on the level and forward visibility of the decision maker's role within the organization, take into account the company, group and/or team culture, the competitive environment, company politics, productivity, available resources and their skills, timelines, budgets, and a number of factors either at the operational, tactical, or strategic level. To make these decisions to move the organization, project, or task forward, companies hire individuals with knowledge and experience in the appropriate focused areas.

If the managing person makes incorrect or poor decisions because he or she does not have the background or experience for the role, then that person is replaced by someone with experience and the capability of interpreting and reacting to the information within the context of the organization's boundaries. But what happens if the underlying information is incorrect? An individual with all his or her insights from previous business experiences, life experiences, and educational background makes decisions based on the information at hand.

The information is data within the proper and focused context. For example (Figure 2-1), "57 people" really does not mean anything without context. If I ask how many people were in the store yesterday afternoon between 3:00 and 4:00 P.M., then "57 people" makes sense. Without context, the data is not information and therefore not of value to the business.

We have all seen movies or television programs where an executive is being reprimanded or sentenced to years of incarceration, and as he is being led away his last words are: "…but that's the information I was given." In order to achieve due diligence, upper management, especially for larger financial institutions, expect and, in many cases, are legally required to have their organizations ensure a high level of data integrity. If the financial organizations of the world crumble and it affects the lives of millions of individuals, and the problem spreads in a domino effect to the national and world economies, then organizations must be accountable for their data asset, or lack of one. This exact issue is the reason for the Basel II Accord for banks and financial institutions as well as the Solvency II Accord for European insurance organizations.

In short, data within the organization is a corporate asset that must be managed with due diligence in a timely and auditable manner, ensuring management the full opportunity to use the data as a fundamental resource in the decision-making process. Whether management uses that information in an appropriate or improper manner is a totally different matter.

Note that the corporate data asset is larger than the scope of a data warehouse but its enterprise management usually starts with a data warehouse project because this type of project usually touches more data and more sources than any other effort other than a full-blown master data management initiative.

Let us say, for example, that you are in the business of selling noodles to the general public from your noodle stores. You have many noodle stores all over the country. You purchase noodles from a central wholesaler and distribute them to your noodle stores nationwide. You typically order 10,000 boxes of noodles every week

Figure 2-1   *Information: data in context*

and blindly divide them up based on the number of store locations and send them on to each store. All is well, especially from that newly opened store you were worried about. Actually, the new store is better than you thought as the new store manager sends noodle order requests each week, so you know everything is fine. But reality strikes when an audit reveals that these are not order requests but stale-inventory updates. In actuality that store does not want more noodles; they have much too much inventory and want less. The store manager has no idea why you keep sending more noodles when he regularly sends inventory updates showing an overflow. The data may have been fine, but if the context of the data is misunderstood, incorrect information is processed, potentially resulting in inappropriate business decisions and actions.

Data and its context are critical to a data warehouse and business intelligence initiative. Data must be organized, structured, and understood in the appropriate business context. Ensure that your project has a seasoned business analyst and a business subject matter expert working together toward determining specific business requirements and converting these into supporting data terminology to understand the underlying data and their inherent sources.

I was involved in a large project with many teams all working toward the same goal. A problem soon became apparent: The goal was somewhat out of focus, as the project did not have a proper business analyst or a business subject matter expert to define and refine the exact goal details. The project eventually failed due to the individual interpretations of business terminology and therefore the eventual business goals. Without a lead business subject matter expert to resolve the business terminology, there was no way to appropriately interpret or relate at a fundamental data level. At the other extreme, I was involved with another client who did supply a business subject matter expert who was an ex-IT business analyst and had moved to the business side of the organization. He was very capable in explaining the business and the phased requirements as well as explaining and understanding data terminology and data modeling. This project was a great success for both the business and IT alike.

Data Quality

Now we understand that business people make decisions by interpreting information gathered from the business environment. This information is data in context. The individual interprets the data using his or her knowledge and experiences. The individual is hired because the company has confidence that he or she has the experience to interpret the data and make appropriate informed decisions.

The company provides data for this individual from their environment to interpret and to make decisions to move the company forward either directly or indirectly. There is then an understanding that the data being used has a high degree of confidence; if not, the company is in trouble, as the decisions are probably incorrect. In other words, the information should have a high degree of data quality, which means that the data can be trusted.

How does data become reliable, or have a high degree of data quality? What is data quality?

Data quality is the consistent and timely integrity of the data components that form the context of the information. It is the usage of the data that is fundamental to the business. Knowing how many customers or products your business has is extremely valuable, and therefore we must know how to define concepts such as customer and product.

Data quality is not just one thing; it consists of many aspects including

▶ Determining appropriate business terminology and relating it to the fundamental data items

▶ Determining usage, aka context

▶ Identifying the universe of values for each data item

▶ Organizing the data components into manageable structures

▶ Ensuring the proper domain values (data types)

▶ Profiling the data

   ▶ Documenting the source

   ▶ Understanding source conversions

   ▶ Understanding data values

   ▶ Determining ownership

   ▶ Documenting data-feed timeliness

▶ Ongoing governance

▶ Security for current and historical versions

Managing the data is the key to proper data quality. Tagging data stewards from the business and technology sides for an ownership perspective is also critical in a data quality endeavor to know who to approach for insights and mediation.

Does the following scenario show proper data quality? A customer enters a retail store and is offered 10 percent off any and every item they purchase over the next two hours if they subscribe to the store's credit card program. The answer is yes and no, as it depends on usage. The reason is that the point-of-sale or sales transaction information will be available to the business that day or next, because it is an important and fundamental measure to the business. But the customer data will probably take two or three days before it enters the system and is therefore available for business consumption. For those wanting an aggregate of sales or inventory levels, the data is of high quality because it exists. For those wanting to perform customer relationship management analysis on new customers, the data is of poor quality due to its tardiness, but only if it is required before the two-to-three-day lag period. Usage and timeliness of the data are critical to a data quality effort, just as much as the data values.

Here is another data quality scenario: I was engaged to help with the data warehouse data architecture for a telecommunications (phone) company. To obtain a better understanding of their prepaid calling cards and to have a real test case of data flow within the organization, I purchased a prepaid calling card and registered with the company to obtain a local phone number. Legally I was supposed to show a driver's license or passport to identify myself to the vendor, but in this particular country no one seemed interested in such legalities, so I registered as Mickey Mouse. Their customer service center was supposed to call back within three days to validate the customer information, but no one called, so on the fourth day I called them. To my amazement, without hesitation or question the call center person very politely asked, "Are you satisfied with the service, Mr. Mouse?" I suggested that we not be so formal and asked to be called by my first name, Mickey, which they did. From a data point of view, the first and last names had values in their system and the data source was their own CAF (customer application form), so how could it be wrong? Again, what is data quality? In this case the quality was appropriate but still quite low—but how could they really know?

As a side note, later that year a bomb exploded in a hotel near that company's headquarters. The device was remotely detonated by a cell phone. I do not know if the mobile phone or subscribed phone number was from the same telecom company, but I am certain the subscriber was untraceable. In this later case data quality was extremely poor. The government has since set strict audit laws about mobile phone subscriber data to enforce a high standard of data quality relating to prepaid customer information.

Since data is a prime corporate asset, data quality should not be just good enough. Set high standards on data quality because your business depends on it in the competitive environment.

Data Vocabulary

To achieve a reliable and trusted data environment, we must first understand what the data is. This may sound simplistic, but this is really the heart and soul of business intelligence and data warehousing. The size or breadth of the organization is irrelevant; what does matter is to identify and define the data components within the organization.

For example, the marketing and finance departments may ask for customer demographics. But each defines customer and demographics rather differently. To extend the previous noodle store example, marketing defines a customer as anyone who entered the noodle store, whether they purchased something or not. This means that marketing includes potential customers under the customer umbrella. Finance considers customers as only those who actually purchased one or more boxes of noodles. The definition of customer for each is different as it includes status, events, descriptive attributes, and associations. Marketing defines demographics, for example, to include anyone over 15 years old. Finance, on the other hand, considers demographics to include any person of any age as long as they purchased a box of noodles.

This example shows several fundamental terms: customer, demographics, product, store, and possibly location. These are business terms. When talking with the business users, always communicate using business terms, but clarify these using data terminology. For example, in the discovery phase, the business analyst or data modeler could discuss and break down the business term "customer" into data components as follows:

▶ A customer is any individual. These are two distinct concepts, as not all individuals will be customers; however, customers will form a subset of individuals.

▶ The individual has descriptive qualities such as: gender, age range, and so on.

▶ The individual may be associated to a location, which is the store location or a residential address.

Data quality cannot be achieved if different groups within the organization define the term differently. Commonality of the business terminologies must be determined, which means the data must be broken down into its underlying components. A definition must be set for each of these data components as well as the business item itself. Best practice and a highly advisable habit is to document data component definitions and use examples for clarity and communicative purposes in each and every instance.

From the preceding example, we could identify the following *business terms*:

▶ **Marketing Customer**   Any noodle store visitor
▶ **Finance Customer**   Any individual who purchased a noodle product

We can also identify the following *fundamental data terms*:

▶ **Individual (name, gender, age range)**   A singular human being
▶ **Sales Transaction**   A retail point of sale event at the product granularity

► **Date and Time**   Gregorian calendar date at the day granularity and 24-hour time period at the hour granularity

► **Store**   A predefined establishment for the sale of merchandise

► **Location**   A physical geographic area marked by a legal postal address (in this case)

► **Product**   A commodity offered for sale within a store

Data Components

A business uses business terminology, while Information Technology uses data terminology. It is important when building a data warehouse to always think in these two distinctions. A business analyst chats with the business users to understand what they want and need in business terms. A data analyst then must interpret or translate these business terms into data terms. In many instances the effort is simplified if the business and data analyst are one and the same person. In reality a data modeler or data architect, especially on smaller projects, plays the business analyst role. Unfortunately the opposite is rarely realized, but if possible this would be ideal as well.

The reason for this translation or interpretation is so that the data components can be determined and some sort of commonality and distinction can be applied. When you understand the data components, it becomes easier to interpret what the business truly requires by eliminating misunderstandings and enforcing a common vocabulary. At the same time, if you translate the business terms into data terms and echo these back to the business, the business has the opportunity to re-evaluate their requirements. In almost every scenario where the business is explained in data terms, the business becomes much more aware of their true needs and is able to more accurately verbalize and document their requirements. This simple effort is critical to any project and especially to a business intelligence effort, which could easily span the entire enterprise, including many disparate operational systems and therefore disparate business terminologies.

Setting an enterprise vocabulary and being able to differentiate and decompose business terminology into data components gives the overall project effort much more focus, which greatly enhances the project's probability of success for both IT and the business unit.

Figure 2-2 is an example of how the business uses the term "demographics" and how this translates into data terms. Again, the usage of the term is critical. In this case demographics represent individuals, individual attributes, addresses, address attributes, and an association between the individual and the address.

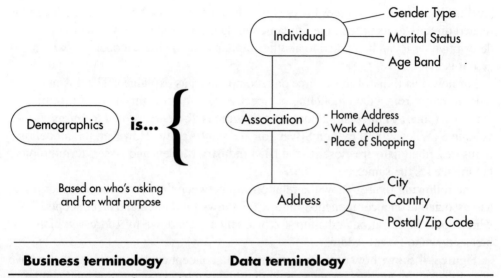

Business terminology   **Data terminology**

Figure 2-2   *Example of vocabulary: business and data terminologies*

During discussions with one customer, the demographics term emerged and the business quickly tried to dismiss it as obvious. Unfortunately for that business user, the business analyst had just finished intense discussions with an epidemiologist business subject matter expert who had just spent half a day discussing the importance of demographic usage within the healthcare organization and its many uses throughout the healthcare institution. Epidemiology is the study of the transmission and control of diseases within population segments and geographic areas. At that point, we were able to guide this business user to a very refined data interpretation of the term, surprising the user as to many possible uses within his department and his own reporting needs.

When breaking down business terms into their underlying data components, an easy method is to think of data in three basic concepts: (a) fundamental, (b) descriptive, and (c) associative.

To use our customer demographics example, both marketing and finance departments think of a customer as a person or individual; this is a fundamental data component. A fundamental data component is basically the object of the discussion or the main point: person, address, transaction, communication, or account.

Another data component in our example is age. Marketing only looks at individuals who are over 15 years of age. I cannot use the term "15 years old" by itself without thinking of the individual in this context. While "individual" is a fundamental data component, "age" is a descriptive data component since it describes the individual or fundamental data component.

The third data component is the association of the customer to the noodle store or to an address as shown in the demographics example in Figure 2-2. Data at its lowest level is always related to other lowest-level data, or else why hold the data? It can be related directly to its parent, the fundamental data component, in which case it is descriptive, or it can be related to another fundamental data component, in which case it is associative.

For now, just think of these three data components as explained. There is much more to these from a data modeling perspective, but for now this level of insight works just fine. An interesting book on this topic is *The Data Model Resource Book*, volume 3 (Wiley, 2009) by Len Silverston and Paul Agnew. However, the modeling terms described here are closer to the IBM Industry Models and Assets terminology, but the idea is the same.

The following figures show the relationship between the fundamental, descriptive, and associative data components. Figure 2-3 shows fundamental data concepts, which could be Location at the top, followed by a breakdown to Address, which breaks down to Postal Address.

Figure 2-4 shows how each fundamental data concept or data component can have descriptive elements. For instance, an individual can have a name, age, and gender.

Figure 2-5 shows how each fundamental concept can be associated with another fundamental concept. For instance, in our example an individual can be related to a postal address. The association can hold information such as start and end dates, or other descriptive attributes relating to the association between the fundamental components. Again there is more to this sort of modeling, which can be applied to a normalized model or a bus architecture model.

The end result is that the breakdown of the business terms into data terms in this manner normalizes the data into a very flexible structure. This type of structure allows the data to be understood at a fine granularity and gives insights into business terminology. This method results in data components that can be used throughout the enterprise in combinations as required. Not only is this applicable to a data warehousing system, but to any other usage within the enterprise.

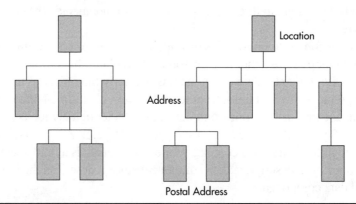

Figure 2-3 *Fundamental data components*

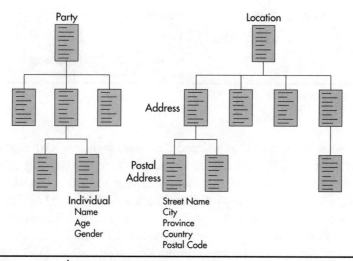

Figure 2-4 *Descriptive data components*

In descriptive form, our noodle store example would produce the results shown in Figure 2-6.

The noodles themselves are products, but this fact has been omitted from the example for simplicity's sake. Of course, it would be great to know other details as well, including the individual's name and the store's address. As mentioned previously, the term demographics can encompass many more data components, such as gender, marital status, income range, nationality, language, and so on. Demographics for one department

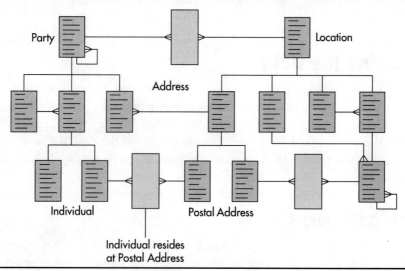

Figure 2-5 *Associative data components*

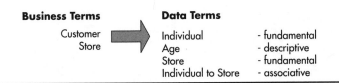

Figure 2-6   *Term conversion*

(or usage) could be, for example, all married Canadians in their 40s who speak English and drive red sports cars. However, in another department (or usage), it could be any individual with an income over 100,000 dollars per year and over 6 feet tall.

Remember, the whole point in understanding the data from the business terminology is to figure out what the business is really doing. When the business uses the data in context in the output portion of the data warehouse, it is recommended to use as much business terminology as possible. The output portion of the data warehouse is the business intelligence domain. Business intelligence should use business terminology as much as possible but in proper context.

To ensure context, each term should have its own description and examples to ensure that everyone knows exactly what the term means. The atomic repository layer, on the other hand, should be modeled in data terms. It is quite possible that numerous nearly identical terms exist, hence modeling at a normalized level to determine the difference is critical. For instance, marketing may have several demographic terms, such as student-demographics, northerner-demographics, and so forth. To differentiate between the generic term of demographics, the term should be decomposed into data components for the data warehouse and should be refined for business use, hence student-demographics or northerner-demographics.

Organizing the Data

For data to be organized, it must be defined and structured. Structuring the data is done through design. Just as an architect creates blueprints when designing a home or building, a data modeler creates a logical data model design to understand the data components and how they inter-relate. Then in the use of the data, a data architect will design the flow of data from its source to final usage including all the touch points along the way.

Structuring the Data

To have an understanding of what these data components are and how they relate to themselves and/or to other data components, we need to make some sort of sense out of the data. This is called structuring the data, and it forms a big part in the development of a data vocabulary, which is a must for a data warehouse system and a business intelligence environment especially if the effort is at an enterprise level.

Without structuring the data, the data warehouse would be quite an unorganized environment. Just as it may be difficult to find a particular tool in a messy garage, in an unstructured data warehouse, it not only becomes nearly impossible to find the required data but difficult to figure out where to put any new data, or worse how one piece of data relates to another. Thus, organizing the data is the key to creating and maintaining a data warehouse system. The better the design up front, the less rework is required in the future, which directly translates to low costs.

Typically a data warehouse system spans the entire organization, which is why it is called an enterprise data warehouse. But even so, the first several initiatives do not scope all the possible data components, as it is quite impossible to implement all at once because there are so many variables to attend to. In other words, you cannot eat all the food at an all-you-can-eat buffet at the same time; you must plan, prioritize, and phase what is most important so as to reap as many rewards as possible as development progresses in a timely manner.

To ensure that data structures on the first effort are still valid in the phases that follow, it is quite important to model, or design, the data appropriately. But how can you know what will happen in the next phase or the one after that and so forth? The answer is in the types of data modeling coupled with the appropriate data architecture.

This is why a data warehouse project should only have experienced data warehousing experts. Do not train resources on a data warehouse project; do this on operational systems, which are typically simpler due to their specific focus. A data warehouse involves understanding many areas of the business, different methodologies based on direction, and may involve the merging or separation of previous methodologies or designs as the next project or effort begins. The same reasoning applies to bringing in operational system experts and expecting them to be great data warehouse resources. These systems are different and require different skill sets. Actually, the same reasoning applies to pure dimensional modelers trying to build a normalized repository design or vice versa. Ensure the proper skill sets for the role at hand.

Understanding the different aspects of a data model and of data architecture can greatly reduce design issues further down the line.

Data Models

Structuring the data is done based on the purpose of the structure, underlying data, and the manner in which the process begins. Is the effort to look at the business requirements in business terminology, or is the effort to look at the underlying data components in IT terminology? We have to know both, but where do we start and how do we start?

Modeling as a discipline by itself is important to the business as it visually communicates the data usage either in conceptual business form or conceptual data terms while being tagged with a level of understanding based on usage. This level of data modeling is very much directed towards understanding what the business wants to look at or what the enterprise data model wants to hold. This is still at a high level with little detail but enough to get a good idea of what we are trying to do.

For example, from the previous noodle store example, when chatting with the business person, a business analyst would ask the purpose of marketing and of finance perspectives—basically what do they want to do and why. Let us say, for simplicity's sake, that both departments want to know the number of sales transactions based on the date the transaction happens, the product that was sold, and the store location based on city, the store itself, and possibly the customer generalities, for which fine details may still be up in the air. Marketing at this point is happy to relent for this exercise and look only at customers who make actual purchases, but the whole question of customer seems to be another topic, so we'll just take it with a grain of salt for the moment.

In this scenario we are looking at the information required by the business. The business representatives further explain that they each want to have simple reporting capabilities where they can look at locations based on regions, provinces, cities, and products by category. Unfortunately no reports currently exist, so we must start from scratch.

For this bottom-up approach, as shown in Chapter 1, Figure 1-10, we focus our efforts on a specific business area, which we will call "Sales." Within the "Sales" focus area of the business we can analyze the business from several angles. Figure 2-7 is a classic analysis model, within the "Sales" business focus area, which is based on specific business requirements.

Since we focus on a particular business area, we start with a Focus Area perspective. Within this focus area are many possible analysis perspectives. We start with a purpose, or goal, which in this case is Sales. The measurement or fact the business wants to look at is placed in the center in a star to represent what is called a star schema. A *star schema* is simply a method of representing a data model for communicative purposes and therefore a simple way of understanding the design from a business perspective. Circling the star are other concepts called dimensions. These dimensions qualify the middle fact (star). In this case, the Sales by themselves are hardly usable as they have no context. Looking at the sales by date, product, store, or location now adds value to the sales measures. Since this is a high-level model, it can be considered a conceptual model; in other words, it highlights the main concepts that are involved in the analysis area.

Note there are two lines per dimension. The first identifies the concept and the second details the granularity. For instance, Date in this example is at the day granularity level.

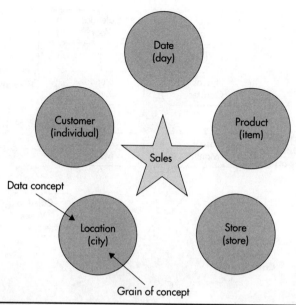

Figure 2-7   *Analysis area model, aka concept model*

We still have to identify the sales measures that will be used in the business reports. For now let us call these "Number of Sales" and "Sales Amount." Typically, measures are amounts and quantities. These measures are not directly shown in the concept model in Figure 2-7 simply because their addition clutters up the model, especially when there can be a number of measures. The measures are detailed in the diagram shown in Figure 2-8.

The dimensions in Figure 2-7 are the fundamental components in a conceptual model. To understand what descriptive details are required for the business requirements, the dimensions, or concepts, can be extended as shown in Figures 2-9 and 2-10. Notice that each descriptive data component, or attribute, is connected to the fundamental dimension. This diagram is simply for communicative purposes; in actuality, the descriptive data components are attributes of the fundamental data component.

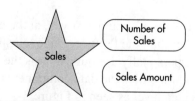

Figure 2-8   *Sales analysis measures*

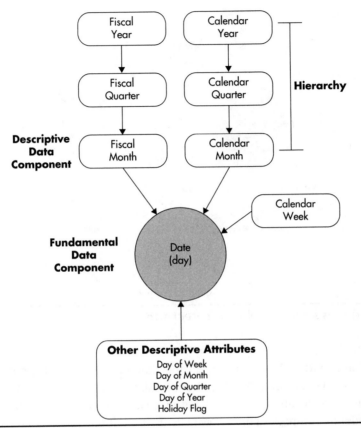

Figure 2-9   *Date concept breakdown*

Typically many dimensions have one or more hierarchies as seen in the Date dimension, which can have fiscal and calendar hierarchies. Also note that the Location dimension has two hierarchies as well, with the province, county, and city belonging to both hierarchies. Hierarchies are used quite often in business analysis. These representations are good communicative and documentation methods to relate the business concepts back to the business to validate the business analysis understanding of the fundamental and descriptive data components and how they inter-relate.

In Figure 2-10, "Internal Region" could easily be at the city or county level, but in this model, it is a level higher than the Province but exclusive of the country.

Another representation I personally use quite a bit is the "pillar" diagram, as seen in Figure 2-11. This method identifies the data components at a high level rather than the metrics at the analysis area level as seen in Figure 2-7.

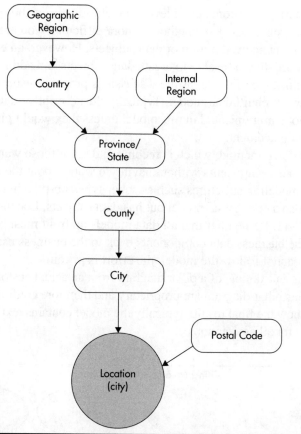

Figure 2-10 *Location concept breakdown*

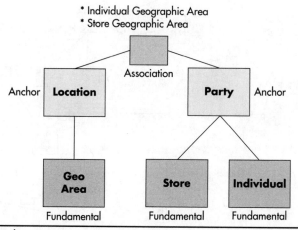

Figure 2-11 *Pillar diagram*

This model starts at the conceptual level and adds details as the subject matter expert interview progresses. This method is more difficult if you are starting from scratch with no preconceived notion of data subjects. However, an experienced data warehouse modeler should be able to create data subjects and add fundamental data components to this type of model as the discussions progress, especially if the data modeler is using a prebuilt data model. Typically the descriptive data components, attributes, are not communicated in this model unless they would give a better understanding of placement.

This is a top-down method, which is recommended for those wanting to understand the data components without having to worry about the exact low-level details or rigid modeling structures such as super-type/sub-type intermediate levels. This model is also a conceptual model but has data subjects, Location and Party, as seen in Figure 2-11. Remember that all data models up front must be able to communicate the business data components back to the business users for validation. If the business cannot follow the model, the effort is in vain.

Figure 2-12 is an example of a pillar diagram from an actual customer engagement. The details of this pillar diagram are proprietary and therefore confidential; however, the point is to show the final result. Typically the model contains text stating business rules, especially for all associations.

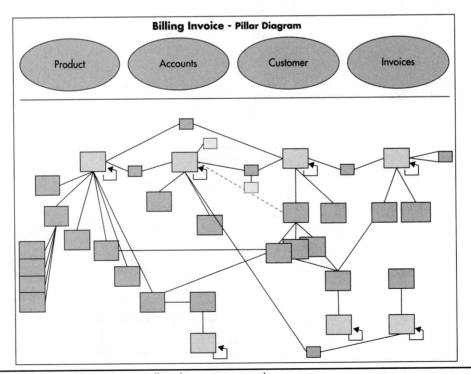

Figure 2-12   *Billing invoice pillar diagram example*

The model starts with the classic data pillars of any business, which generally are: party, product (including services), and location. *Party* is a high-level view of all individuals or organizations, *Product* anchors all the different products and services, and *Location* anchors concepts such as postal addresses, geographic areas, email addresses, and so forth. Every business under the sun requires these three basic pillars of data. These pillars hold up the business activities, which are the transactions or events. Retail businesses have as their primary event point-of-sale transactions, as in our noodle store example. Phone companies have call detail records (aka CDRs or phone calls or text messages). Insurance companies have claims. Every business, no matter what they do, must have these types of basic underlying pillars, hence the "pillar" diagram concept. Of course, there are other pillars depending on the line of business as well as other events.

To focus the business analysis discussions, business subject areas can be highlighted; these are the ovals on the diagram: product, accounts, customer, and invoices. These categories help by giving a perspective to the viewer as to the business areas discussed in developing the diagram. Note that these categories are not all-encompassing from the individual business area perspectives.

Data Architecture

With all the pieces defined, the next component of a data warehouse and business intelligence solution is to understand the actual flow of data throughout the data warehouse system. This is a major component of data architecture.

This is not to be confused with the technical architecture of a data warehouse, which involves the servers, database management systems, operating systems, middleware, software, business intelligence tools, and so forth.

Data architecture typically starts with data as required by the business. The reason for this is to limit the scope of the effort. If you are doing a full top-down approach, the effort would be to find all data in the organization and model it in an understandable data model to see how it all fits together. This would be a huge undertaking, so to be more realistic, this is done in a phased approach based on business subject areas. A data warehouse is not a data dump; every piece of data should be required by the business. If you are doing a bottom-up approach, which is based on business requirements, again a focused phased approach is required, and this is called *focus areas*.

Since all efforts are specifically to support the business, there must be some sort of business value for every deliverable. In other words, if the business is to spend money on a project, they expect to receive some sort of return on investment; this is why a business perspective must be taken for each effort.

When you are determining the underlying data for either approach, data architecture is involves a number of areas such as:

- ▶ Where the data is from: source system (not always a simple task)
- ▶ Who owns the data: data steward
  - ▶ Data profile
  - ▶ Data values
  - ▶ Data definitions
- ▶ Data format
- ▶ Full data technical details including database, platform, and so on
- ▶ Data quality
- ▶ Data availability
  - ▶ When is it available?
  - ▶ How often is it updated?
  - ▶ Are there any dependencies?
- ▶ Source-to-target mapping
- ▶ Transformation rules
  - ▶ Merging rules from multiple system
  - ▶ Delta processing
  - ▶ Temporal changes
- ▶ Data volumetrics
- ▶ Security
- ▶ Lifecycle
  - ▶ Retention period
  - ▶ Regulatory requirements
- ▶ Backups
- ▶ Data models
  - ▶ For capturing and holding
  - ▶ For usage and performance
- ▶ Distribution
- ▶ Usage
- ▶ and everything in between!

Based on all these areas, it is easy to see why a distinct role is required for a data architect. Projects should start with two main roles: a project manager and a data architect. Without a data architect, the project teams—DBA, data modelers, reporting team, ETL team, and source system team—are not being coordinated at a data-flow level. Project managers are tasked with ensuring project planning, ensuring resources, removing political hurdles—essentially, keeping the vehicle on the road and moving toward a particular destination. The data architect ensures that the silos are all functioning in tandem with coordination between roles and phases—the mechanic ensuring that the vehicle is doing what it is supposed to do.

Data architecture can also be thought of as the design of the overall blueprint for creating the data warehouse from a data perspective. There are many aspects to a data warehouse and alternate ways of building, each with its own implications. This book discusses the many facets of the design and how to arrive at something tangible and usable.

Data architecture and data warehouse architecture in this sense are synonymous, but in many instances the latter includes technical architecture as well.

As explained in Figure 2-13, the following are typical data architectures for data warehouse systems.

▶ Bill Inmon's top-down or repository-based approach
  ▶ Central and normalized data warehouse repository
  ▶ Data marts sourced from the repository
  ▶ Subject-oriented
  ▶ Staging environment used for transformation purposes
  ▶ Can become a large project effort if not subject-specific
  ▶ Can be time-consuming
  ▶ Good if strong IT involvement
  ▶ Not so good for departmental mini-IT shops
▶ Ralph Kimball's bottom-up or data mart–oriented approach
  ▶ Conformed dimensions
  ▶ Denormalized
  ▶ Bus architecture
  ▶ Data marts can be sourced directly from operational systems via staging environment
  ▶ Can get caught in a cycle of producing data marts and not conforming to enterprise bus architecture

- ▶ Can get caught in a reporting-only environment scenario
- ▶ More data redundancy means possibly more disk space required
- ▶ More data marts, more difficulties
- ▶ More accepted than top-down approach
- ▶ Hybrid approach
  - ▶ Conformed dimensions
  - ▶ Central normalized repository
  - ▶ Both working together as needed depending on phases and strategic goals
  - ▶ Best of both top-down and bottom-up worlds
- ▶ Other approaches
  - ▶ Distributed or federated
  - ▶ Independent data marts—similar to bottom-up
  - ▶ Interconnected data marts

Mr. Inmon advocates using a central data repository design to hold all the data in a structured normalized manner. Access to the data is typically via data marts, which

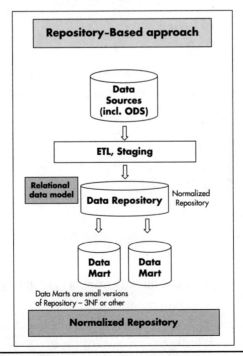

Figure 2-13   *Data architectures*

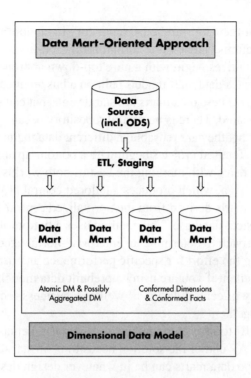

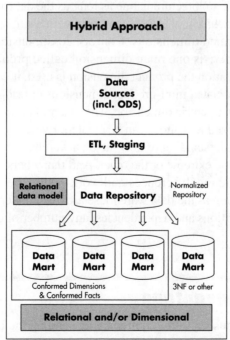

Figure 2-13 *Data architectures* (continued)

are simply a subset of the data warehouse repository in an optimized for use structure. These structures can be third normal form (3NF), star, or snowflake designs. Many IT initiatives begin with a pure top-down approach.

Mr. Kimball advocates data mart models built on a bus architecture, which is simply conformed dimensions. These data marts are star designs but can snowflake out, although this is not desired. There is no central repository because all dimensions are conformed, meaning that they are reusable in different data marts as needed. Most business requirement–focused projects begin with a bottom-up approach.

The hybrid model deals with merging the best of both worlds into one. It uses a normalized central design, which produces a tailored central physical database and uses conformed data marts derived from the normalized central design and populated from the central physical database. This method uses a bottom-up approach along with a top-down approach to determine an enterprise-normalized vocabulary and design while tailoring the effort for specific performance and usage by the business. This approach is excellent if you are using a prebuilt data model, which usually has a normalized repository or central design as well as a business focus area perspective with both mapped together.

These days many BI tools prefer straightforward star schemas. This means that the reporting and OLAP end of the solution needs to be in star data mart format, while the source of the data marts can be in whatever design desired.

Either method of data architecture is fine as long as the data architect is fully aware of the implications of each. Initial efforts can begin with a single or several focused data marts with conformed dimensions. Conformed dimension for "product", for example, means that there is one main dimension called product, and anytime anywhere in the organization the product dimension is used, it will always be the same. There may be other associated mini-product dimensions or bridged dimensions, but there is one main product-centric dimension. Then later after several controlled data marts, a central normalized repository can be created. Everything depends on your philosophy and your understanding of how the data warehouse is to be built. Many data architects lean to one extreme or the other. And many believe a hybrid approach is just right. Understand the differences and work within the area you feel most comfortable with. As long as the data warehouse architect understands all the building blocks and their implications and dependencies, any number of development avenues can be undertaken.

Competitive Advantage

Building a data warehouse system requires understanding the business analytic requirements and the underlying data at an enterprise level. Of course, there is a competitive advantage for the organization to have such an organized environment, which many companies value dearly. The question now becomes how fast can efforts ramp up and time to market, so to speak.

Data Model Build or Buy

One particular method of organizing the data is to purchase a prebuilt data warehouse and/or business intelligence data model. Such a model can save considerable development time and effort since the vendor already went to the trouble of structuring the data in a methodological manner. The idea is to use this sort of data model to kick-start the enterprise effort, which can otherwise be quite an undertaking, especially if you are attacking a data warehouse from a full top-down perspective.

The following list presents the type of questions to think about when considering a prebuilt data model:

► Who built it?

  ► Does the vendor have a history of data modeling and a customer reference base?

► What is the underlying data architecture?

  ► Is the data model stand-alone as a repository, data mart–specific, or part of a larger solution?

► How deep is the solution around the model?

  ► Does it cover not only your line of business but the area your project is focused on?

  ► Does each object have a definition? Do not purchase a model with no entity or attribute definitions!

► How should it be used?

  ► As is

  ► As a reference

► Is it flexible?

  ► Can it be extended?

  ► Just because it is a big model does not mean it covers all of your business. Can it be extended, and what is involved in doing so?

  ► Can it be scoped?

▶ Large models typically mean that there is way more than what is required in the first phase of a typical project. How can the required areas be scoped to generate a physical environment of just the required entities, attributes, and associations?

▶ How can a scoped version be merged with a later scoped version? If you are doing a phased approach, how can the next scoping be merged into the first scoping?

▶ What is required to convert from logical to physical?

▶ Real usage

  ▶ Is specific tooling required? (Erwin, Powerdesigner, IBM IDA, other)

  ▶ How often are releases available?

▶ References and how they are using the model

  ▶ How many models were sold in your particular industry (banking, insurance, retail, telecommunications…)?

  ▶ How many in your line of business are doing the same effort as yourself?

    ▶ If 20 items were sold for retail but no one is doing distribution, ask why.

▶ Is maintenance required and what is included?

  ▶ If you are paying for maintenance, be sure the vendor is producing new model versions. There's no use paying for maintenance each year if the vendor only produces a new version or minor changes every two to three years. Ensure that the maintenance contract details specific vendor efforts such as adding regulatory features and so forth, and specific target dates.

▶ Consulting services

  ▶ Does the vendor offer consulting services to educate the purchaser on model content and best practices?

▶ On the buyer side

  ▶ In-house skills and resources available for the project and new data model.

Purchasing a pre-existing model can be a real time-saver and really advance a project's current and future efforts. Pre-existing models need to have fundamental entities, descriptive attributes, and show how all inter-relate (associations). In addition, everything needs to be documented. Never purchase a data model if the entities and attributes are not fully described; the more examples used in describing each item, the better the model. Remember, a data model is a communicative device to explain how the business functions from a data perspective—not necessarily the business processes themselves, but the underlying data and how they all interconnect. Because a model is a communicative tool, it may be modeled visually in a particular fashion but implemented quite differently, so vendor consulting and education services are quite important at first use.

Prebuilt models can be complicated simply because they hold lots of information. Remember that prebuilt data models span lines of business as they pertain to organizations around the world. A telecommunications data model may only contain prepaid calling card information, but you want billing information. Be sure the data model covers your specific business needs.

Here's an interesting point I learned some years ago regarding the size of a vendor firm: Corporations are like ships; the large ones take much more time in turning and taking new direction while smaller vessels are quicker to react to trends, corrections, and can build tailored solutions in record time. Just because a vendor is smaller than the competitor does not mean their product is less worthy. Silicon Valley produced many small startups that turned into billion-dollar corporations.

Prebuilt models come in many different flavors:

▶ **Very specific data mart or data usage focus**   Invoicing analysis or customer relationship management pertaining to geographic location only

▶ **Business solution focus**   Retail inventory

▶ **Data warehouse repository focus**   An IT or data management perspective focused on data in the enterprise rather than business intelligence usage

▶ **Overall data warehouse and business intelligence focus**   Full business focus areas, enterprise vocabulary (integrated data dictionary), atomic enterprise repository, data marts (3NF and stars), such as IBM Industry Models

▶ **Technical architecture focus**   Tightly integrated with DBMS, optimizer, reporting (Teradata)

Prebuilt data models can save months of effort if used properly. For the larger models, be sure to obtain services when purchasing the data model. These vendor consultants will explain the data model usage and purpose, and help guide the data architecture of the project. But it's best to understand where you need help. Just having an expensive hired hand without direction other than "help please" is carte blanche for the consultant to decide what should be done. As mentioned before, physical implementation may be quite different from a design model, so be sure to discuss data architecture and the pros and cons of different physical implementations.

Another alternative method is to build a data model yourself. Beware of this method, because doing something incorrectly in the design phase can have a huge impact later during the build and implementation phases or when adding to the design in the next phase. This is the same for any up-front effort. If the business analysis is incomplete, this will have a negative effect on scoping, which will spread in a domino effect to the design, build, implementation, and final deliverables.

A proven prebuilt model will have worked out the fundamental data components and their complex interdependencies. Even if such a model is not completely used, it can act as a reference point. The same cannot be said if you build on your own.

A data warehouse effort can be quite complicated, whether you build from the bottom up or the top down or take a hybrid approach. Data modeling done wrong or poorly up front will affect the overall result in all of these cases. Figure 2-14 shows an example of the impact of poor data modeling.

Just as with purchasing a prebuilt data model, the in-house data modeling experts must know how to model a data warehouse solution. This means they must be aware of how to model a data warehouse repository and data marts. Each is designed for different purposes; data warehouse repository is to capture and hold data, while data marts are for end-user usage and performance. Be sure to have seasoned data modelers who understand both methods and can help in the data architecture of the overall current solution as well as positioning for the overall strategy.

Mentoring the Business

The previous sections covered the data, its importance, its quality, vocabulary, and components to understand how to organize the data. To jump to the next level, we should be interested in what to do with the data, or rather, what the business wants to

Poor Data Modeling almost always results in lots of rework:
>
> RE-ANALYSE requirements
>
> RE-DESIGN data models
>
> RE-CREATE database
>
> RE-WRITE ETL scripts
>
> RE-RUN ETL
>
> RE-LOAD database
>
> RE-OPTIMIZE database
>
> RE-DESIGN data marts and BI output
>
> RE-BUILD data marts
>
> RE-WRITE reports
>
> RE-RUN reports
>
> RE-TRAIN business users
>
> RE-DOCUMENT
>
> RE-DO production maintenance procedures

Figure 2-14   *Data model failure impact*

do with the data today and tomorrow. What are the business strategy and typical operations? When the business uses the data in context to obtain an understanding of how the business or a business component functions, IT should be there, as this is a major portion of business intelligence. The data warehouse supports business intelligence by holding and organizing the data and making it available to the business in a timely manner. The business intelligence portion supports the business by allowing the business users to dynamically access the data at will. IT should be tightly coupled with the business to understand requirements and direction and not simply sit around waiting for the next support order to trickle in.

The people who support the business from a data perspective, typically under a business intelligence umbrella, should really want to be a part of the business itself. These people should not simply wait on the business but help the business by being proactive. The reporting team and business analysts should not be pure IT resources, but a bridge to and for the business. These roles should try to understand the business operations and add value by interpreting the business needs. In short, a business intelligence effort in the organization spans the business and IT. Business decides what they require and IT supports them. However, if IT can learn the business, becoming familiar with the business events, causalities, direction, and milestones, BI could help the managers run the business better and more effectively through the use of data insights.

Every business intelligence team should have dedicated personnel for each major business value chain. These resources should attend regular meetings with the business representatives to get an understanding of the business direction and expectations. This gives both business and IT a chance to understand each other's requirements, schedules, and dependencies. Being proactive will give IT a chance to plan efforts and resources appropriately to fully support the business initiatives. This relationship should evolve to the point where the business wants the BI person to work with them—this is how important and integrated the role should be.

Business intelligence should not wait on the business; if it does, there will always be a state of reaction and stress wondering if the next e-mail or phone call will be a two-minute effort or a four-week effort. Juggling these on-the-spot requests can really add up and really play havoc with BI planning efforts.

The following list describes some BI best practices:

▶ The BI team should not wait on the business—BI is not a restaurant.

▶ The BI team should not be in a constant reaction mode.

▶ The BI team should be responsive but in a planned state.

▶ The BI team should be actively involved in the business.

▶ The BI team should be contributing proactively to the business.

> ▶ The business should be asking the BI team for insights.

> ▶ The business should be planning with the BI team.

> ▶ The business should share the costs and overhead of the BI team up front and ongoing.

> ▶ The BI team should monitor business involvement as it grows to understand their own future resource requirements.

> ▶ The BI team should be centralized: center of excellence.

The BI team is a subset of the overall data warehouse efforts. Once the data warehouse is implemented and production support takes over the daily oiling of the bolts, ensuring that the machine ticks along nicely, the data warehousing team can focus on other technical, data, and business areas. This is not to say that the data warehouse team is dismantled; it simply means that the goals change. The number of overall team members can be reduced, but because a data warehouse is a system, it will still require a core group to support it. The business intelligence specialists, however, should remain but should be switched from a delivery mode to a proactive mode in partnership with the business.

Data warehouse efforts may be distributed (matrix managed), but the BI portion must be central. Data warehouse and business intelligence should form part of the overall business performance management effort.

CHAPTER 3

Reasons for Building

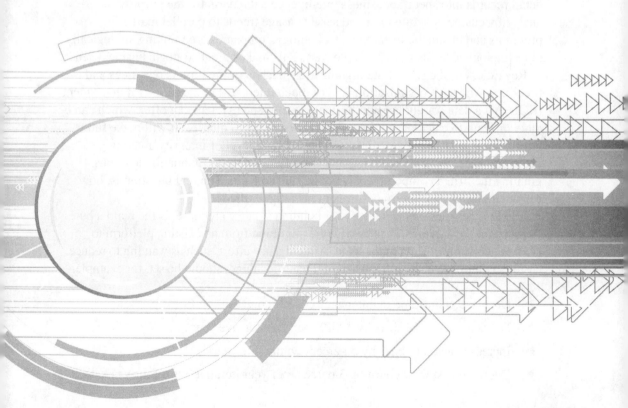

There are many reasons to build or not to build a data warehouse or business intelligence solution. Large blue chip organizations most definitely are interested in creating one central vocabulary and therefore a "one version of the truth" data environment. This is simply because the business is so large that it takes quite an effort ensuring that everyone dealing with apples is indeed dealing with apples and not oranges. Essentially, every organization typically has massive quantities of raw data that needs to be analyzed for trends, associations, predictions, baselining, and so forth to give insights and competitive advantages.

On several occasions I have been involved with organizations that have realized the value and impact of proper data management and analysis at the onset of their venture and commissioned the creation of a data warehouse and business intelligence system while the organization was in its infancy. Before their doors opened and any services were provided to the general public, these startup organizations decided to position themselves advantageously in their marketplace with the ability to analyze service usage, network usage, and customer acquisition and churn as part of their business strategy. For example, at one telephone company we designed and architected a data warehouse using their network and billing systems to capture call detail records into specific business intelligence data marts for the purpose of analyzing customer acquisition and service usage trends to parallel marketing programs and channels. In essence, technology companies are thinking strategically in technological terms right from the start. This makes great strategic business sense.

Regardless of the size of the organization, each is limited by its resources and timelines. And each organization is very much interested in the return on investment (ROI) that a data warehouse and business intelligence system can offer, which can be quite difficult to calculate. A data warehouse is easy to qualify: It will make future efforts more reliable because data will have a high level of integrity, making decisions more accurate, realizing and solidifying the data foundation and thus granting the firm a competitive advantage, and so forth. The real question is, how can a data warehouse return on investment be quantified?

The ROI depends on the strategy for building a data warehouse. Is the build a pure IT focus for cost savings, such as with the migration from an existing platform to another? Or is the effort a pure business intelligence effort, such as wanting to reduce customer churn? Whatever the reason, a quantified target should be set, for example:

▶ Decrease mainframe maintenance costs by one million Euros per year

▶ Decrease software costs by $250K per year for five years

▶ Increase customer base by 5 percent within one year

▶ Decrease customer churn by 3 percent per year iteratively for four years

Perhaps calculating the average or estimated average revenue per user (ARPU) multiplied by the number of customers retained or increased can quantify a revenue potential. Forecasting sales based on a baseline or trends is another possible method of estimating revenue increase that can be attributed to insights gained from a data warehouse environment. The trick in this case, as with any other corporate asset, is to determine the potential revenue gain or cost reduction based on capitalizing the data warehouse. If the gain or savings outweigh the development costs and capital expenditures, then the data warehouse is viable from an ROI point of view.

It is important to reiterate, however, that tagging a fiscal perspective to a data warehouse effort may be difficult. Determining the fiscal savings that will result from standardizing the corporate data vocabulary or centralizing data from disparate sources into one central environment may be quite difficult, if not impossible. One perspective is to understand the reason for building the data warehouse and business intelligence solution. By gaining a clear insight into the type of environment to be built, you may find that costing and revenue are simpler to identify and calculate. At the least, understanding why your data warehouse system is being built gives insight into how to approach the project.

Popular scenarios that have brought about the development of data warehouse systems include

▶ Migration from existing platforms

▶ Centralizing diverse data warehouses

▶ Consolidating diverse data marts

▶ New initiatives

▶ IT just-build-it scenario

▶ Data floundation scenario (yes, "floundation")

The following section details popular scenarios for building or not building data warehouse and business intelligence solutions, along with insights involved with each.

Platform Migration

Building a data warehouse based on a migration objective can be due to a re-platforming strategy. This usually happens when a data warehouse grew from legacy systems, most likely on a mainframe operating system that has been operational for years. The strategy now is to move to mid-level servers. The main reason is usually to reduce cost or because the mainframe is being decommissioned. In many cases, the monthly maintenance cost of the mainframe is more expensive than the combined cost of moving to a new platform and purchasing all new software. This is an excellent opportunity to purchase prebuilt data warehouse data model, database, disk, and so forth.

Business Continuity

From a pure business point of view, since a data warehouse system and all the trimmings already exist, there are expectations of business continuity. This means that the organization has been operating based on currently developed reporting programs, databases, loading routines, and so forth on the legacy system for some time. More importantly, the business has stabilized on current reports. The data may have levels of doubt, but it must be assumed that since the legacy system has been operational and the business has been receiving regularly scheduled reports, the business has been functioning from some baseline one way or another. It is this regularity and current baseline that are quite important. Deviating drastically from this current level can be devastating to the business, and therefore a sense of business continuity must remain.

A migration from one platform to another means many technical changes, which may lead to changes in the reported information. It is not unusual to change programs or completely rewrite programs during a migration and find that the results are dissimilar. Differences could be due to an undocumented bug fix from years ago that has not migrated properly or a misinterpretation of underlying program logic, but either way, the resulting output may change. To make matters worse, the resulting difference may not be noticed at the initiating program level but at a dependent program downstream. In other words, data may be changed from one program, but you might not realize the change until down the line from another program's output.

The end result is that the final reports may not be reporting figures in the new system that are identical to those produced from the legacy system. If an audit trail is possible, then there is traceability for report line items, but if not, there may be embarrassing moments for upper management because there is no way to determine how figures were aggregated or derived.

Reverse Engineering

Another major effort with a re-platforming scenario is in reverse-engineering the current data warehouse system to understand how it was built, which is always a major undertaking. In my opinion, reverse-engineering is always a more time-consuming effort than rewriting programs from scratch.

A worst-case scenario is that many legacy systems have poorly documented program specifications, if any at all, and in most cases, updates or corrections have not been recorded over the years. With one particular customer, we had COBOL program load modules that lacked source code. In other words, the program was running and working, but there was no documentation of the actual program code itself. No one knew exactly what the program was doing. It ran once a year at year end but it was undocumented—very dangerous for the business. If for some reason it had stopped running, possibly due to improper data values, data format, or whatever, it would have been fatal to the business reporting environment.

Reverse-engineering is a fact of life in certain instances and must be done. Efforts must include time to investigate what processes actually do, how they do what they do, and re-create them in the new language, possibly on a new platform. This takes time and effort. Nearly every attempt I have witnessed has been underestimated, which translates to budget overruns. The end result is that the project to migrate from the legacy system to a new platform takes considerably longer than anticipated, requires more people than anticipated, and costs more than expected. Outsourcing such efforts is an option that has proven to be quite successful at times and dreadfully unsuccessful in other instances.

In conclusion, reverse-engineering efforts can be costly and at times impossible. However, if the legacy system is documented and the logic of the existing software can be determined from the programs, then a reverse-engineering effort is feasible, but it will take time and effort.

Data Quality

In most instances, higher costs are not simply due to a migration effort but due to data quality issues, which always arise. Data quality at times seems to be the root of all evil in a data warehouse. Chapter 2 discussed what data quality is, but how far should efforts go in correcting them for the task at hand? Data quality efforts usually take time to resolve because a profiling must be done, an owner must be found, and management must decide on corrective action; bypass, fix at the source, fix during ETL, and so on. Even though best practices dictate that all data quality issues should be corrected where they originate, fixing data in a source system may be impractical and may at times be resisted by the source system management. Hence executive management must facilitate and decide on the course of action, and the data warehouse manager must then design and build accordingly.

In most migrations of legacy systems to another platform, data quality issues are a large portion of the efforts, especially if the legacy data warehouse system is quite old. Years ago there was less of an issue about data quality because the data was focused more toward a single usage and in many instances from a single source. Now with the understanding of the importance of sharing data throughout the enterprise and therefore the sharing of disparate sources, many important issues arise, such as vocabulary and data values. A complicated legacy issue of data quality is with the reuse of data fields. Old COBOL programs used 77 level redefines, which means that a data field could be in one instance referring to the value X and in another instance referring to the value of Y. As such, data sources can in effect be mixed together and difficult, but not impossible, to separate.

One customer had a legacy source feeding their legacy data warehouse. A particular loading program looked for an "X" in position 286 of the source file. If the "X" appeared, certain specific logic would be performed. No one knew what the "X" represented or how it came to be. When this was brought up in a management meeting, it turned out that the director of the source system was the person who coded this logic ten years earlier. Unfortunately she did not remember exactly what it represented or why it existed, just that when it was used, the results seemed more appropriate. This data quality issue had a downstream dependency and as such was let to die another day. But what would happen if this step suddenly no longer showed up in the source file? Would existing reports be affected? All data quality issues should be documented and investigated. Do not leave such issues outstanding to be fixed later.

Parallel Environments

In nearly all projects doing a platform migration effort, the business always, for some reason, believes they can run the old mainframe system and the newly built system in parallel for only a short time, such as a month or two, before dropping the legacy system. This has never happened in my experience, as parallel existence usually lasts for a minimum of three to six months depending on the reporting granularity: daily, monthly, or quarterly.

Think of it this way: The business has been using the legacy data warehouse and has been making decisions based on its output for some time. If data quality issues arise, the end result may be that key performance indicators (aka measures or metrics) can change. This means that the business may no longer be working with the same facts, thereby impacting the decision-making process, which could mean a drastic change in business operations or direction. In these cases the business may decide to put a hold on the switchover to figure out why there are such differences between the legacy and the newly re-platformed systems.

Running both old and new systems in parallel for a planned duration is a good idea. I find it is always a good idea to have more than one or two parallel comparison months. For example, if the granularity of reporting is monthly, it is probably a good idea to have at least three to six months of both environments running in parallel. I find organizations that run both old and new systems for such periods are much more confident when they decide to pull the plug on the legacy system. The reason is that the first month typically shows unforeseen discrepancies. If all goes well and all issues are corrected, the second month can validate the corrected results. The third month would double-confirm whether all is going well and give management the due diligence required to complete the migration to the new system. In this case three months would be satisfactory, but more may be necessary if other substantial discrepancies appear.

Several years ago a large bank migrated from a legacy mainframe data warehouse system to a newly platformed system. Unfortunately, even with all efforts to resolve data quality and reverse-engineering issues, they still found themselves in a situation where their old and new systems did not report the same results and they could not figure out the reason for the differences. If they had blindly accepted the situation and reported their new financial accounts to the general public, which included several large mutual funds, their stock value would surely have dwindled due to their financial statements being drastically different from one reporting period to the next. In this case, management did decide to delay the data warehouse implementation until differences could be reconciled, which took only another couple of months.

Added Value

When overruns begin in a pure re-platforming approach, it is typical to solicit an end-user project. By running both the migration effort and adding value to the new system for a specific purpose/customer (aka end users), the budget for the new project can help fund the over-budget platform migration effort.

This business-savvy approach can also add steam to the entire data warehouse effort as more business people are jumping on board. There is the added complication of managing different programs, but the project can be extended while producing more internal marketing effort. Typically a re-platforming effort does include new business intelligence endeavors, but usually the BI effort must wait for the data quality and reverse-engineering efforts to complete.

Data Warehouse Centralization

The idea behind a data warehouse centralization objective is to gather all the information from the data, processes, architectures, and uses from several pre-existing data warehouses and merge them into one central environment, aka system. This effort can be logical or physical in nature.

The migration of several data warehouses in a centralization objective can include a re-platforming effort as one or more of the existing data warehouses can be on disparate servers and on different or similar operating systems. The idea here is twofold; centralizing on one platform would reduce hardware and support costs in a physical scenario and allow for a central data strategy to take root under both logical and physical scenarios.

These types of centralization scenarios are typically undertaken when corporations acquire other corporations or when two or more data warehouses have been created in a single organization and are now being merged.

Corporate Merger

In a corporate merger scenario a doctor's visit is first in order. This means that before doing anything, an intense examination of each data warehouse must be done. Is each data warehouse at the departmental or enterprise level? Are sources similar or completely new? Should the plan be to stick with the parent architecture and strategy, go with the newly acquired solution, or a hybrid of both? Of course, the physical examination spans the overall business as well, including a resource skill analysis as well as a technical architecture evaluation.

In-house Merging

For in-house merging of systems, chances are that either one of two events occurred. Either it was noticed that costs to run two or more full data warehouse systems were ridiculously high, and/or business decided that having all data in one central environment, as is the primary purpose of a data warehouse, is best for the organization. In many cases, departments are politically motivated to create their own business intelligence solution, especially in the financial and insurance sectors. Executives in these organizations are very much dependent on their annual bonuses, which can be quite lucrative and therefore a push for their own results regardless of other divisions' results and efforts becomes a full-blown data warehouse solution at the department level.

Central Design and Local Usage

In other in-house merging scenarios, an organization may span the globe with hubs all over the world. For these organizations, a strategic vision is to consolidate the corporate asset into a central design, integration, and data environment. This may or may not necessarily result in a central database repository, but possibly in a federated or satellite data warehouse solution with a centralized design and centralized coordination. Individual locations may administer their data warehouses while the designs and architectures are controlled centrally, thus ensuring an enterprise data vocabulary, distribution of reporting strategies, and therefore financial accounting standardization and insights.

In either scenario, a discovery project must be done before any efforts on consolidation take place. There must be awareness of each environment being merged, in order to determine the underlying data components, processes, architectures, usage, and so forth. The major point to these approaches from a business perspective is to centralize all the data knowledge into a common area accessible by all involved parties. This means that everyone would be talking apples and apples rather than apples and oranges. From an IT data perspective, the main objective is to create a common vocabulary and structure the data accordingly to create an enterprise standardization.

This approach typically begins with an IT investigation with or without business support. In fact, the effort is an overall business function, but the first step, determining what assets are under the roof, becomes an IT initiative. The efforts that follow become a business decision on how to proceed based on enterprise usage and value. This is usually not a just-build-it approach (which will be explained later in this chapter), as it becomes part of the enterprise data-strategy direction and requires business sponsors and representatives going forward.

Data Mart Consolidation

With this scenario, several departments have their own data mart environments. Sources may or may not be the same, and reporting is typically different, but there may be some sort of conformity with the underlying data.

The data warehouses can be managed purely at the business department level, or partly administered by Information Technology. In either scenario, it has been determined that the impact of having these independent environments is becoming a liability and is no longer in the best interest of the departments themselves or in general to the organization.

Perhaps the business departments have their own mini-IT shops and feel that pulling data from many source systems is becoming quite difficult and complicated. At this point the business feels that if IT could manage and support the physical environment overall, it would be more advantageous. IT has the people who know how to extract from the source (aka operational or functional) systems and are better suited to design and build a more robust environment than the mini-IT shop in the end-user department. The end-user resources typically include business analysts, report writers, and maybe a junior database person.

This scenario varies from light to heavy in terms of data warehouse development. The idea is similar to the data warehouse centralization strategy, but in this scenario the data warehouse environment may not really be created yet. The business mini-IT shops may currently be doing analytical reporting, but not from a robust strategic data warehouse perspective. They may be using departmental data marts scoped and tuned only for their own purposes. Reporting in this scenario is typically done via Microsoft Access and Excel. Data design can range from home-grown dimensions and fact tables, which are completely independent of any conformity, to a hybrid of star, snowflakes, and third normal form modeling along with tables that just seem to work. On the other hand, designs can be proper conformed dimensions and nice star schemas but unconformed to the other department data marts.

This scenario is normally seen in smaller departments which use MS Access and Excel quite heavily. There are usually one or two key technical people who grab the data from several source systems and massage it into something they consider usable by the business users. This approach is business usage–heavy, with many reports already developed and in use. The problem is that, in the worst case, there are many redundant reports, which a good BI tool could possibly merge into one nice cube. See the discussion in Chapter 1 in the section "BI User Presentation."

These types of departmental data mart systems are usually from first data warehouse efforts. They were developed to hold historical transactions, since the source systems typically only held transactions for a short current period. Usually there is some sort of general aggregation to get the data ready for everyone else in the department so they can do as they wish. Unfortunately this means that the real business usage requirements are not always 100 percent known. After three to four of these types of data marts, the administration becomes difficult and IT is asked to assist with some sort of centralization and population effort. Of course, data quality issues seem to be popping up all over the place as end users are simply used to data being incorrect or incomplete, for instance, by the period's adjustments.

Other scenarios are multiple departments each having their own data mart environments. Some may be at the level already mentioned; others may be more advanced. Either way, the development approach here is to understand what the business is currently using from a reporting perspective and then to extract the data components. This means understanding the business terminology, or vocabulary, and converting to fundamental data components. A conformed dimension model may be a perfect fit for these types of efforts along with bus architecture or a normalized logical design to integrate into an enterprise model.

The positive aspect about these environments is that the business may already have pretty good business and source analysts. Since they had to fend for themselves for so long, they usually know a thing or two about the business usage and the source systems. The head business analyst in these scenarios usually becomes the department subject matter expert—but be careful. These analysts may know the data and what the business does, but they do not necessarily know what the second or third guy down the line does with the results.

The downside of these scenarios is that the business usually wants to keep control over their environment development to a certain extent. This is especially true if the business is using advanced BI tools. There is a feeling that the business analysts can design the data requirements themselves and IT should really serve the business. It is important for IT at this point to become involved in the business to ease them out of managing the data, in order to determine the real business requirements and usage. The business intelligence effort here is not simply to move population efforts over to IT but to work together in building a true BI environment from usage back to design, then to sourcing, and finally to overall build. A data architect should be very hands-on in these types of efforts. At the same time it is important that IT does not take over the initiative, trying to bypass the current business side analysts and jump directly to business users without them. This would cause riffs and political hindrance overall.

Focus on the solution for the first efforts, not on who owns what or on petty political issues. Get to a tangible and usable solution that adds value to the business in as short a time as possible in the most structured manner causing the least pain. Once the solution is in place, the business users will realize the positive benefits from the new system which will foster a closer partnership between the business technical people and IT, granting the opportunity for IT to get more than just a foot in the door.

New Initiative

The "new initiative" approach is, or should be, a partnership between the business and IT. Typically the business is interested in creating a business intelligence solution for reporting and possibly an advanced solution involving dashboards and scorecards. The business may have a reporting environment, but essentially this is considered a "start from scratch" effort. The idea with this scenario is that the business has a strategy for timely and accurate reporting to analyze the business fundamentals and reduce costs and increase revenues.

For supply chain readers, this is called a *make-to-order effort*. The project is to build a data warehouse to support a business intelligence scenario in a timely manner with a focus on value added to the business. The great advantage of this scenario is that the business is willing to support a new development project and is typically much involved with the project effort.

The start of a new data warehouse initiative frequently involves much hype from both business and IT, with everyone anxious to begin. Initially there is much forgiveness in timelines, since it is understood that no one has built such an environment in the organization before. Progress may be somewhat slow, but within reason because resources are still learning the ropes and differences between data warehousing and the current transaction systems. It's always good to bring in a seasoned external consultant in the initial phases of such projects.

IT is tasked with carrying out the project effort to build the environment with full business support. This means that IT can integrate this effort into an enterprise data strategy with best practices. However, focus must not be lost, as the goal is to add value to the business. Also be careful not to fall victim to scope creep. At this point, the word is out and expectations are high, and as such the scope is being added to—just one more piece of data for one or two more reports, which will make a huge impact. Carefully phase the initial efforts and contain the requirements. If a data warehouse effort was never attempted in the organization before, beware that the first phase of a data warehouse requires much foundation to be built. Add value for the initial business usage, but realize that considerable effort will be on foundation building. If a data warehouse was attempted before, and most likely failed—which is why it is restarting from scratch—be aware of why the first time did not succeed, and again limit scope creep.

If the effort is for a department-level solution, then the project is usually focused on data marts and sourcing, with data architecture keeping an eye on enterprise standards. If the effort is beginning at the department level but sanctioned at the executive level for an overall enterprise strategy, then the project becomes a full-blown enterprise data warehouse initiative with initial efforts to support the requesting department. Both types of efforts are actually the same, but each has a slightly different focus. The first focus is on specific business value with IT ensuring conformity to vocabulary, data structures, and data quality while applying best practices. The second focus is much more centered on ensuring an enterprise data warehouse and business intelligence strategy for the entire organization while delivering a specific business application in the first iteration.

Executive championship at the CIO level is highly required to ensure that both of these scenarios are able to control future development to keep the data warehouse aligned as the one central version of the truth. If the first scenario turns into a data mart consolidation effort or the latter into a data warehouse centralization effort down the road, then the initial enterprise strategy was lost up front. The data architect, project manager, and executive management along with the business sponsor must all work towards an enterprise solution.

A caution point of a new initiative could be that the business does not fully understand the design phase, aka logical data modeling, and believes that building is simply creating database tables and populating them with data. Intentions regarding data quality issues are good at first with the goal to fix all problems, but as the project progresses and more data quality issues arise, the priority for fixing the data diminishes, especially if the project timelines are closing in. The underlying view is to build fast, even though common sense says it may take a while. There should be awareness and effort to not let this evolve into a data floundation effort (which will be explained later in this chapter).

A new initiative can be to reduce load on operational systems with the creation of a specific optimized environment designed for reporting or OLAP analytics. In all cases the design would be to allow for simplicity of use while ensuring that all data from disparate source systems is gathered in one central area with security and data quality in place. Efficiency may also be realized from special data structure designs, as these differ between a business intelligence system and a transaction-oriented system. An enterprise central go-to place with conformed vocabulary with coordination of administration and usage is a real competitive advantage to an organization, and a true corporate asset.

New Initiative: Dynamic Reporting

By far the most popular business intelligence project is IT taking on the role of a hired development team with little business involvement. The DW team is asked to build a BI solution for specific reporting needs. The project is a pure build of specific reports in a dynamic environment enabling drill-down or drill-up. The effort is a business intelligence focus but leans towards a pure data warehouse perspective simply because the IT effort is blindly given a number of reports. The solution is to give the business a dynamic view of their data in a predetermined report manner via OLAP visualization.

The idea behind this scenario is that the business will have the ability to look at specific reports at will and to analyze the data based on the reporting boundaries with drill-down and drill-up capabilities. A potential drawback of this scenario is that the data warehouse team is not acting as an active part of the business solution. In this scenario the team is simply taking on the task of figuring out how to make the effort work. The team should really be involved with the business to not only determine how to deliver a new reporting environment but also to analyze and create a proper and appropriate reporting solution for the business purpose. Many data warehouse or business intelligence efforts fail because of the way this type of project is approached—do not be a restaurant waiter and simply take the order: Work in the kitchen with the chef to determine the meal best suited for their clientele. At minimum the designs for the reports should be based on more than just the specific reports at hand and take into account the underlying data associations.

In this scenario the team may be given a number of reports, possibly 100 or 120,000 reports as in my previous example, and asked to build a data warehouse to support these. What is your first step? Typically you would try to organize the reports into some sort of bundles, aka business focus areas. But there always seem to be handfuls that do not quite fit one area or the other, so the reports are prioritized into different types of internal bundles: simple, mediocre, and complicated. Then the effort is to analyze each area in a phased manner one after the other. The perception of the report priorities is based on a once-over as to the amount of differing data the reports contain. Then each report is discussed with the business, which becomes a bit annoyed at such a lengthy process, and eventually the items at the bottom of the pile are just tagged with a priority ranking. Sounds familiar!

Finally the actual analysis effort begins, which can be quite time-consuming. This first phase is to analyze and discover the underlying data components of each report. Typically the reports themselves are a mixture of other reports either from existing systems or derived from Excel. The business typically includes additional "added value," which essentially is a "wish list" of reports accompanying the ones they already use. The refined list of reports becomes the initial deliverable goal, and the major aspect of the effort is to determine the underlying data components and structure them in an optimized manner for effective usage. In many instances, the business supplies simple report specifications that are unclear and need refinement, and the business SME is hardly ever available, making the analysis effort nearly impossible and delaying scheduled timelines. Ensure that report specifications are documented up front before strict timelines for analysis and development begin.

This scenario also fits into many of the other reasons to build scenarios. Platform migration, data warehouse centralization, and data mart consolidation typically all have this scenario in some fashion within its scoped boundaries.

"Just Build It"

This data warehouse strategy is purely based on an IT approach. In supply chain management, this is called a "make-to-stock" project with hopes that after the environment is built, demand for consumption will flourish. Typically this effort originates from the data architecture, database group, or a new IT manager who has seen the benefit of a data warehouse and is convinced the organization should head in this direction whether the corporate strategic direction dictates it or not.

A just-build-it scenario is a pure top-down approach based on designing a central data layer to identify all the data within the organization. Of course, there is some sort of prioritization in this approach to ensure that the fundamental data of the organization is captured. This usually involves the main transactional data of the organization along with primary subject areas, aka data pillars. For example, within a telecommunication organization, the main data components for the majority of departments are the call detail records (CDRs). Hence all CDR details will be captured, which includes called and calling telephone numbers, the carriers involved in all calls, duration of calls, cost of calls, time of call, type of call (voice, SMS, data, and so on), along with the fundamental pillars: customer, product, and location data. For retail organizations, the first just-build-it effort would focus on the point-of-sale transactions: product identification, sales amount, number of items sold, store, and so forth.

The good thing about a just-build-it approach is that IT has vision and is doing something positive for the organization for the long run—or so they believe. The bad thing about this approach is that IT is building at their leisure with no particular business usage focus. This means a very low budget, and the project is probably the senior data guru's or manager's pet project. Typically IT is on a quest to find support within the business community from a middle management perspective without upper management buy-in.

In these scenarios a home-grown data model is typically created. If the model is built with flexibility in mind, all will be fine. If the model is built based on "boiling the ocean," meaning trying to analyze all data at once, the effort will burn out simply because too much is being attempted at once. You will probably hear about how such an effort was attempted several years ago, or they tried that but it became overwhelming and resources became quite busy, so they had to drop it. These efforts tend to work out best when a prebuilt data model is purchased and followed to give structure and organization to the effort. If an enterprise data model is home-grown based on one project effort, it may be discovered that the model has to change for the second, third, and following projects. The end result is that an enterprise view slowly erodes because of the constant redesigning. A prebought model allows for some sort of up-front structure to see how elements can be placed and gives a good methodology for organizing the data going forward. More information on structuring data models will be presented in Part II of this book.

These just-build-it efforts can also get a bad reputation, as they are constantly marketed within the organization in an almost preaching fashion. Business users become tired of hearing what they should do and tend to shy away. Mind you, once a sponsor is acquired, focus can be achieved and development can move forward quite rapidly.

When it comes down to the fine points, a just-build-it effort is costly and unfocused. If such an effort is to create an enterprise vocabulary and enterprise logical data model with no reporting aspects, no database environments, no ETL efforts, just a data design exercise sometimes with data sourcing, sometimes without, then the attempt is well placed. Remember, a data warehouse is supposed to add value to a business. If the effort includes the building of an enterprise data repository, it may seem like a good idea but has no ROI association and therefore has no business usage or value. Which area should the data modeler work on: customers, products, or events? If the IT strategy is to build such an environment, then there should be sponsorship, a budget, a focus, and therefore business value. If this is a manager's initiative, there may be an opportunity cost in resource assignment and effort that may oppose the current business initiatives.

Data Floundation

Yes, this is spelled correctly.

Data floundation refers to data within the data warehouse behaving badly; in other words, a fumbling struggle at ensuring best practices for data. This approach is not recommended and unfortunately exists more than it should. The idea is that a specific area of the business will ask to have their data requirements added to an existing data warehouse initiative, which may already exist or may be in its first stages of life. In the latter case, the data warehouse manager is usually thirsting for business support and extra budget, which makes the project especially vulnerable to any sort of recognition and therefore to a data floundation situation.

The business simply wants to get something going fast as it probably has its own business intelligence program already under way. There is no regard for data modeling, enterprise vocabulary, or synchronizing with existing efforts because all will be thrown away in several months when the budget gets approved for a full proper business intelligence effort—or so they say. This causes an awkward struggle for IT as to whether or not it should ensure data quality, best practices, and data architecture. Do not be taken in by this scenario, whether it is intentional or not. The data warehouse should always stick to its rules of proper project management including data analysis, data model design, data sourcing, data mapping, data quality, and implementation procedures. Throwaway systems have a funny way of sticking around for many years. Nothing is worse than having a throwaway project break all the rules and then stick around for a while. It's kind of like having an uninvited guest at your party who just showed up and will not leave.

These types of data warehouse additions are generally advocated by the business because they have no resource availability and are willing to pay IT for a quick and dirty effort. This gives added funding to the data warehouse budget and allows for a quick buy-in, but over the long haul, data floundation efforts hurt more than they are worth. In short, do not become involved in these types of initiatives. Let the business know that all data warehouse and business intelligence efforts must follow best practices up front.

If the business area is new to data warehousing and business intelligence, there may be a level of ignorance as to the complexity of building such an environment, hence contempt for data management. For some reason there may be a feeling that data is available in source systems, which is accessible, and all that is required is to pull it into a new database designed for business intelligence. Then reporting can easily access the database and begin reporting. Of course if the data is bad, it will be fixed as the project determines. This simple view causes so many projects to fail because the business is absolutely unaware of underlying efforts.

In many instances, data warehouse projects have allowed such situations to occur where the business gets their foot in the door and additional data components somehow creep in. Then another and another and, in a worst-case scenario, this situation results in a completely new data source that should require analysis, data quality initiatives, and other efforts pertaining to the addition of a completely new source system. Another worst case may be the business deciding to pull out as the effort and cost is becoming more than anticipated. This reflects poorly on the data warehouse environment, and the problem spreads in a domino effect to other departments that do not want to be involved in the enterprise effort at this point. It becomes a wait-and-see type of scenario for other business areas, which may affect the progression of an enterprise data warehouse initiative.

In another particular instance somewhere between a "just-build-it" and "data floundation" scenario, efforts went a step beyond the simple data perspective. One organization believed that if they purchased servers, a database license, a fancy leading-industry data model, and the latest BI tools, all they would have to do is literally load the data and everything would work out. This IT department was directly under the CFO, who asked why the data warehouse team could not just "push the button" and generate the reports. He also expected his data to be perfect since the business was functioning, so how could the data quality be an issue? His expectation was that if any data quality problem existed, it would be fixed once inconsistencies were seen on the reports. Needless to say, the project ran into a number of show-stoppers.

The point is that all data warehouse project efforts really should follow best practices that have been proven time and time again. Do not use the data warehouse system as a pass-through system to simply hold data. A data warehouse is created firstly based on a standard vocabulary to identify all data components. Secondly, a data warehouse is created to contain common structures to hold cleansed data.

Reasons for NOT Building a Data Warehouse

There are a number of reasons to build a data warehouse, such as:

- ▶ Reducing operating costs
- ▶ The current system cannot handle the overhead
  - ▶ Servers' capacity, data volumes, or usage
- ▶ Disparate systems, causing reporting inconsistencies
- ▶ Vocabulary issues, causing data and reporting inconsistencies
- ▶ Creating a central one-version-of-the truth environment for data analysis
  - ▶ Data, vocabulary, data structures
- ▶ Simplicity of usage

There are also a number of reasons why a data warehouse should not be built or should be put on hold. These range from technical to political to practical reasons. The following section presents a number of reasons why you might not want a data warehouse effort to proceed.

Poor Data Quality

If the historical data is of such poor quality that it cannot be fixed, then building a system to hold this historical data is futile. Data quality in context is critical to the business; therefore, if the business cannot use the data, then there is no reason to build a system to hold it. However, if the strategy going forward is to correct the data quality in the operational systems, then designing for the future is a good objective.

Lack of Business Interest

If the business community lacks interest in a data warehouse project, and a data warehouse effort is to add value to the business, then, once again, moving forward is a waste of resources. This just-build-it scenario is an opportunity cost to the organization because resources could be deployed in other more pressing areas. From a sales point of view, do not create a supply before the demand exists.

On the other hand, if the business is resisting a business intelligence solution, there may be a political reason, such as they are currently developing in their own environment and do not want to participate in an enterprise effort.

Lack of Sponsorship

Project sponsorship is very important to a data warehouse or business intelligence project, especially from an IT perspective. If management, especially executive management, is unwilling to sponsor the effort, why waste resources? In other words, if management does not see a successful outcome, then why should IT spend the budget?

Unclear Focus

Many projects produce lots of hype about building a business intelligence system to add value to the business, but the business cannot seem to come up with a tangible ROI example. If the business is not 100 percent clear on their goals, the luster will eventually dull and the project will fizzle out. Do not begin a business intelligence effort without a clear purpose. Otherwise, how will you know when you have attained your goal?

Sufficiency of Current Systems

Perhaps the business does have a clear focus in their requirements. And the reporting needs can be handled by the current transactional systems. In this case, even though a data warehouse strategy is clearly beneficial in the long run, using the existing system is good enough. Why spend the money on a new car to go to the corner store when the store is next door? If the platform, servers, database, and maintenance resources can handle the new requirements, stick with what works. Remember, you are looking for a solution for the business, not a make-work or technical curiosity effort.

Refer to the "Frequently Asked Questions" section in Chapter 1.

Lack of Resources

If your organization does not have the proper skilled resources, then embarking on a data warehouse project may not be the best direction at the present time. Many organizations do not have IT as a core competency and therefore do not have the proper resources experienced in building a data warehouse solution. In this case hiring new staff, external consultants, or outsourcing may be a better alternative than trying to build in-house.

Unstable Environment

The economic forecast is not bright, the business sponsor is unsure of forecasts, or the business is under review for a buyout. In such unstable situations, even though the projection for the organization and specific added value to the interested department is high, the current environment may not be conducive to such a large new project. Perhaps a management reorganization is about to take place or is currently taking place. An unstable environment is not a time to embark on a new system development. A data warehouse is not simply a project but a system. Projects come and go, but systems have lifecycles and require continuous administration.

Too Costly

An initial data warehouse development project can be quite costly. If the organization is falling on hard times, the current budget may not allow for the expense. Perhaps a reverse-engineering effort may be costly, perhaps the learning curve is too high at this time; maybe hardware and software costs are too high, or ramping up resources is too costly.

A data warehouse has a business objective to add value to the business. The business therefore should have a goal, preferably a tangible ROI. If the ROI is not achievable in the required fiscal period, then perhaps a data warehouse system is too costly at this time to begin or to continue. If the initial goal of profit or ROI is not achievable due to development issues, perhaps stopping the effort is a proper direction.

Poor Management

If the data warehouse effort has been under way for some time and it seems that scope creep is gaining too much ground, technology is not handling the solution as expected, resources are not producing as expected, and timelines are being pushed out far beyond the expected finish date, then perhaps the project is not being managed properly. With poor management, a project can take turns on a dime and never seem to advance to predetermined milestones. If the project is overly task-oriented rather than business-focused, perhaps management has become too involved in the underlying tasks rather than driving the vehicle. This may be a good reason to halt development and re-evaluate direction, strategy, and future efforts.

Data Warehouse and Business Intelligence Strategy

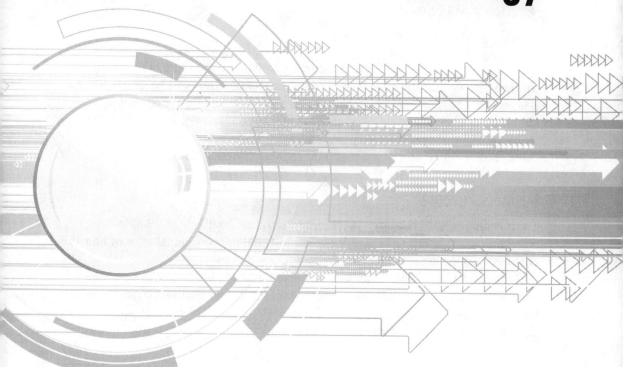

The data warehouse and business intelligence strategy is a plan based on two perspectives, that of IT and that of the business unit. Both perspectives must be considered, as success for only one means failure for the other. Ensuring that both groups have input to the plan and both guide the development based on what is realistic and practical in the given timeframe with the given resources in the current corporate culture is a best-practice strategy for a data warehouse and business intelligence effort.

Business Intelligence Strategy

When creating a business intelligence plan, first thoughts should be to get a usable solution up and running quickly to support the business and to ensure that it follows a data architecture strategy, hopefully an enterprise data architecture strategy. To get to this point, a good idea is to understand the business in terms of several fundamental factors:

▶ What is being built and why

▶ How it will be used

▶ Overview of a planned solution

Perhaps a level above all these is the realization that if the thought is toward a business intelligence solution, then the data warehouse effort will be geared toward business usage rather than an enterprise data management–only perspective. Enterprise data management, aka master data management, while a value to the business, is in this context an important supporting element to the business intelligence strategy as it forms part of the underlying data structure.

Business Purpose

The most important initial step in building a business intelligence solution is to determine what the business is trying to achieve and the conceptual view of how this goal will be used in the business decision-making process.

If the project has a detailed project charter, efforts have been spent in determining purpose, expected usage, and value. The last chapter in this section (Chapter 6) gives a brief view into project charters, project scope, and statement of work. In scenarios lacking such documents or low on content detail, the business analyst must determine the basic business purpose of the project and its fundamental details from the business community which can be quite time consuming.

A clear vision of deliverables must be established at the onset of the project efforts. The details may be out of focus, but the vision must be solid. For example, creating an environment to produce specific weekly reports based on the integration of data from multiple systems is an excellent goal. If low-level report details are lacking or unknown up front, this is fine for such a high-level planning phase. Later steps will be to determine the reporting details and stabilize on a central vocabulary, among other tasks. At this stage in the strategy planning, the goal is to determine what is required and why, with a view toward usage.

It was rumored some time ago that a very large Asian telecommunications organization had a business goal of reducing costs associated with their text messaging services—a solid outlook. Through in-depth business intelligence analytic efforts, the organization was able to determine that a certain customer profile was actually costing more than it contributed to the revenue base. Through a second focused BI effort, the organization was able to correlate service usage, billings, and customer segmentation to isolate a refined customer base and usage pattern. This latter effort resulted in the repackaging of the product, eliminating certain aspects popular to this unprofitable customer base and influencing their churn propensity, which resulted in a shift to a competing service provider. In so doing, the organization was able to massively reduce the costs of the focused service and much more effectively understand and market to more profitable customer segments. The initial plan had a clear and solid vision, which transformed into a focused goal that drove efforts. Later phases dove into details, resulting in a positive and successful outcome.

Business Usage

The second influencing factor toward the overall solution is the intended usage of the resulting product. To paraphrase: understanding what the business wants to accomplish will help the evaluation process in determining an overall solution, as will an understanding of how the business intends to actually use the solution. If the solution is report-driven, will the reports be produced and emailed to users (aka the batch method)? Will the end users want to drill down to finer levels of detail depending on analytical insights and requirements? Or is future usage intended to be more of a look-and-discover effort based on pure data insights? Understanding the business purpose from goal to practical usage is the driving factor in determining an effective business intelligence strategy.

Active business intelligence, which excludes batch reports (aka old static what-you-see-is-what-you-get reports), is based at one extreme on simple business reports and queries with the ability to drill up and down into the data granularity. Viewing the data from different granularities, for instance at monthly, quarterly, and yearly aggregations, gives the business valuable insights all combined into one dynamic reporting environment. Figure 4-1 shows different types of typical business intelligence usage.

Along with these reports and queries is the freedom and flexibility for the business user to manually query the data themselves but within the business analysis area boundaries. This is all analysis-driven, aka based on predetermined business requirements data.

The next step in a business intelligence environment is the ability to view the data in a more communicative fashion, which is the OLAP perspective: graphs, pie charts, and so forth. This gives added insights from a more communicative and comparable perspective. It is much easier to see proportions from a pie chart than from rows and columns of data.

At the other extreme of business intelligence is the ability for the advanced user to mine the data directly. This is called "data mining" and is a purely data-driven effort in hopes of discovering associations between data. This scenario gives the business user a wide view of the data. Unlike the queries from the analysis-driven context, which are limited to specific dimensions and measures, data mining allows the user to delve into the data as needed to determine insights based on data discoveries. Database designs for data mining can vary drastically from report and query designs; hence, knowing the business usage of the solution is critical for the planning, design, and development processes. Typically data mining has a much wider access to the underlying data within the database, whereas analysis-driven reports and queries are more limited.

All business intelligence solutions are designed and planned to empower the business user with data in a manner that will support their business decision-making process.

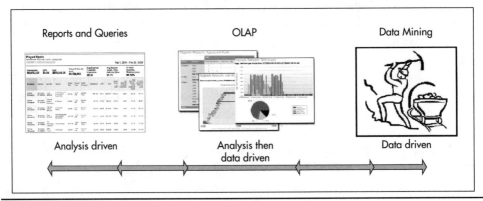

Figure 4-1   *Analysis-driven vs. data-driven business intelligence*

Architecture Overview

Armed with an understanding of what the business is trying to realize and why the overall solution has been formulated, the business intelligence effort has purpose. In addition to understanding the goals, how the business wants to access the information can give great insight into a general BI architecture in the performance and user presentation layers, as seen in Figure 4-2—a focused view of Chapter 1, Figure 1-9.

The performance layer is essentially data marts tuned for usage. The design or macro phase of a project is to determine data mart design, while the build or micro phase optimizes the design for specific usage. Both layers include elements such as database management system (DBMS) and business intelligence tool considerations. At this point the project is in the design phase and in the perspective of the performance layer, aka the data mart layer, thoughts should be toward data with a usage perspective. The design at this point usually centers on a star design if the business is expecting a user-empowering, analysis-driven solution. As a side note: the build phase may determine that the physicalization of the designs may be best implemented in an alternate optimized structure closer to a normalized or snowflaked structure rather than a star structure. More information on this topic will be presented in Part II of this book.

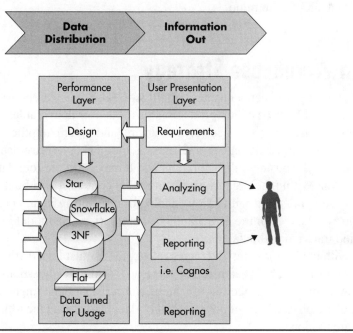

Figure 4-2   *Performance and user presentation layers*

The user presentation layer is typically oriented around a BI tool such as Cognos, Business Objects, Microstrategy, or Crystal Reports. Reports generated by these tools are all about the end user's experience or usage. While the performance layer has to do with designs for speed of data delivery, the user presentation layer has to do with communicability and ease of use tailored for specific usage.

How the business wants to use the data, the format being presented, and the timeliness of receiving the information will determine the presentation layer and impact the performance layer. If the business is happy with receiving static reports, the performance and user presentation layers will be architected in one fashion. However, if the end user requires graphics with the ability to drill down into the different levels of data granularity, then a completely different architecture within these layers is required. Design the architecture based on communicating a solution with expected usage and build based on actual usage, which includes database table indexing, data volumetrics, data partitions, data granularity, number of users, and realistic usage patterns.

Another area to consider is the BI tool being used. Most BI tools work well in aggregating lots of rows. A star schema with dimensions and lots of fact rows is great for most BI tools. Connecting one star schema with another via conformed dimensions can really slow these tools down, as would snowflaking dimension designs; therefore, when architecting a solution, do so with simplicity and specific BI tool capabilities in mind.

Data Warehouse Strategy

The distinction between a business intelligence and data warehouse strategy in this context is that BI is based on producing business user deliverables, while the data warehouse goal is to only focus on structuring and organizing the data. A data warehouse strategy is an effort in designing a logical enterprise data model to gain insights into the business data components. It may form the foundation for several applications within the organization, but in this context it will be the basis for a data warehouse application with its physicalization resulting in an enterprise data repository. The data in the data warehouse enterprise data model includes reference data and transactional data.

As with the business intelligence strategy, there must be a distinction between architecture and usage. Then based on these two factors, key questions will discriminate between effort levels: Is the solution at the enterprise or departmental level? Will the initial phase physicalize a repository and/or data marts? And the ultimate question is: when are we done?

Usage

The first step is to determine, as discussed in the previous section on business intelligence strategy, the purpose of the effort, which impacts how it will be used. Is the current project to create a data warehouse repository that holds all required data in a structured and organized manner? Or is the effort to create a vocabulary or taxonomy and data model for the enterprise, not knowing how it will be physicalized? Either way the first step is in ensuring that the goals of the effort are understood, and then an appropriate architecture can be selected.

In a business intelligence effort, the project begins with a bottom-up approach where business usage and purpose requirements are understood first, followed by sourcing of the supporting data. If the project is based on a data-driven effort, a top-down perspective is initially taken within a limited scope. The scope is limited to set a boundary on the breadth of effort, and it gives a realistic perspective to the project. A hybrid of both top-down and bottom-up approaches can be undertaken, which is actually the best of both worlds. A hybrid approach works best when purchasing a model because the data is already structured and defined. The task is then to become familiar with the new data model and decide whether to use it as a guide or directly, which includes scoping and extending the model(s) as need be. A hybrid approach, however, requires business end-user usage, which may not be fully understood or possible in certain scenarios, which is why a pure data warehouse, aka an enterprise data model effort, is undertaken.

For technical-driven projects such as a platform migration, data warehouse centralization, or a data mart consolidation effort, efforts are usually more geared toward a central version of data on a specific database. This effort begins with a technical analysis and a top-down view. The other scenarios, as described in Chapter 3, "just-build-it" and "data floundation," are also top-down scenarios. These all deal with organizing the data, but unless the planners know how the system will be used, it usually ends up with a large, fully normalized repository optimized for capturing and holding data rather than for extracting and using the data. If data marts already exist, they are assimilated into the data warehouse enterprise data model and conformed to a central vocabulary.

Of course, there are a number of reasons to build a data warehouse, and hopefully they are all geared toward the business. But for some projects, the build reason is simply to organize and align the data within the organization. In this case the business effort is simply to get a view of the multitudes of data components in a structured manner for future business analytics, operational data stores, business processes, or whatever the application usage is expected to be. The point at this stage is to determine why the data warehouse is being built, and cast that in stone. Of course, as other business units come on board or other insights are achieved, a change in direction will occur, but for now solidifying a clear and current vision is important. It is very typical to hear about the many reasons why a data warehouse project is in existence, but when asked what is the current driving requirement, many cannot reply with other than generic data warehouse or business intelligence best-practice concepts. Without a clear and current purpose, chances of success are low as there is no tangible and realistic goal to focus upon.

DW Architecture

This is not the actual building of the data warehouse system; it has to do with choosing a strategy to design, develop, and possibly build the data warehouse repository. It's the same idea in building a house; first decide what is required, and then make designs based on dependencies and boundaries. Will there be one or two floors? Should the entire first floor be constructed this year and the second floor next year once a new budget is approved? The point is to set the guidelines up front to understand and agree to the basic deliverables. The actual project plan with milestones, resource allocations, and all the trimmings can be drawn up later; the first effort is to decide on a purpose, which is dictated by usage.

To begin, set a base foundation of understanding the goal. Typically the purpose of having a data warehouse is to centralize corporate information. Remember, information is simply data in context; therefore, the centralization concept is identification and organization of data in a structured manner. The reliability of this data is then referred to as the "trusted and central single version of the truth" environment for the entire organization. The basic premise of a business intelligence system is then to connect the business with this trusted, timely, and single-version-of-the-truth data environment in an optimized and usable manner for business consumption.

Data warehousing began as database environments but has evolved into a system that includes architecture and the business intelligence, aka business usage, aspect of the data. Over the past decade, at least, data warehouse projects have been divided into two camps: a BI project, which is a business and IT partnership, to build a requirement and usage perspective, and a data warehouse project, which is the classic data-driven effort. Both efforts are based on data as the foundation. The first is geared toward a focus on specific usage and underlying data structures with IT helping the business determine the best solution, while the latter is geared toward the data foundation to support the business. Perhaps a better way of saying it is that the latter is geared more toward development of an enterprise data environment.

As with the construction of a house or any physical structure, the first step is the blueprints, to get an understanding of what is required. These blueprints consist of two levels: data flow architecture and technical architecture. Starting the process by creating diagrams has proven to be the best approach, as it quickly communicates the plan. A document is then produced explaining the diagrams in detail once the concepts are understood.

Data Flow Architecture

The data involved in the data warehouse system and the anticipated route, flow, or motion of the data within is data flow architecture, normally called data architecture. Data modeling deals with organizing and structuring the data into data models, while data architecture deals with the sourcing and movement of the data to its target structures, which are typically the data models.

Data warehouse architecture has two perspectives: logical and physical architectures. In a nutshell, the logical aspect is the identification of the data components and how they inter-relate within one data model and between data models. The physical aspect is how the logical architecture is implemented. Of course, the physical design and implementation is highly dependent on usage and logical designs.

Figure 4-3 shows the distinctions between logical and physical designs. A number of logical data models are shown: data source systems, data repository, and data mart models. Other types of data models can include data interface models and data staging models. In many instances the overall business data is modeled in a normalized fashion without regard for any specific application. That said, in most cases there is an underlying application usage influence or flavor. Figure 4-3 shows a one-level data architecture for specific data warehouse applications.

In the initial stages, the data architecture should give insight into the basic pillars of data for the first perceived phase of the project. What data will be involved? All customer and all product data or only specific aspects of the fundamental areas? Where is this data from? Which source systems will be involved? These questions can all form part of a preliminary analysis of reporting requirements connecting back to source systems. This is a simple view of data architecture in a nutshell.

Data architecture applies equally to both business intelligence and data warehouse strategies. It has simply been pointed out in this enterprise data model/data repository section.

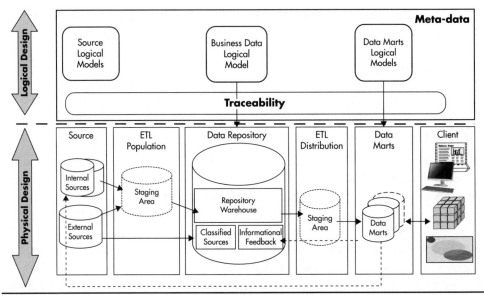

Figure 4-3   *Typical simple data warehouse architecture flow*

Technical Architecture

Technical architecture is the physical data architecture and the tangible aspects of the physical system. This includes databases, operating systems, middleware, involved networks, servers, software tools, and so forth. Will the system have its own machines or share a central server? What business intelligence tool will be used? What ETL tool is available? How will data be delivered from source or to data marts?

Again, technical architecture applies to both business intelligence and data warehouse strategies equally.

Creating this technical architecture at this point may seem premature, but it is necessary to get an idea of how the solution will look along with possible costs. This all forms part of the initial inquiry stage of a data warehouse project. Changes may occur as the details are revealed during the project evolution, but in general the overview should be fairly stable.

A simple method of creating a first-draft technical architecture is to create a second diagram identical to the data architecture diagram and add the technical aspects. Or simply create a simple technical architecture diagram and highlight the technical aspects. Then continue adding to the diagram as more hardware and software items are known (see Figure 4-4).

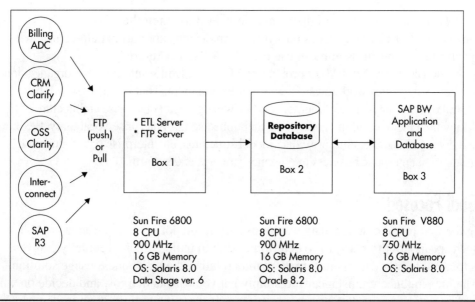

Figure 4-4   *Simple technical architecture diagram*

Focus and Success

All data warehouse and business intelligence projects have the same concerns: Is the design a good fit for the current usage? What are the boundaries of the scope, and when is all completed and successful? The following sections present brief discussions on these topics.

Enterprise or Line of Business?

Is the data warehouse initiative IT-driven or business-driven? IT typically has the knowledge and overview to build enterprise designs, while business units build for their specific usage. Both groups are involved in building the data warehouse, IT as the architects and construction workers and business as the end users or customers. If one group builds by themselves, success will be one-sided. Both groups need to work together ensuring that the business has a usable solution, which helps with their decision-making process while ensuring that the data asset is managed at the corporate perspective. Data is a corporate asset and should be designed as such. If the focus is purely on only one business unit area, project funding is not going toward the other areas within the business and the entire central one-version-of-the-truth strategy fails.

If business builds within their environment only, then the effort is not enterprise-based. If IT initiates the effort, then designs are purely data-centric with hopes that any business unit can use them "as is" in the future.

A good strategy, and the best probability of a successful solution for the organization, is when both groups work toward a win-win environment. That is, business will have a central usable analytical environment and IT will define an enterprise architecture of the data, which includes all the good items mentioned so far: enterprise vocabulary, flexible and open architecture, enterprise data model structures, an enterprise data foundation strategy, an enterprise business intelligence strategy, and so forth.

Goal Focused

In the first phase of a new data warehouse effort, do not get too carried away. I have seen six-month projects just to determine what to build, which eventually evolves into a full master data management roadmap rather than a business usage solution. The idea in this circumstance is to simply get your ducks in a row and decide on why and how to build the data warehouse system. If there is funding for an in-depth evaluation of the organization's strategic direction and creation of an enterprise roadmap with all the trimmings, then good for you. The idea should be to figure out the story line for building the data warehouse given the resources, timeframe, budget, management support, data quality issues, and political or cultural environment. These parameters can and will affect the build, but the end result should be a tangible solution and a tangible usable data warehouse environment. Selecting specific goals and remaining focused on delivering a usable solution is the best recipe for success.

Success: When Are We Done?

Many projects begin without properly defining a target goal. Usually it is expected that at the end of the project all will be well and therefore success is imminent simply because the project exists. Why would a project begin if there is no expectation of completion and therefore success? But we all know that when we're working with multiple groups and departments, one may claim success while the other sees the final result as a complete failure. The best thing to do for a data warehouse effort, data-driven or business intelligence–driven, is to qualify and quantify the definition of success up front.

There are usually two groups involved in a data warehouse build or expansion: the business unit and IT. Each group should be able to claim success at the end of a data warehouse project. To be realistic, each group should be claiming success for each milestone during the project. Do not wait until everything is designed, built, and released for usage before claiming success or failure. The project should have milestones, and each milestone should have a success-or-fail status. There is no such thing as "kind of" successful; there is only yes or no, success or failure for each milestone. Of course, plans and milestones can change for any number of reasons, and as such, the definition of a successful completion may change. Again, beware of scope creep and unnecessary additions, especially in the initial efforts.

In the end, if IT builds a data warehouse system and is quite happy with the results, they may claim success for themselves. For instance, if an enterprise data warehouse was to be built, the design itself may be very useful in structuring the data for the organization, but the build for the specific business usage was not. Hence the design is successful but the usage was a failure. Another example can be that an initial scope was to build a customer relationship management (CRM) system, but there were so many data quality issues that a customer could not be properly defined for the intended usage. The design may be wonderful, but the usage is not possible at this time until the source systems clean up the data. Hence the solution design is successful but the build is a failure.

The point is to break down projects into milestones for IT and the business. Think of the project in chunks, not just as one final delivery. Both groups should gain levels of success throughout the project lifecycle.

Efforts should not deviate too much for one group at the expense of another. This happens quite often with scope creep. Initially everyone agrees to delivering X, but as the project progresses, the business wants just a little more; maybe another table, or perhaps to include, for instance, customer addresses, which was not in the initial scope. Or maybe there is a request to include some other data area to leverage some newly discovered insights, even though this is not an initial requirement nor agreed-to scope. Remember the reason for building the data warehouse in the first place and be true to the goals and scope. If two groups are building the data warehouse, there must be coordination in this symbiotic relationship and accountability.

A data warehouse system is completed only once the agreed-to goals are attained by all parties involved. Only at this point is the project as a whole a success.

Where to Start?

Step one in determining where to start is to determine what is to be built—as has been said many times so far in this book. Does the business unit want analytics, or is the purpose to organize and structure the data throughout the organization, or a combination of both?

In many instances I have seen projects stuck in the "get'er done" syndrome. In these cases the business and developers just want to get whatever data is required to build specific reports to satisfy the business users. This is all well and good if there is no regard for enterprise modeling or creating a flexible environment that can be added to as other requests from the same or different business units emerge. But the whole idea behind a data warehouse and business intelligence effort is to cultivate the corporate data asset. So the question is where to start with an emphasis on producing something tangible for the business while ensuring a data management strategy for the entire corporate data asset.

Several decades ago when I started my career, I focused on creating business reports. When someone wanted something, I always started from scratch to build a new report. There was no regard for organizing or structuring data, as data was from the same one environment. As far as I could tell, the world was in that one database. But when I had to compare pension payroll entries with human resource details, efforts became more difficult because identifiers were different, data types were not consistent, history was not always retained, and data was on two distinct, unrelated systems. If only I had known the virtues of a centralized single-version-of-the-truth data environment back then, my headaches would have been minimal.

Let us make certain key points right off the bat. The first is based on whether the purpose is to create reports or structure the data, or both if possible—my experience suggests to always consider both—a reporting environment otherwise known as the user presentation layer with a performance layer and an organized layer or central repository design layer. However, specifics will come from project requirements. The second point is, do we want to create something only for a department (single purpose) or design for the enterprise (whole company)? My experience suggests to design at the enterprise level but implement at the department level. Obviously, designing for the entire company cannot be done all up front, but the intention is to model the whole company at some point in the future in a phased approach. The up-front design will therefore allow add-ons and extensions without having to redesign from scratch at a later stage.

For BI

For business intelligence, aka creating a business data access environment, the first step is to determine the type of BI environment based on usage.

- ▶ **Batch reports**   Static reports
- ▶ **Dynamic reports**   Being able to drill down or up into different levels of data granularity, for example, looking at the year, then the quarter, month, and so forth
- ▶ **OLAP reporting**   Same as dynamic reporting but with more communicative presentations: pie charts, graphs, comparison diagrams, and so on

▶ **Data mining**   Data structures whereby the advanced user can use SQL queries to traverse the data as needed

▶ **Specialized: dashboards and/or scorecards**   Preplanned specialized graphic reporting showing many business measures in one central spot, typically for management to refer to for current business movement

This is a pure bottom-up approach, or in other words, this is what the business wants, so let us have a look and figure out how to make it.

If a data warehouse or business intelligence environment already exists, then discussions with the data warehouse architect are a must to determine the best approach based on what already exists and what must be newly incorporated.

Looking at the simple data flow architecture, the overall plan can follow the data layers. For BI, start from the bottom or end of the data flow with the deliverables, which are typically the business reports. Decompose what is on the reports to find the data elements and model from required data. Then trace this data back to the source system to understand its origins.

The same logic applies for any report, OLAP, dashboard or scorecard, and data mining environment. First determine the data requirements at a fundamental level, and then all descriptive components as you go along with the associative aspects of how the data inter-relates.

For DW

The first step in a data warehouse project, which is not business intelligence–focused, aka no specific environment for the business user, is to decide on the purpose. What is the effort?

▶ To create a central enterprise data vocabulary?

▶ To model the business data to determine how all interconnects?

▶ To logically model a data warehouse repository to capture and hold all historical data?

▶ To create a physical data warehouse application repository for specific historical data?

▶ A combination of several of these?

Since this scenario is data-driven, the goal is to determine the fundamental data elements and how they interassociate along with their descriptive aspects. A good method to use here is the pillar diagram mentioned in earlier chapters. This method gives a simple way of determining the data components and how they inter-relate in a simple and communicative fashion. Plus an added bonus is that no specific modeling tool is required—just a piece of paper (to begin with). The source at this point is not the end reports but the data itself. The pillar diagram helps with identifying what the business requires in documenting multiple sources into a common understanding. Typically, source systems are the starting point for a data-driven modeling effort.

How to Start?

At this point there is an understanding of what is to be built and an idea of where to start the efforts. Let's have a peek at the details. Later chapters will discuss this in more detail.

For BI

If the business has existing reports that they wish to include in the DW/BI solution, then obtain the reports and decompose them into their data components.

Figure 4-5 is an example of a business report that has been decomposed. At this point it is not necessarily known whether the components are pure data components or business terminology. The point is to determine the report components and how they relate to other report components. Later we can refine the dimensions and measures further.

The data components for the report shown in Figure 4-5 are discovered and placed on a dimension and measure cross-reference matrix as seen in Figure 4-6. This process should begin to help identify the underlying data components.

Daily Net (Product) Sales (Northern Region)

Day Week 44	Net Sales 2008	Net Sales 2007	Variance 08 vs 07	Customers 2008	Variance 08 vs 07
Monday	€ 22,485,104	€ 21,359,944	5.0%	345,987	3.0%
Tuesday	€ 14,303,432	€ 15,303,432	−7.0%	356,743	−1.0%
Wednesday	€ 17,506,111	€ 14,506,111	17.1%	233,111	11.0%
Thursday	€ 18,099,000	€ 17,099,000	5.5%	387,111	4.0%
Friday	€ 19,876,323	€ 19,456,123	2.1%	298,000	20.0%
Saturday	€ 25,999,345	€ 24,999,345	3.8%	401,222	1.0%
Sunday	€ 12,456,111	€ 11,456,111	8.0%	212,000	5.6%
WEEK	**€ 130,725,426**	**€ 124,180,066**	**5.0%**	**2,234,174**	**4.6%**

Dimensions

Time Period	Year, Week, Day
Region	North
Product	Goods not services
Store	All northern stores

Measures

Net Sales	Derived from Point-of-Sales transactions
Net Sales Variance	Derived (Net Sales 2008 - Net Sales 2007) / Net Sales 2008 * 100
Num of Customers	Given from source
Num of Customer Variance	Given from source

Figure 4-5   *Sample report decomposition*

Dimensions and Measures / Reports	Scenario	Year	Quarter	Month	Week	Day	Store - Name	Store - Number	Region	Division	LOB	Brand	Product Type	Product - Name	Product - SKU	Product - Size	Product - Fin Hierarchy	Product Color	POS Gross Sales Amount	POS Return Amount	Number of POS Transactions	COGS	Profit Margin
(count)	0	0	0	1	3	1	0	1	3	3	1	0	2	2	2	0	0	0	1	1	1	1	1
Weekly Sales					×			×	×	×	×								×	×	×	×	×
Weekly Shipment				×	×				×	×			×	×	×								
SKU Performance					×	×			×	×			×	×	×								

Figure 4-6　*Sample dimension vs. report cross-reference matrix*

Once all the known reports have been analyzed and placed in the cross-reference matrix, commonality can be determined. Efforts can then be prioritized based on the most common dimensions and measures. This gives a good insight into underlying data requirements, prioritization of efforts, and phased deliverable expectations.

Note that not all reports are necessarily done at once; depending on the number of reports, a subset can be analyzed, for instance, departmental or customer segmentation reports.

The next step is then to map the discovered data dimensions and measures to the source systems; basically, find out where the data is from. Since this overall effort is not only based on pre-existing reports but also on newly required reports or "wish lists" of new reports, there are usually gaps, which means the data source, as shown in Figure 4-7, is not identifiable.

This gap analysis is quite important. If the business wants a piece of data that is expected to be in source system X but is not there, what will the architect, designer, and/or developers do? Taking in a new source system is always an added cost in time, understanding, and participation, which may add to the overall timeline and cost. Hence a gap analysis is quite important to determine whether all the data is where it is supposed or thought to be.

For DW

Begin by looking at the business value chains. These are the main business process areas within the organization. Then identify the fundamental data components such as customer, product, and the main events of the business, which is typically what

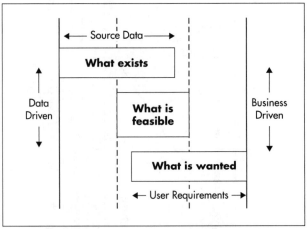

Data-Driven vs. Business-Driven Approach

Figure 4-7   *Determining gaps*

the business does in that area. For a telecommunications organization (phone, cable, video), the main data is the call detail records; for the retail industry, it is inventory and point-of-sale transactions; for the health-plan provider industry, it is medical claim details and pharmacy claims; for the insurance business, it is policy and claim information; and for financial services, it is investments and financial transactions. Of course there will be issues of exactly what data to capture, for example, should customer or patient address information be obtained or not. Without specific business usage requirements, these types of questions will be constant annoyances to the project effort.

Another consideration at this point is whether to build or purchase a data model to help with the enterprise data modeling efforts. If you are building from scratch or using a pre-existing in-house data model, there is always the real possibility that the design will not take into account one aspect or another, thus causing much rework down the line. If a pre-existing model is used, its initial purpose was probably for a specific application and not conducive to an enterprise effort. As mentioned earlier, if you are purchasing a data model, how deep is the data model, and does it cover the business value chains of your organization? Prebuilt industry models are great as a guide and, with extensions, can be used as the foundation to the overall business.

The main point for a data warehouse data-driven effort is to ensure that all data components conform to a single enterprise logical data model. This ensures a common vocabulary and definition, and is understood as it relates to other data components. This is also the start of a data quality awareness, which is key to ensuring trustworthy and shareable enterprise data.

Build with a methodology rather than just arbitrarily. Create a methodology and conformity will follow.

Analyze the Current Environment

Just as a doctor listens to a patient describe his or her health problems and then follows up with an examination to determine the patient's current state of health, once a data warehouse project's purpose, objectives, and boundaries have been determined, there will be a need to analyze the environment within the organization. The effort will be to determine the current state of the business regarding the data source systems, the technical environment, and the resource skill base to establish the appropriateness of the current environment to fulfill the project tasks and goals.

The environment assessment will be guided by the expected project deliverables and the project approach. If the project is focused, for instance, on inventory analytics, the inventory source systems will be assessed.

Enterprise Modeling

One approach to a pure enterprise data model design approach is to break up the organization into chunks. Then break these chunks down further. The chunks are subject areas and the further breakdown is known as concepts. The concepts are then broken into fundamental, descriptive, and associative data components, as described in previous chapters.

As mentioned earlier in the book, to help with a data view of the organization I created the pillar diagram method. The idea behind the pillar diagram is to silo the data into categories: Locations, Parties, Events, very similar to the way IBM data models are created. The point is to model the reference data and the key transactional data components to help with the transition between data discovery and data modeling. Do this for key business processes and/or data sources, and later merge into one version to ensure that everything conforms to the same terminology.

Very high-level anchors are the key. Then tag the leaf-level fundamental data components to these anchors and show the generality of how they interconnect. This allows a high-level view of the data models using data terminology. And it allows processes to be decomposed, showing their underlying data components as well. Business terminology can be added as well to show placement and potential future items to decompose into data components.

There can be a number of data components between the anchor, as shown in Figure 4-8, that is, Location or Party, and the leaf level, that is, Post Adr, Store, or Person, but these will be left to the data modeling effort. Pillar diagrams are only to represent the business topic at hand in a manner that can be understood by technical IT data people and nontechnical business people.

The pillar diagram was developed by using the following logic: Every business needs certain types of data or information as a foundation for the business. People and organization information, address information, product/services information,

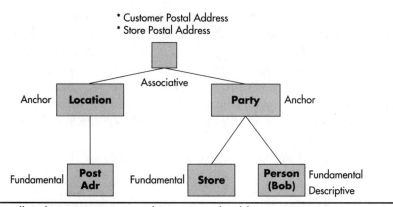

Figure 4-8   *Pillar diagram: Person and Store Postal Address scenario*

certain asset information, and contract or agreement information all form the basis for every company's data foundation. These are the basic pillars of information for any organization. Then depending on the line of business the organization operates within, there are different types of events that are supported by the underlying basic data. In other words, the fundamental data pillars support the company's events. Retailer events are promotions, point-of-sale transactions, supply orders, inventory depletion, and so forth. Telecommunication companies (telephone companies) events are distribution and sales of equipment, prepaid minute cards, promotions, and telephone calls (better known as usage of service, since usage can be voice calls, text messages, data usage such as internet, ringtone downloads, etc.). Insurance company events include claims, crimes, accidents, property damage, and so forth. Banks have marketing campaigns, ratings, transactions, orders, settlements, and others. None of these events can exist without one or more of the fundamental data pillars: party, location, product, agreement, asset, and so on.

Project Phasing

Just a few brief words on development: one of the fatal areas in a data warehouse project is insufficient or poor planning. One aspect is not knowing how to phase the project. *Phasing* is the process of creating segments of work that have a start, effort, and end with a defined deliverable that moves the overall project forward. These segments need to be clearly understood by those engaged and those awaiting the outcomes.

While most project plans contain tasks and milestones, most do not realistically phase the efforts. Building an enterprise data warehouse system is not like a regular project; this type of project spans a lot more of the organization. As such, it involves more unknowns and hence more risk. To reduce the risk, a data warehouse plan should focus on delivering small fundamental solutions first followed by tangible end-user solutions.

Regardless of which approach is being used, begin with analysis. Like a doctor who tries to resolve a patient's illness, gather all the factors, analyze the situation, make an assessment, and finally provide a solution. You will notice there may be a gap between what is desired and what is available. This gap analysis is quite important to understand as it gives a realistic insight into actual delivery potential; refer back to Figure 4-7. In a data warehouse it is important to design a proper data foundation up front for the expected business delivery. Hence the first phase should be fundamental data tagged to specific business requirements.

The first delivery phase may seem to be geared more toward IT, but this is to be expected. Before you can deliver a sturdy and reliable analytical reporting environment, a data foundation must be established. Build the basic data pillars first. If the business reports are known and a cross-reference matrix was used, there should be a good understanding of the common dimensions. The dimensions can be grouped in pillars, and the focus should be on designing these basic pillars first. Business can do pillar insight analytics such as customer segmentation analysis and product analysis.

▶ Phase 1 then involves analysis followed by design of basic pillars, followed by build and population of these basic pillars.

▶ Phase 2 should then add more tangible value for the business by including scoped events. For retail, that would be point-of-sale transactions, and for telecommunication organizations, the call usage.

Of course, much depends on the resources available and their ability to understand the business, data components, and how to overlap these two phases, making delivery of each phase distinct as well as coupled to give the business some sort of tangible and usable result as soon as possible.

How Long Will It Take, Revisited

The big question now becomes: How long will it take to build a data warehouse solution?

Before the build can begin, the first step is preparation. Do not simply begin building in hopes that all the pieces will fall into place. That may happen, but chances are that the project will fail before the pieces align. Step one is to prepare, which is why the first part of this book is called "Preparation."

▶ **Step 1:** Determine what the project wants to accomplish, and document this as the primary goal. At the high level a qualitative goal is fine: Build a data warehouse that centralizes all historical data from the source systems, which will be used for analytical processing to enable the business to better understand their environment and make informed decisions to move the organization forward. Remember, the goal should be defined from both a business and IT perspective.

▶ **Step 2:** Be more specific and set the boundaries, still at the qualitative level with an introduction of quantitative elements. For instance: capture all point-of-sale transactions from the POS system and hold them in a central data warehouse for specific market basket analysis to determine which top 500 products typically sell with which other products. And of these, compare the top 100 most profitable products. This should produce an analytical environment within seven months, for instance, to allow business more insight into these product sales by store and by region on a monthly basis. POS sales are the foundation to the organization's existence and ongoing health. From these insights future efforts will look at customer behavior, and inventory control to ensure adequate stock levels without being overextended needlessly. The last part of this step will consist of discoveries in identifying customer segments, distribution analysis efforts, and vendor management analysis efforts.

These two steps lead the overall plan. In our example the first tangible business usage is expected in seven months.

▶ **Step 3:** Investigate the business environment at a high level to identify any business process issues. Can all products be identified? The POS system only holds an identification number and name per product. Do more details exist so that we can better understand the type of product, the size, color, packaging, and so on? Are other systems required for the missing data? Are there any issues with pricing or the duration of information held in the POS system? A major focus is to discover if any obvious gaps exist that would hinder the effort. The last part of this step is to determine who can act on this information, how they would receive it, and a rough insight into the effort it would take to build.

One cannot go shopping without a general idea of how much is available to spend or the general cost of the goods. As with any other project, the quantitative aspects must now be realized. What is the expected timeline for building the data warehouse solution? How many resources would be required, and what new assets, if any, are required?

This is very difficult to pin down at a high level. So much depends on what type of data warehouse effort is planned: the availability of resources, resource skill level, cost of data models, cost of new servers if any, installation of new hardware and software, outsourcing costs, scope of expectations, and so forth.

If everything is in place, the general pieces of the puzzle for a new build effort might include:

▶ Business analysis effort with full-time focused business SME: three weeks.

▶ Source system discovery and data profiling: two weeks in parallel with data modeling.

▶ Data modeling is central to the data warehouse; experts should be able to scope a purchased model on a small fundamental scope in six weeks.

- ▶ A DBA can create a database from the data model in two weeks.

  - ▶ Other DBA or infrastructure efforts can run in parallel throughout efforts.

- ▶ BI report creation can easily take four weeks.

  - ▶ Software installation can run in parallel with other efforts.

- ▶ ETL programming is 70 percent of the solution.

- ▶ Testing and implementation can easily take two weeks.

This totals approximately 28 weeks, which is in the seven-month timeline. Of course, this is a rough estimate and expects everything to go rather smoothly. Typically, if data quality issues surface, these can take time to rectify and may involve either source system changes and/or rethinking in the overall solution. Many activities take place in parallel, but many still require a waterfall approach; one must finish before the next begins.

Again, this is a very rough estimate based on a small scope with no additions along the way. There is an expectation that all resources are senior, no hurdles hinder progress, and there is a clear view of the final result. Overall solutions can possibly be done in shorter time or can take quite a bit longer. Everything depends on the scope and business usage expectations.

The next step is to determine feasible and realistic milestones followed by detail tasks and activities. Even though it may be difficult at times, quantitative forecasting is a must as the planning progresses into details.

Points of Interest

The following topics are points of interest applicable to all data warehouse projects no matter what phase they are in. There should always be concern about typical reasons for failure in order to avoid them and gear all efforts sternly away. The latter topic deals with basic project values, which are especially useful on a data warehouse effort.

The reason for adding this section in the data warehouse strategy portion of the book is to highlight what not to do and what to beware of within a data warehouse project. If strategy is about making a plan, then knowing which avenues to divert away from is in itself useful information and forms part of the overall mentoring context.

Typical Failure Reasons

I have been using a slide in my presentations for years stating that 65 percent of all data warehouse initiatives fail. I think it initially came from the Gartner Group, but I looked recently and could not for the life of me find the official source. Nevertheless, from all my personal experiences, there is a high number of data warehouse failures. But this depends on what success and failure are deemed to be within the organization, as discussed in previous sections.

For all the initiatives that do fail, there seems to be some commonality, as described in the following sections.

Lack of Vocabulary

▶   If terminology is not completely analyzed, confusion and misunderstanding of fundamental data components terms will result. For instance: what is a customer? What is demographics? What is a product? Context within different departments will define these basic terms differently, as seen in previous discussions. Without a proper vocabulary, how can development be expected to define and structure the data correctly?

Lack of Business Participation, aka Clarification

▶   This is tightly coupled with the "lack of vocabulary." If a data warehouse solution is being built for a specific business usage, the business and IT must be very clear on terminology and expectations. I was involved in building a data warehouse solution for one of the largest retailers in the United States. The requirements were confusing, so terminology clarification was requested. The only person who could answer the question was a product buyer, but since the buyer was unavailable, an aide was tasked to answer all questions. Needless to say, building a house for one person based on another person's description is always a recipe for failure.

▶   Best practices suggest that when building a data warehouse for business usage without business participation, you should create a mock solution, that is, a report, and define each data component. This allows the business to see exactly what is to be developed, and redirection can occur if necessary up front before any development efforts begin.

Excessive Focus on IT

▶   Sometimes there is a belief that if a specific product is purchased and implemented, all development issues will fade away and the final data warehouse will magically appear. One customer once seriously asked which button to press to create the data warehouse. Unfortunately the world has not advanced to the point where all can be accomplished with a simple software product. There are tools that will speed up efforts, such as a computer, extra CPU, more disks, a prebuilt data model, a reporting tool, but in general there is no magic. Business requirements must be understood and itemized, a specific solution must be devised, designs must be created, data must be mapped to reports, and development must then build to support the solution. In short, business requirements must be understood and only then can efforts to convert these into a tangible system be built.

▶ Another major IT focus issue is the overly obsessive academic approach to structuring the data. In many instances projects are overly focused on designing an enterprise data perspective rather than a business solution. While an enterprise data repository is a good strategy in most data warehouse efforts, overly focusing on the repository rather than the goal in a business-focused project may lead to overall project failure.

Data-Driven Projects

▶ While this type of approach may be fine if you are designing an enterprise data architecture, building a data repository without a usage focus means that efforts may be wasted in unnecessary areas. Why spend months designing a repository, identifying sources, and building customer segmentation data into a repository if there is only interest from the finance department for external reporting?

▶ Always build with usage and purpose in mind. If there is no business sponsor, chances are that the project is IT-based with no real purpose in mind other than to build now and hope that maybe someone will want the project later. Of course, there is a massive assumption that all data required later will fall within this unfocused build stage.

▶ It's best to identify real business needs and build based on these.

Lack of Experience

▶ Many believe that a data warehouse is just another project and IT should be able to handle it. If no one in your organization has ever created a data warehouse before, hire a seasoned data warehouse resource or bring in a consultant at the planning stage to guide initial development efforts.

▶ If in doubt, bring in consultants to audit the direction and efforts to ensure that initial focus has not drifted.

Insufficient Planning

▶ An underestimation of effort, duration, budget, hardware, and resources is also a big cause of data warehouse failures. First in this category are effort and duration. It is not unusual for an inexperienced organization to plan the first phase of a data warehouse project within a two- or three-month timeline using their top business analyst and database resource. Unfortunately, this is simply a precursor to disaster. I have never seen a successful data warehouse effort in less than six months. Determining business requirements, refining these requirements, extracting appropriate data components, determining source, profiling the data, resolving data source to requirements analysis, resolving data quality issues, designing the vocabulary and data structures and all the intricacies of building the database, the programs, scheduling production jobs, end user training, and deployment take time. Do not underestimate the effort required. And of course, business always wants just a little more, which adds to timelines.

▶ I once had a two-hour discussion with a new vice president of data warehousing who was planning on having a data warehouse system built in two months. After a lengthy in-depth discussion on architecture and all the involved components, the plan quickly changed to six to eight months given the company's environment and culture.

▶ Spend the time to make a plan. Look at the potential gaps within your organization and determine how these can affect your timelines. Get an external opinion by hiring an expert to review the plan.

Lack of Executive Support

▶ Without high-level management support, there is no champion, and the project typically fails due to perceived lack of importance within the business community.

▶ Executive support should come from the business and then from IT. There is no benefit to IT in having a data warehouse environment. Sure, a migration effort can reduce costs, but in the end the business will have to spend time ensuring that the results are the same as before to ensure business continuity.

▶ IT owns the design and build, but the business owns the final solution.

▶ From years of experience, the author advocates the creation of a data warehouse executive within the organization to own and champion an enterprise data warehouse at all management levels. Currently financial institutions are leading the way with the creation of a vice president of data warehousing or business intelligence role.

Lack of Proper Resources

▶ More data warehouse projects have failed due to poor resourcing than any other reason for failure. I have seen directors of business intelligence confused about basic terms such as "data mart," a junior OLTP data modeler heading an enterprise OLAP data effort, a mainframe DBMS DBA in charge of all technical details including logical data modeling and report writing without any experience in these fields whatsoever, and project managers who only know how to create project plans with no idea what the individual tasks really are or how they inter-relate.

▶ If the resources are not available in-house, hire experienced people. Do not simply accept resources because they are available within IT or highly enthusiastic about the project. Would you hire an eager first-year dental student to perform your root canal simply because he or she is available and inexpensive?

▶ Ideally a data warehouse should initially have experienced data warehouse resources in all roles. A data warehouse effort requires advanced skills from individuals who can understand how one effort relates to the next and the one after that and so forth. This becomes quite apparent in offshore efforts where junior resources are typically used. In offshore scenarios this is expected as the cost is low, but the architect and management must have solid data warehouse experience.

Data Quality

▶ Tied with or closely following "lack of proper resources" as the top reason of failure is data quality. Data quality is the evil of all evils for an enterprise data warehouse initiative. Many believe that their data is perfect or has very few issues. I have only seen one organization that had practically no data quality issues. Every other customer has had some form of data quality issue that has caused delays with the project timelines. Several organizations had such poor data quality that their data was actually unusable. The business was run intuitively because there was no way they could rely on the actual data values. I am constantly amazed at how many organizations can actually operate given the level of poor data within their operational systems; the systems used daily to ensure fundamental business continuity.

▶ Every single bit of data must be looked into. All values must be investigated. For instance, gender type should be Male, Female, and maybe Unknown in most circumstances. If it is discovered that gender type contains Male, Female,

Married, and Single, then a data quality issue exists and efforts must be guided toward understanding and rectifying this issue. Hence every data warehouse project must have a data modeler to understand and design the data components.

▶   In real estate it is said that location, location, location is the key. In a data warehouse we say: data quality, data quality, data quality!

Basic Values

In summation, both a data warehouse strategy and a business intelligence strategy should strive for several basic values, which can act as a basic guide in all areas of development and in all aspects of the projects.

Keep It Simple

Plan with simplicity; everyone should understand what is being delivered in plain and simple terms.

Think Big, But Act Small

Plan the architecture strategy and deliver in small, controllable phased portions. This facilitates win-win scenarios and therefore high positive visibility for growth.

Do What Is Right

Do not flounder. Do not take on poorly planned projects that do not offer the proper support or are throwaway. Build based on the corporate data strategy and ensure integrity throughout the data warehouse.

Manage with a Bias for Action

Make things happen, be innovative, find ways to deliver, find ways to resolve data issues, and help others to help you.

Continuous Improvement

A data warehouse system must continuously be oiled. Be involved in finding ways of ensuring that the corporate data maintains a high level of quality and impacts are minimal. Corporate change control and impact analysis of source systems is an ongoing effort.

Be Extremely Focused

Always remember that the data warehouse, while typically an IT administration, is for the business. Facilitate a helpful environment to empower the business users. Don't be bullied, but be focused and helpful.

Be Transparent

Let everyone know what is happening and why. Be completely open to suggestions and consider alternative approaches to issue resolutions.

Add Value

In addition to being focused, add value to the business. This forms the initial foundation for performance management. Be part of the business; understand the business in order to add value to their efforts.

Risk Minimization

Coupled with continuous improvement, a data warehouse manager and architect should be continuously finding ways to reduce the unknown variables within the project. This includes data quality, design flexibility, ensuring proper backups, ensuring resource support, reducing run times, and so forth.

CHAPTER 5

Project Resources: Roles and Insights

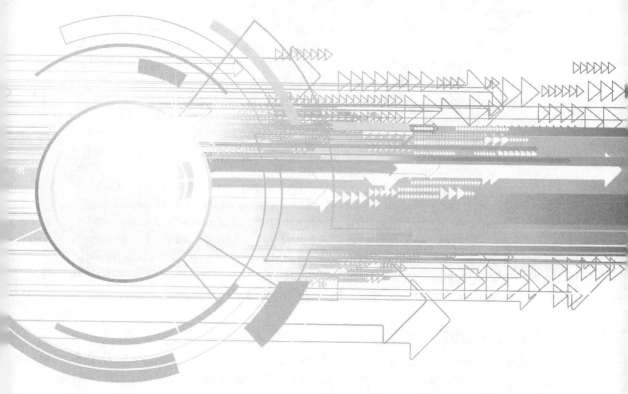

This part of our discussion on preparing to build a data warehouse and business intelligence system deals with the most important aspect—the people. The fundamental building block of the organization, department, or team is the individual. Before individuals are brought on board a project, management must decide which roles the project requires, and only then can individuals be assigned to these duties.

Key Observations

As the organization grows, there are more roles and therefore more levels of authority, which means an increasing issue of achieving control, and therefore coordination of tasks becomes difficult. Smaller organizations do not have so many levels of authority, so individuals can perform tasks more informally based on their best judgment. In larger organizations, the levels of authority tend to control tasks and therefore add formality to roles and tasks. This is one of the main reasons why smaller organizations can bring new and innovative products to market much faster than larger corporations, and why larger organizations are afflicted with much bureaucracy.

To mitigate bureaucracy, organizations create divisions within the ranks. As the organization grows, the divisions become hierarchical from the executive office down to the department and subdepartment levels. At the lower level, the organizational grouping is typically formed at the level of functional expertise; for example, database, data modeling, data architecture, ETL team, BI team, and so forth. In many cases, individual departments buck this structure by creating their own line-of-business mini-IT teams consisting of a senior analyst and several empowered junior resources. The idea here is to alleviate cross-departmental bureaucracies in hopes of enabling speedier business intelligence insights. However, while this may be a necessity if the IT department is slow or unresponsive and the business unit must advance at any expense, this setup goes against core competencies of the line of business. Organizations with several mini-IT shops are prime candidates for a centralized business intelligence team. On the upside, the mini-IT shops are run by business managers who know and understand the data-driven business requirements for their departmental reporting needs. These are the important business individuals who can really help an enterprise business intelligence effort move forward.

Project Teams

Project teams are at the lowest level of the hierarchy, as they typically take on the fundamental building tasks of the organization. Because projects have a start and end date, individuals are taken, or borrowed, from their respective functional groups to work together on the project. This is typically called a *matrix reporting scenario* because the individuals report primarily to their functional managers and to their project managers. Large global organizations have the added luxury of sharing individuals from different countries remotely or by physically relocating the individuals temporarily to a central site.

Resources report to their department managers but act as a group within the scope of the project. As such there is usually a level of dominant competitiveness as individuals strive to take their place in the pecking order of the project based on their personalities and insights. Individuals with the most years of experience within the organization and within their area of expertise tend to take on more authoritative roles. This is not to say that their role on the team gives them the power to take on such authority, but there always seems to be a shuffling toward a ranking of dominance within the team that tends to result in a leadership order. This all forms part of the group formation and development steps:

▶ **Forming**   Members try to determine their roles and dominance in the team.

▶ **Storming**   Resolving conflicts as the team members find their place and common ground.

▶ **Norming**   Creating trust and openness as a group culture sets in.

▶ **Performing**   Goal and task achievement focus.

Typically on any project, as in any organization, it is not necessarily the person in authority who gets things done, but the one with the power who knows the levels of authority and can work the bureaucratic chain successfully who gets things accomplished. Individuals who have been in organizations for a longer period of time tend to have many social connections, which works well for an enterprise project, especially when it comes to sourcing data and inquiring into data issues. It is essential to keep these in mind while building a project team.

Initially when a project plan is developed, the roles are identified and hence a role culture develops that emphasizes the duties of the role over the individuals since the roles are not always filled at this point. In a data warehouse or business intelligence project, since roles should be filled by experts who are typically senior-level individuals within their expertise, the culture quickly becomes a task culture.

Senior Expertise

In the author's opinion, only senior-level IT expertise should join a data warehouse project. Junior resources should tune their craft and expertise on operational systems rather than on an enterprise-level effort such as a data warehouse system. The reason is that a data warehouse system requires a strategic-level design since it covers the enterprise as opposed to a functional area within the organization. From my experience, those who have built enterprise-level systems should begin data warehouse system projects to ensure a high level of flexibility in the design, and tailor the physical implementation with the ability for growth as the system expands over time. Once the fundamental phase of a data warehouse system has been created, then junior-level resources can join to manage the operational aspects and ongoing ad hoc requests.

The term "senior-level expertise" refers to an individual with senior-level ability to innovate and has the experience of having built a data warehouse system before. In this context, the reference is not toward, for instance, a data modeler with 20 years of experience who is very silo- or task-oriented. If the person does not have a sense of innovation or finds the task of innovating difficult, that person would be a liability. A person with an open and flexible professional attitude and years of technical skills is the type of person being referred to as having "senior-level expertise." It is assumed that a person at the senior level of expertise should be able to extrapolate and design in new fashions appropriate to the business requirements. An individual who has done the same thing the same way for 15 years is typically not a person open to viewing the enterprise in an abstract manner, thus allowing flexibility to their craft. This is the author's personal guideline but is in no way a rule. Under such limiting circumstances, engaging an experienced external consultant to lead the initiative and mentor in-house resources is a good approach in shifting attitudes and introducing new methodology and innovation.

It has been this author's experience that if the data warehouse team is resourced with junior-level resources and the team is somewhat consensus-driven, the project will progress at the speed and strength of the slowest member. To build and maintain a high level of synergy, especially in the initial phases, all resources should have as senior a level of expertise as possible. With such a level of experts, management must create a "can do" culture and allow the members to manage their daily tasks as necessary. The upside of a project with members at the senior level is that progress can be quite fast, and the result can be quite innovative and add great value to the business. The downside of such a resourced team is that control can be difficult for management; hence the manager must be flexible and able to work with a creative team.

Leadership

Another factor in such an environment is to ensure that the team plays well together. Senior-level resources can turn inward and build based on their beliefs and experiences, which may go against the grain of the group. Management must ensure and reinforce direction and goals without seeming repetitious or parental. Hence the project manager must take on a leadership role without seeming authoritative and manage based on common sense and the best approach for the scenario at hand while empowering the individuals within their own roles.

Silicon Valley was a great example of allowing the creative aspects of individuals to flourish by removing unnecessary bureaucratic constraints. Projects began by ensuring that the environment was fully conducive to a team spirit and effort, and then tasked individuals with specialized goals where the individual was free to determine the best path they knew. A group discussion would allow creativity to analyze the avenues and evolve into several possible avenues. Then leadership would plan and present their best direction to move on. As development progressed, nothing was cast in stone, thus allowing modifications here and there to enhance the effort and resulting product. As we all know, in a short period of time, Silicon Valley produced many major advancements in the computer industry and several very successful organizations based on this open expert-level culture.

On one particular project, many members had to commute two to three hours to the office and several hours back home each day. Adding the typical eight to nine hours of work made for a very long day, and yet the manager introduced a sense of urgency up front by asking the team to stay late and work overtime to meet the milestones on a regular basis. This definitely did not show proper leadership and immediately put the team into a push-back state of mind. Many demanded that the project plan be reviewed so as to have a more realistic timeline without impacting their social lives so drastically. The culture became more relaxed when this was done and by allowing people to work from home periodically. This really moved the emphasis toward the work rather than a lifestyle change and proved to be quite successful. You cannot bring your goods to market if your horse won't move. If you keep the team happy and do not add too many hurdles, overall efforts will be simpler. This leadership quality applies to any type of project, not just to a data warehouse effort.

These days with cross-social cultures and globalization, managing an enterprise-specialized project such as the development of a data warehouse system can be quite difficult. Managers increasingly need more knowledge and skills in cross-culture interactions, multinational teams, and global alliances. Of course, this is over and above the need for the manager to understand the fundamentals of a data warehouse system and the generalities of each development silo: design and architecture, ETL, database systems, data distribution and population, performance layer, user presentation layer such as business intelligence aspects, metadata, physicalization and optimization areas, and so forth.

In any management role, it is the manager's task to instill a culture suitable for the project goals given the team members. It is critical that the manager is not just a timekeeper or task planner, but a people person dedicated to influencing the activities and efforts of the group toward goal achievement given the current boundaries and limitations. Too many projects fail simply because management was purely creating a project plan and emphasizing the management of tasks rather than leading the overall effort. Some overmanage by holding daily status meetings and micro-manage by trying to resolve individual member technical issues on the spot. Others are not 100 percent dedicated to the project and fail to recognize hurdles or to communicate with team members, thus leaving individuals with no sense of leadership. Management must be completely allocated and consumed by the project. There is more than enough work for one full-time manager on any data warehouse or business intelligence project. Management must plan, organize, control, and motivate to achieve project goals, hence a full-time, one-project focus role is an absolute. A good data warehouse project manager clarifies the path and leads the way.

Project Sponsor

Good managers are difficult to find and yet every project has one. The project sponsor is a must to ensure that the project is moving along appropriately—that the project is attaining its milestones and is heading in the proper direction. The difference between the project sponsor and the project manager is that the sponsor's efforts push the project forward within the organization. The project manager pushes the project resources in attaining the project deliverables. However, to ensure that the manager is making progress, the project sponsor must also keep an eye on the project progress. If the sponsor is marketing the project within the organization, it is in his or her best interest to also act as a recurring scheduled project reviewer.

Leaving the corporate investment to a single manager is not a wise strategy. If the project is reviewed by the steering committee only once a quarter, this means that the project can be completely off course for several months before someone pulls on the reins. The project sponsor must regularly review a data warehouse project, especially the first iteration. There used to be a television program in my neck of the woods about building homes. Each week the show would feature a do-it-yourself homeowner who was rebuilding a major portion of their house. The show usually started with the homeowner discussing their well-thought-out plan with budget and timelines. As the show evolved, construction would fall victim to no-show construction crews, rain delays, unavailable construction material, failed inspections, and so forth. Eventually the house would take twice as long as anticipated at twice the cost. The point is that no matter how much up-front planning is done, there will always be delays that the project manager may or may not be able to control.

The project sponsor must be aware of these events on a regular basis to determine the proper corrective action at the strategic level. Unusual as it may be, one project decided to completely stop development due to timeline overruns. This halt gave time to the planning team to re-evaluate the overall effort and goals. They later restarted the project, because it formed part of an overall five-year strategy, but this time with a more solid focus on foundation and scoped deliverables based on absolute requirements. Always ensure that your requirements are tangible and quantified. This will help management plan and control the project efforts. Lead the effort with presence, communication, and motivation, influencing activities toward achieving specific attainable goals.

Data Warehouse Executive

Since most organizations cannot operate without insights from their data, this elevates the importance of a data warehouse and business intelligence system within the operational aspects of the corporation. With data recognized as a corporate asset, many organizations are creating an executive-level role giving enterprise responsibility for this fundamental and critical organizational asset.

Financial institutions, especially, are creating vice president–level roles specifically charged with owning the data warehouse system and creating optimized business intelligence solutions in partnership with the operational lines of the business for in-depth analytics. Focused analytics give organizations insights and a competitive advantage in the marketplace. BI technology enables companies to look forward in their key business processes to identify potential trends, operational insights, and opportunities within the context of the business usage.

Team Structure

Each organization operates differently, but there is a common theme throughout when it comes to resources for building a data warehouse system. Figure 5-1 shows a three-tier architecture: executive sponsor level, project management level, and development team level.

While the following section describes the major roles in a data warehouse and business intelligence development project, there are usually a number of resources in each area, depending on the size of the effort. For instance, it is not unusual for a large project to have a number of data warehouse architects: a technical architect for database and servers, a data architect to ensure data aspects, and a solution architect to oversee the entire system solution being built. Conversely, small organizations have been known to take on teams of three to four people in which each member wears many hats depending on his or her skill level. In most organizations, external consultants are brought in at the onset to mentor the team on the initial efforts.

Executive Sponsorship

To begin we look at the top of the organization. Executives within an organization are similar to drivers of an automobile. They decide on direction and route. If a data

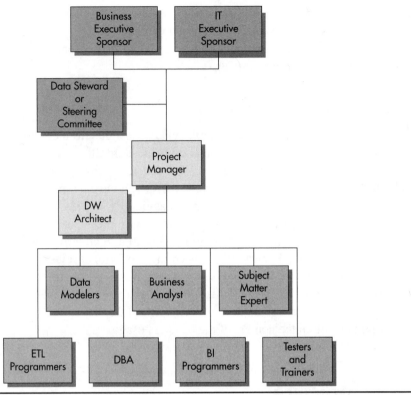

Figure 5-1   *Data warehouse basic resources*

warehouse initiative is from a managerial level, this is similar to a passenger hoping that the proper direction and route will be taken. To ensure that a destination is reached, the driver must agree to drive there. He may not know the proper route, but if there is agreement on the destination, the passenger can navigate and direct the vehicle with the driver. A data warehouse initiative must have a driver, aka executive sponsorship. Without this there is no real push for business usage, which defeats the purpose of building a data warehouse system.

Because a data warehouse is built by IT and used by the business, there needs to be sponsorship within both areas. One without the other is just not a good idea. Having an executive-level sponsor from the business and a CIO or VP of IT is the ideal scenario. Barring this potential, a steering committee can be formed with business and IT management, preferably vice presidents and directors. Having a committee with only manager-level resources is just an organized effort at hoping that all will be accepted at some later date. I certainly would not want to join a firm with a data warehouse committee that has no executive members.

The executive sponsors must have enterprise vision to understand and plan for the organization as a whole. These people must have company-wide insight in order to guide based on the organization's strategic direction. The sponsors must have authority to define priorities and enough influence to get things done. If there are data quality issues in an operational source system, the executive sponsors must be able to persuade and influence the source system owner to make the necessary changes in a timely manner.

The sponsors are responsible for reviewing project progress, achieving milestones, resolving key issues, championing the effort throughout the organization, and most importantly, ensuring a continuous budget to fund the effort. The sponsors are the people who set realistic expectations from a business solution perspective.

Without an executive data warehouse sponsor, regardless of the reason for building a data warehouse, the probability of the effort succeeding is very low. Without an executive sponsor, the effort may begin with high spirits but will eventually fade away due to lack of interest.

Data Stewards

Most organizations typically have an executive sponsor and business ownership or data stewards. There is usually one data steward per business area, who may also be that area's subject matter expert (SME). This individual is responsible for ensuring that the data objects (that is, data components, definitions, and examples) are represented within the data warehouse. While the data warehouse repository is administered by IT, it is initially owned by the data warehouse sponsors. The respective data marts and reporting area contents are directly overseen by the business data stewards. The data steward is the main point of contact for specific business areas from data to usage and from requirements to strategy.

Data stewards normally take responsibility in being aware of changes to the operational systems and the potential impacts these may have on the data warehouse system. Coordination of changes is essential to ensure that the daily data warehouse processes, especially the capturing of source system data, run smoothly. This role is also responsible for business metadata and therefore ensures a level of data quality. Data quality issues within the data warehouse must be resolved by the data stewards, who lean heavily on the data warehouse executive sponsor(s) for support.

Basic Resources

For any data warehouse initiative, there are certain fundamental resources that need to be on the project team:

- ► Project manager
- ► Data warehouse architect

- ▶ Business analyst
- ▶ Business lead (subject matter expert)
- ▶ Data modeler
- ▶ Database administrator: DBMS and application level
- ▶ ETL programmer
- ▶ Business intelligence (report and analytics) programmer
- ▶ Application tester and user trainer

The following sections describe these resources in greater detail.

Project Manager

A project manager (PM) is a must and needs to be dedicated to the development and coordination efforts of a data warehouse. Do not share the PM resource with other projects. The project manager is not simply a timekeeper; this person must be active within the project on a daily basis to coordinate effort, remove political obstacles, and ensure the direction of the project. This role coordinates the design and creation of the data warehouse system and manages all the side projects associated with the effort if the side projects do not have their own program manager. This includes data quality efforts, reverse-engineering projects, data discovery efforts, and so forth. This is a full-time role. To make this role part-time removes leadership and invites defiance within the team. As with any PM role, this person is responsible for implementing executive direction, resource issues, customer and sponsor relationships, and handling all delivery expectations.

As a general guideline, no person should work alone because they all form part of the larger picture, which is the data warehouse system. The author advocates the buddy system, where each person can perform sanity checks with the other to ensure that both are performing effectively within their areas. Hence the data warehouse architect role.

Data Warehouse Architect

The data warehouse architect works hand in hand with the project manager. While the PM is responsible for managing the design and delivery of the final product, the architect is responsible for the detailed development of the final product.

The data warehouse architect role initially begins as a data warehouse solution architect creating the overall solution at a high level. This role also entails the technical architecture, which determines the physical environment: servers, disk space, middleware, general distribution architecture, BI tools, and so forth. Once this technical aspect is determined, the role turns to a data architect, who is to ensure the proper design, storage, flow and optimized usage of the data.

The architect establishes the technical vision for the data warehouse system and should be able to easily partner with each role, hence the importance of the buddy system. The architect may or may not determine the technical infrastructure, but will most definitely design the overall data flow solution with input from resources on the team. To rephrase this role, the data warehouse architect will consult with each role on the team to help as much as possible with direction and best practices while creating the full data flow architecture. The best background scenario for a data warehouse architect is having risen from a technical background including ETL, DBA, data modeling, and business reporting—jack of all trades and master of most.

Business Analyst

The role of the business analyst is to determine the business requirements via business user interviews and to organize the resulting information. The business analyst is responsible for creating the functional specification for the final product—the analytical environment and reporting requirements. This person must be familiar with data warehouse concepts and should have a good understanding of the data model. Alternatively, at a minimum, if no data model exists, the business analyst should be able to create a pillar diagram to show fundamental data components.

This person will work with the data modeler in understanding and modeling the business in data terminology. The business analyst should also be able to produce a dimension and measure cross-reference matrix from the business reports to discover and document the requirements. This business analyst will at first work closely with the business SME to discover the business and the requirements, then with the data modeler to document and model the data components, then with the ETL programmers to ensure that business rules are followed, and finally with the business intelligence programmers to design the final end-user product. Of course, the data architect will be involved with the business analyst quite a bit initially as the business requirements are being discovered, in order to determine an overall strategic solution.

Business SME

The business lead is the subject matter expert and will work side by side with the business analyst to relay the business requirements, business processes, and business rules to the data warehouse team. This person will also be the lead for the source system analysis and will work closely with the data architect and data modeler in source system discovery and mapping. Later the SME will work with the business intelligence programmer lead at times directly or via the business analyst or the data architect to ensure the final product. Testing and training will also be tasks for the business lead if no specific tester/trainer is available.

Data Modeler

The data modeler is responsible for modeling the data warehouse repository and the data marts logically (design) and must understand the implications of the physical design. This senior role involves being well versed in data warehousing and understanding the data model implications, strategies, concepts, and dependencies. In many projects, this person also acts as the data architect if he or she has a strong technical background and has been involved in numerous data warehouse implementations. If the data model is purchased, this position should be filled initially by or in conjunction with the vendor consultant and transitioned to a local resource as the model becomes more familiar.

This person works hand in hand with the data architect (if a different role) and ETL programmers as the data modeler helps create the specification for the ETL processes. The role also works with the DBA to relate the data model from design to usage, and the business intelligence programmers to relate the underlying data and design usage. Of course, the business analyst and the data modeler are in a symbiotic relationship from the very beginning of the project.

DBA

The database administrator, DBA, is required to transform the data model design, aka logical data model, into a physical or optimized data model. All databases are designed for usage and therefore optimized for specific access. The data warehouse repository is physically designed for capturing and holding historical data, while the data marts are physically designed for data retrieval.

There are two types of DBA roles: DBMS and application. The DataBase Management System (DBMS) DBA is tasked with ensuring that the database system is operational and available for use, which includes data backups. In many small and mid-level organizations, the DBMS DBA is also responsible for ensuring and administering the infrastructure (servers). The application DBA is more involved in ensuring optimized data loads and retrieval for specific business usage. The application DBA should always review ETL processes and data extraction queries. Both the application DBA and the DBMS DBA along with the data architect (data modeler) are involved in the physical setup and design of the database. In many cases, the data architect may lead the physical data model efforts with the DBA adding indexes, partitioning, and so forth.

ETL Programmer

ETL programmers are focused on capturing the data from the source system, transforming it in whatever manner is necessary to load it into the database. In many organizations, this function is outsourced. The technical architect, data architect, data modeler, and DBA are usually involved with the ETL programmers to ensure that they understand the requirements and that the programs deliver the required data components into the designed database. This role is also involved in delivering data from the data warehouse repository to the data marts. In the data modeling phase of the data warehouse, ETL programmers are tasked with performing data profiling of the source systems. Data profiling is quite important to the data modeler, who must know if each table column holds the expected data or not. For instance, suppose that gender type in a source system holds 1 for Male, 2 for Female, and 3 for Married individuals. The latter result shows a data quality issue, which might not be known if data profiling were not performed.

In many instances, the source system analyst is also the ETL lead and may be involved with the physical database design with the DBA, as their role is very aware of volumetrics.

BI Programmer

The business intelligence programmers, or report programmers, use the underlying data marts to support the business reports determined by the business analyst and SME. This area has high visibility from an end-product point of view and must be managed carefully. The business typically wants to do whatever they fancy with the data at hand, and the reporting programmers must create solutions that allow for the maximum flexibility to ensure end-user usage and support. These individuals are experts at using at least one of the BI tools such as Cognos, Crystal Reports, Business Objects, and so forth.

This role is at the front lines of a data warehouse solution and must be quick at producing and flexible in what they produce. The BI program team needs an experienced programmer at the helm. This group works closely with the business analyst, SME, data architect, and DBA. The lead BI programmer can take on the role of a BI architect in many organizations. The BI architect in many instances also sets up the BI tool and environment as well as taking on the strategic BI lead and data mart designer role. The data mart designer works hand in hand with the data modeler, who centralizes and coordinates data design integrity.

Unit Tester and End-User Trainer

Before any application can be delivered to the business, someone has to test it to ensure that it operates as designed given the actual production-level data. This person reports back to the project manager any defects to be reworked. The same person usually becomes the end-user trainer. Since the individual is fully versed in the BI solution, this person usually ends up performing face-to-face training with the business end users.

Other Roles

Once established, the data warehouse system will require other ongoing resources such as a change control coordinator, which at first should be handled by the project manager, data architect, or business analyst. Also, an ad hoc reporting resource will be required to help with all those one-time end-user requests and initial data mining efforts.

Periodic Reviews: Progress Audit

It is highly advisable to review progress regularly. This is an ongoing task for the project manager—not to simply ask which tasks have been completed and which have not as a timekeeper would, but to be involved in the detail issues and progress. The executive sponsor will also need a realistic briefing on progress.

Many organizations who periodically bring in external expert consultants to review progress do successfully reach their goals, moreso than those who do not. As I have seen while participating in many progress audits, the builders of these projects seem to be well aware of issues and direction of their efforts and pay attention to criticism with an emphasis on corrective action. If you just continuously build projects without an appreciation for review and corrective action, you are relying on the mere hope that all will evolve successfully. Some of these projects do succeed, but most ignore obvious pitfalls, believing success requires simply longer hours and more effort.

In one particular project with 150 individuals, there was a concern about delivering on time. Everyone was quite occupied; the dedicated manager was continuously busy in meetings, the three architects were rushing all about, and yet there seemed to be problems with delivery due to loading issues. The author did a two-week audit and found several issues: Individuals changed roles every two months, and therefore not one person understood the overall data flow. The idea of moving people around to different positions was interesting but not recommended. A data warehouse needs experts in specific fields. ETL programmers should not suddenly take on the role of a data modeler if they have no experience in this domain. Secondly, with so many people working at the same role for short periods, insights from past efforts were lost. In the end, we had to draw a simple data flow architecture on a white board for a particular focus and interview the leads of each group to obtain details of the built processes. In two weeks we resolved the data flow issues, properly documented the load processes, and were able to remove redundancy, resulting in considerably reduced database load times.

Center of Competence

Since a data warehouse is a system, it will live on after the project to build it completes. An infrastructure team will be required to support the production environment, as with any other system, and a BI team to manage the ongoing business inquiries.

Typically a center of competence (CoC) is set up to manage and enhance the business intelligence system as well as handle ongoing business ad hoc queries. The CoC should consist of a business liaison, which is the role of a business analyst. The center must also contain the business intelligence report and query writers. While most modern-day BI tools give business users the ability to dynamically query the data environment themselves, the business users can only use the table views as defined in the BI tool. When queries go beyond the current data views, the BI programmers, aka report writers, must service the business community in their data quests. To support the efforts, ETL programmers may also form part of the center of competence to extract from the central database repository to create new data marts as needed. Typically, the ETL programmers in the CoC will not pull data directly from source systems because this involves much analysis to determine ongoing feed timings, data quality issues, enterprise data modeling integration, volumetrics for database disk space storage, and so forth.

A center of competence is a call center for business users in the business intelligence forum. The CoC can help with questions regarding the data components, ad hoc queries, or any other IT help regarding the business intelligence areas. The center should include technical-savvy personnel skilled in data query technology and knowledgeable in the business for CoC customers. In turn, the center of competence works toward ensuring

▶ **Data management** Data structures, definitions, data quality, metadata management, and stewardship

▶ **Information delivery** Data marts, analytics, training, ad hoc requests, and overall business support

▶ **BI coordination efforts** Best practices, standards, BI expertise, technology and vender management, and so forth

Write-It-Up Overview

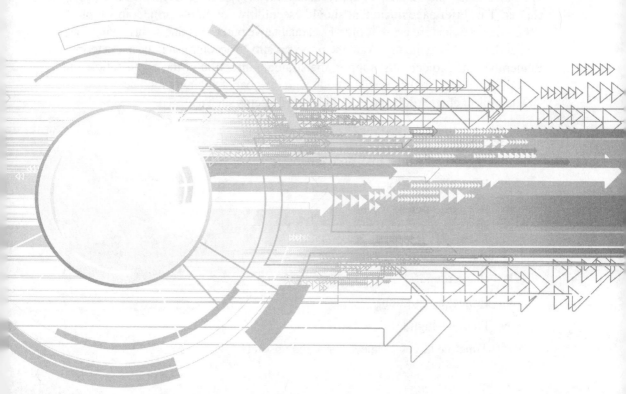

To get a data warehouse project going, the business group must identify the boundaries or details of the project as they pertain to the organization, to the business unit, and to IT from technical and business perspectives. The business group can be a business unit or IT. These details must be documented and presented to upper management for funding in the context of the corporate goals and strategies in the form of a basic business case. Think of a teenager asking his or her parents for money. Their first response would be: why, how much, who will be there, when will it be done, what time will you be home, and so forth. In business terms the funding request will be met with the same sort of questions: purpose, benefit, cost, timeline, resources, return on investment, and so forth.

The following is a brief point form chapter giving insights into project charter, project scope, and Statement of Work documents, of which at least one or all three are used for any given project.

Project Charter

The first step is a presentation to upper management, typically documented as a project charter. This brief page document should essentially define the project in simple terms—bullet points are great. A high-level qualitative purpose is fine at this point. The goal at this level is to identify what the project wants to accomplish in business terms. Remember, the project must support the strategic direction of the organization and should be marketed to the executive body with the goal of attaining funding.

The project charter document should include items such as

- Project name
- Stakeholders (by title, role, and/or name)
  - Executive sponsor
  - Business sponsor
  - Project manager
- Overview
  - Background
  - Project description
  - Phases—high level
  - Timeline target—expectations and absolute

- ► Objectives
  - ► Reason for doing the project
  - ► Metrics—what the project is looking for or to do
    - ► By phase (if more than one)
    - ► Ease of use
    - ► Timeliness
    - ► Response times
    - ► Lowering costs
    - ► Other
- ► Assumptions
  - ► Limits or boundaries
    - ► Defined or imposed
  - ► Focused areas
  - ► Concerns
  - ► Inputs
  - ► Outputs
- ► Deliverables
  - ► Documents
  - ► Data models
  - ► Data architecture
  - ► Additional findings (changes on initial goals)
- ► Cost and ROI
  - ► Estimate of timeline
  - ► Estimate of resources
- ► Key expectations
  - ► Executive support
  - ► SME availability
  - ► IT specialists
- ► Approval required to start, aka signoffs
  - ► By sponsors (executive, business, and IT)

The project charter can be a difficult document to put together but should be required because it starts the funding process for the project. One important and difficult aspect to estimate is the cost and return on investment details. These are problematic since the ultimate business impact could be seen in a number of business areas and costs can be highly variable in each area. There are many aspects of costing, but for resources costing, aka resource cost estimating, perhaps the following scenario is useful. Pick general base resource rates for cost calculations, for example, $100K per year for in-house resources and $200K per year for consultants; then determine the overall cost based on the estimated timeline for the project—remember, this is a high-level estimate. For example:

▶ Three in-house resources * $50K (for six-month duration) = $150K

▶ Two consultants * $50K (for three-month duration) = $100K

▶ Total *estimated* resource cost is $250K over six months.

Return on Investment is quite another challenge. First: is the data warehouse system or business intelligence focus 100 percent attributable to a business ROI? If more noodles in the noodle stores were sold during a targeted time period, were these sales 100 percent attributed to the data warehouse effort? Are the sales 100 percent attributed to the cost of the BI effort? Probably not, since there is no absolute method of determining this relationship, but there is a high probability that the effort did have an impact, and therefore a percentage of the business revenue, profit, cost reduction, and so on, can be attributed, but how much?

In conclusion, a project charter is a brief "vision document" to communicate the project and boundaries. Some like to include more information including team members, project schedules, milestones, change control procedures, and so forth. Whatever the details, the point is to have a project charter to explain the foundation of the project. It can also be used to form the foundation of a managing contract, especially if the company is using an external consulting firm to resource or perform the development efforts.

Project Scope

Another document used to supplement the project charter is the project scope document. This document gives more details on the project as a whole but is typically only a few pages in length.

The project scope details what is in and out of scope, how a change is performed, and usually includes the many risks associated with the effort. While the project charter is used to get the point across with due diligence to upper management for funding and as a communicative tool going forward, the project scope document is a refinement of the details. In short, this document highlights high-level rules on what will and will not be included in the project efforts along with the associated risks.

In many cases the project scope is integrated in the project charter. Others merge it into the Statement of Work as seen in the next section, under "Scope of Work."

Statement of Work (SOW)

The Statement of Work document is the one document most visible to the project team. This document lists all the fine details of the project including the team members: project manager, business subject matter experts, business analysts, technical architect, data architect, data modeler, DBA, BI architect, ETL developers, report developers, source system analysts, and so forth.

Once the project is defined by the project charter and refined by the project scope, the Statement of Work sets the playing field: project plan, resources, timelines, milestones, completion criteria, and each deliverable. Responsibility matrices are also used to correlate roles and responsibilities.

A Statement of Work within an organization defines all aspects of the project. A Statement of Work with an external organization, for instance, a consulting firm to manage and develop a project, is geared more towards a contractual obligation on deliverables within time periods. Both can include the technical environment requirements, location of work, timeline of the project, exact deliverables, acceptance criteria, regulatory requirements or guidelines, specifications, special requirements, risks and risk mitigation, payment schedule, and other areas.

The Statement of Work usually includes the following points:

▶ Project name
▶ Stakeholders (preferably by name and title)
  ▶ Executive sponsor
  ▶ Business sponsor
  ▶ Project manager
▶ Objectives
▶ Scope of Work
  ▶ Inclusions
  ▶ Exclusions

- ► Approach
- ► Description and sequence of work modules
- ► Dependencies to unit of work
- ► Key deliverables and milestones
- ► Resources
  - ► Team members
  - ► Roles and responsibilities
- ► Project plan
- ► Management approach
  - ► Change management
  - ► Issues and problem management (log and escalation)
  - ► Risk assessment management
- ► Progress communications
  - ► Executive meetings
  - ► Management meetings
  - ► Team meetings

Note that assumptions and estimates are not included in a Statement of Work. Since the SOW is an actual plan, all details are fact-based. The project charter has estimations of timelines, costs, resources and so forth, but the SOW is supposed to be an accurate representation of the project efforts. Assumptions can, however, be communicated as risk items within the project scope document under the "management approach" section. The idea is that if x happens, a solution of y is possible, or milestone re-evaluations will be required, or the following scenario will reduce a specific risk.

For instance, two business subject matter experts, sales and marketing and inventory, shall be available to the project two days a week during the four-week analysis phase. Should this not occur, the project may be delayed xx weeks. To alleviate the risk, a time schedule will be agreed to and distributed with the business SMEs to facilitate exact meeting dates and times.

Any changes to an agreed-upon statement of work should be evaluated individually to determine their overall impact to the project timelines, deliverables, scope, cost, and so forth. These changes are tracked by individual change requests as they occur.

PART

II

Components

This section discusses the ingredients of a Data Warehouse system to support the corporate asset and Business Intelligence efforts.

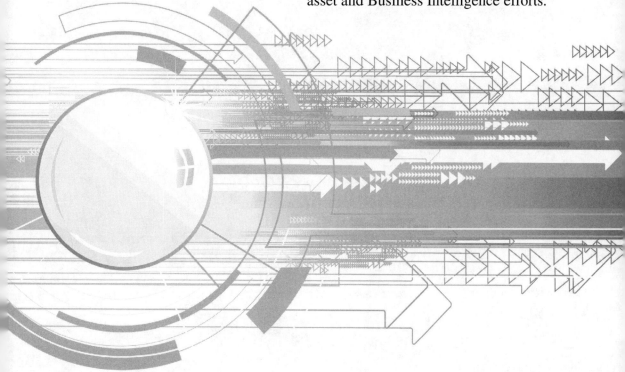

Business Intelligence: Data Marts and Usage

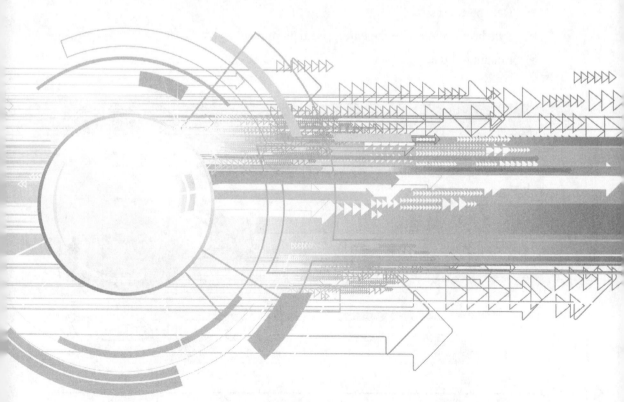

W e start this part of the book from the perspective of the business usage, as most data warehouse projects are focused on tangible business deliverables. Looking at the basic data architecture of a data warehouse system, as shown in Figure 7-1 and as previously mentioned in this book, our focus for this chapter is on the last two layers: performance and user presentation layers. These form the "information out" or usage of a data warehouse system, typically for data analysis of some sort or another.

Depending on your role within the project and/or usage of the business intelligence solution, you may be interested in any number of IT operational or business information aspects, such as

▶ The information on the final reports

▶ The performance or speed of obtaining the report information

▶ The underlying data mart designs with dimensions and measures

▶ Volumetrics

▶ Indexes

▶ Data partitions

▶ Synchronization with the enterprise data model

▶ Loading of data

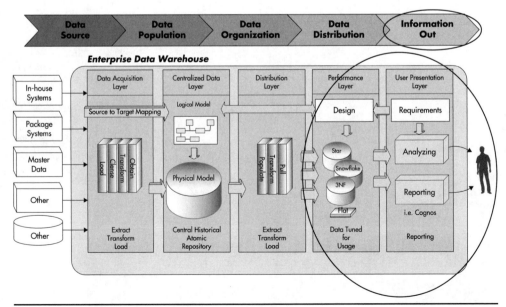

Figure 7-1 *Data warehouse architecture: data flow*

- ▶ Quality of data
- ▶ Source of data
- ▶ Granularity of data
- ▶ Association of one data mart to another
- ▶ Operational support

and the list goes on.

This chapter reviews several of these topics with a focus on components. The idea is to discuss the basic areas of business intelligence from a design and build perspective with insights on best practices, along with the implications of one design or build path over another.

Why Model the Data?

To assist in the development of a business intelligence solution, the underlying data should be organized and structured in such a fashion as to facilitate the querying and usage of the data. This is called a *data model*, which is an abstraction of individual data elements and how they relate to each other. It visually depicts how the data is to be organized.

If the data queries are known up front, then the data can be structured in a fashion that greatly enhances the effectiveness of the individual queries and the ease of use for the business user. If the exact business usage of the underlying data is not known, then the risk is developing structures that are not conducive to how the data will be queried, which almost certainly guarantees poor performance and probably low usage of the final solution and therefore a poor ROI.

In business intelligence solutions, the data model designs are typically data marts designed in a star, snowflake, or third normal form fashion. Data marts are slices of the overall corporate data model designed for a specific focused usage. If the corporate enterprise data model were an apple pie, the data mart would be a single slice of the pie.

A data mart is a data model specifically designed for ease of use by the business user, which is optimized with performance of usage in mind, and its contents should be obvious to the business.

If the data is modeled by a central team within the organization, then an enterprise vocabulary can emerge, thus ensuring that all data models conform to the same vocabulary. If the data is modeled by separate departments without coordination, then distinct vocabularies usually emerge. "Customer" can be called person, individual, member, guest, or whatever else. And different descriptive attributes can be merged into the same entity: current address in customer, family members in individual, and so forth.

A key to a corporate data model, no matter what its usage, is the conformance to a single vocabulary to ensure consistent terminology and an understanding throughout the enterprise. For instance, is a customer an individual or is an individual a customer? Is an employee a customer, is an employee an individual, or is the individual a customer and an employee? Perhaps the model has individuals who can have roles as customers and/or employees depending on the distinctions and usage. Determining a consistent vocabulary and structuring the data in a flexible manner is an important aspect of a data warehouse design, and it is also the recommended approach.

Each data mart model should be designed for specific groupings of use both in regard to the need for speed of retrieval and intended information usage. This means that the effort is not only in determining what data should be in the data mart but also in determining its granularity, amount of history, dimension designs, and measure designs. Should the sales data be for each point-of-sale transaction or summed up at the day level per product by store? Should the customer information hold the customer address? Should the data mart hold current year sales or all sales over the past five years? Of course, a data mart can be used for multiple purposes; for example, to determine the number of distinct customers who purchased a certain product last month or total sales this past quarter, which depends on the dimensions, measures, and granularity. Design for a specific purpose and hold to that strategy. For instance, design a data mart and call it something appropriate such as "Current Year Daily Sales," and also include a brief description such as "current calendar year daily product sales, based on POS sales price, per store up to the end of the previous month." Use the data mart as needed, but within the boundaries of the designed context.

A query is performed on database structures, which in turn are based on a data model design. The latter is known as a *logical data model*, while the database structures are known as a *physical data model*.

Types of Data Models

Figure 7-2 shows many different data models but is by no means a complete view of all types of data models. The vertical arrows make a distinction between logical and physical data models.

Data models include the following types:

▶ **Logical enterprise data model**   Also known as logical business data model, this is a conceptual data model to capture all the business data in a non-application-specific format at the enterprise level. The idea of this data model is to set a vocabulary and to structure the data at an atomic level showing one and only one home for each data item in the enterprise. This is not data-warehouse-specific.

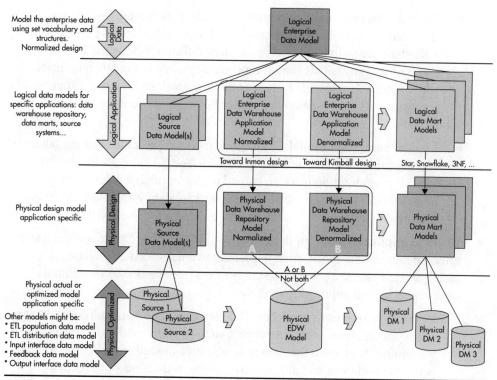

Figure 7-2 *Data models*

▶ **Logical application data model** This level of data models is specific to an application, which may be source systems, data warehouse repository, data warehouse data marts, process models, and so forth. For our data warehouse purposes, Figure 7-2 shows the following types:

    ▶ **Logical source data models** This would be the logical version of a source system. Usually, unless built in-house, this model is identical to the physical database tables and their columns. This model would map to the logical business data model to show compliance with the overall enterprise vocabulary and to ensure that the enterprise business data model has all aspects defined. Data is an asset to the organization; therefore, all data should be modeled at the enterprise level.

    ▶ **Logical enterprise data warehouse repository data model—normalized (A)** The data warehouse repository can be modeled in a third normal form, Inmon style, or in a denormalized Kimball style, which is described in the next bullet point. Most data warehouse repositories are modeled in this Inmon 3NF fashion.

▶ **Logical enterprise data warehouse repository data model—denormalized (B)**   Same as the model described in the previous bullet point but in a Kimball denormalized design. A main difference between Inmon and Kimball designs is that Inmon represents history at the attribute level while Kimball represents history at the row level. More information on this comment will be presented in Chapter 8, which discusses enterprise data models.

▶ **Logical data mart models**   This data model represents what the business users require for their particular focused usage. In many instances this logical representation is a star, snowflake, or normalized design. This model should stem from the logical enterprise data warehouse repository data model and conform to the logical enterprise business data model.

▶ **Physical application design data model**   This level of data models is a step after the logical data models and is geared toward a specific database management system. Such a model may or may not be one-to-one with its counterpart logical application data model.

▶ **Physical source data models**   This model is usually the physical database tables and columns of the in-scope source systems used to feed the data warehouse. It maps to the logical source data models, usually one-to-one per entity and table and attribute to column. Names may differ between logical and physical, but as long as they can be mapped to each other, then all is fine.

▶ **Physical enterprise data warehouse repository data model—normalized (A)**   This normalized data warehouse repository model can be one-to-one with its logical version, but this may be impractical for implementation and usage. Therefore, in most cases this physical version contains collapsed logical subtypes and associations depending on expected input and volumetrics. This type of data model is tuned for capturing and holding data for many years.

▶ **Physical enterprise data warehouse repository data model—denormalized (B)**   A denormalized repository design. This data model, as with the normalized version, is tuned to capture and hold data for many years if using it as a repository base. If you are approaching the overall enterprise repository from a conformed dimension perspective, this model can be just reference data with the transactional measures directly in the data marts. There are several variations on this design at the repository or staging levels.

▶ **Physical data mart models**   The physical version of the logical data mart design. While most business reporting and business intelligence tools prefer this to be a star schema design, it is possible and practical at times to physically represent the star as a snowflake or perhaps a normalized data model at the physical level. This depends on how the data mart will be used, but generally the physical data mart is a star design.

▶ **Physical application optimized data model**   These data models are exactly what the database management system will be using to create tables, columns, indexes, partitions, and so forth. The physical design data model is how the database tables are planned to be built, while the optimized physical data model takes into consideration indexes; anticipated number of rows in the tables; database partitioning; usage, which is anticipated CPU consumption depending on usage frequency; and I/O, which is the anticipated number of database pages being swapped in and out of memory, again depending on expected business queries on the underlying database tables.

▶ The optimized physical data models are based on the initial physical design data models, which are based on an earlier logical data model. The logical data models all conform to the logical enterprise data model, or enterprise business data model. All data models are designed by the data model team.

▶ Logical data mart models can be initially designed by the BI tool designers or architect but should conform to an enterprise model to ensure consistent vocabulary, data types, and data quality expectations (especially with data value expectations; for example, gender is male or female and marital status is single, married, divorced, or separated, rather than a combination of both intermixed). All physical models will need much input from the database administrators to ensure proper technical architecture and setup based on planned expectations.

Design of Data

The planned usage of data determines the type and design of the data model. The type of data model is the context in which the data is held (data marts, data repository, and so on) and the design is the fashion in which the data is structured (star, snowflake, 3NF, and so on).

If the goal is to set an enterprise vocabulary for the corporate data asset, then the type of data model is a logical enterprise data model and the design is one of many, as discussed in Chapter 8. If the goal is to capture and hold enterprise data for long periods of time under a distinct vocabulary, then the type of data model is an enterprise data warehouse data repository and the design can be normalized or denormalized. As in the context of this chapter, if the goal is for a specific business intelligence focus, then a data mart is the type of data model required and the design depends on the specific usage. In this context, a business intelligence focus is a subset of the enterprise data warehouse data model.

Typical types of business intelligence usages are

▶ Multidimensional analysis

▶ Data mining

Multidimensional Analysis

Multidimensional analysis is so named because it is based on a star schema that has a central fact table holding all the required measures and dimension tables, as seen in Figure 7-3. The great aspect of a star schema is that it is very easy to understand and use. Simply select a dimension to qualify the measures and aggregate as desired.

Multidimensional queries are based on the business wanting to look at measures based on specific dimensional analysis. A data model is created and structured for a

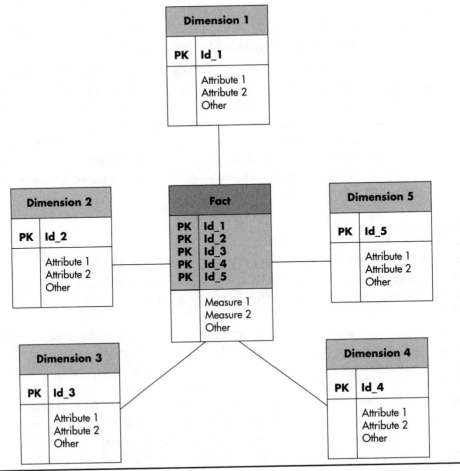

Figure 7-3   *Star schema design*

specific business analysis focus, and is therefore analysis-driven, and when used, it is data-driven because specific dimensional data parameters are chosen. For instance, the data mart may be designed specifically for a retail store sales analysis, and a query may filter the product dimension to look at only measures relating to power tools, for example.

Since a data warehouse collects data mostly from operational systems, the data is "used." This means there is a temporal aspect to the data, which can span as long or as short as desired. Therefore each data mart typically has a time, or date, dimension. This refers to the time of data creation in the operational system, the time of load, and the time of aggregation or summarization. Each is important to the user community especially if the data is seen as perishable. The level of the time dimension is one granularity aspect of the fact table measures.

Star dimensional data models, or star schemas, are based on dimensions with a relationship to a central fact table. These are normally shown as sets of dimensions that surround the fact table such that queries can be stated graphically and design can follow, hence the design looks like a star. These types of models have distinct dimensions that are denormalized entities or topics. For instance, everything about product might be in one dimension and everything about customer would be in another dimension, called customer. There are several deviations to a star schema, the most popular being its physical separation into static and dynamic portions of dimension table for performance reasons.

A variation of a star schema is the snowflake schema, shown in Figure 7-4. Snowflakes are in the same type of data model as stars, but the dimensions are more normalized. The more normalized the snowflake, the more it could potentially revert to a fully normalized, 3NF, data model.

Figure 7-5 shows a typical drill-up and drill-down example based on date. A business usage may be to know all of a certain parameter, such as sales for the year, and then drill down into the sales by quarter, month, week, and finally by day. Or the usage might be the opposite; the business may be looking at day details and want to roll this up to the year level to get an annual view of the business.

A multidimensional analysis report or query in this context is considered dynamic since the business user can decide on the granularity of a dimension and therefore change the report. Granularity in this context is the year, quarter, month, week, or day. Years ago, before multidimensional designs and BI tools, this one dimension example would have been five distinct static business reports.

The potential for multidimensional analysis is tremendous. Imagine the design having six dimensions, and you can drill up or drill down from each dimension as desired. This is a huge empowerment for the business user and tremendous insight into the data for analysis, which is one of the main reasons why business intelligence and data warehousing became such a popular topic.

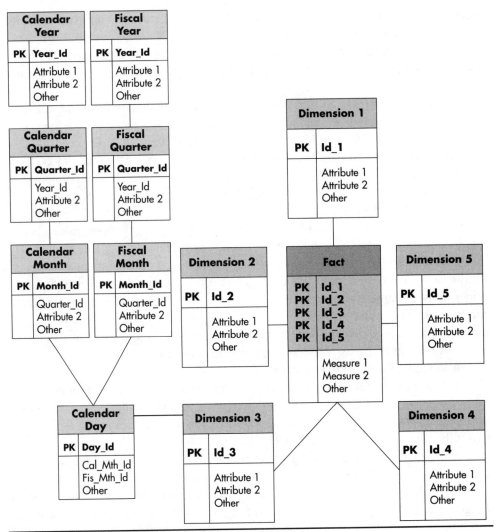

Figure 7-4 *Snowflake schema design*

Figure 7-6 shows a Sales Analysis data mart with six dimensions. Four of these have differing levels of granularity. All together these are considered one dynamic area of analysis or one "dynamic report." When I started in this business, this one analysis area example would have been produced from over hundreds of reports or queries. Since that would be impractical, the business users had to decide which dimension granularity to select to produce only a handful of reports. As compared to today's business intelligence technology, prior insights would only have been a partial view of the underlying data aggregation.

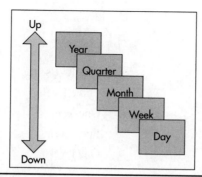

Figure 7-5   *Drill-up and drill-down example*

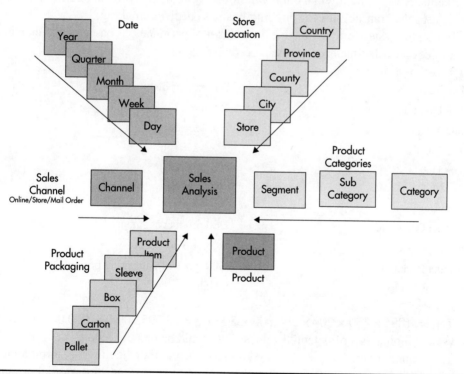

Figure 7-6   *Dimension hierarchy example*

Report calculation would include these levels:

Date	Five levels
Store Location	Five levels
Product Categories	Three levels
Product	One level
Product Packaging	Five levels
Sales Channel	One level

Each dimension level can create a report with one level from each of the other dimensions, so total dimension permutations could be: $5 \times 5 \times 3 \times 1 \times 5 \times 1 = 375$ reports. It is easy to see how multidimensional analysis really empowers the business user, giving a single person the ability to run 375 reports as in this example, in moments. And the data, via a data warehouse system, could be added to daily with the latest sales transactions for ongoing business decision making.

To take this a step further, imagine the number of permutations based on the individual data values of each dimension for the preceding example:

Date Year	3 (years of history)
Date Quarter	$3 \times 4 = 12$
Date Month	$3 \times 12 = 36$
Date Week	$3 \times 52 = 156$
Date Day	$3 \times 365 = 1095$
Store Location	350 stores
Product Categories	200 product segments
Products	200,000 products
Product Packaging	500 types of packaging possibilities
Sales Channel	3 values

Total = $1095 \times 350 \times 200 \times 200{,}000 \times 500 \times 3 = 22{,}995{,}000{,}000{,}000{,}000$ potential rows or combinations of potential values. This could be one big report!!

The chances of each region having all products and then having each product in every store and each sold for all sales channels are nonexistent. Plus, not all products are in all 200 product categories and perhaps not all product items were actually sold in the time period, so while the maximum number of potential rows is theoretically possible, the actual maximum number of rows is the total number of items sold in three years.

Data Mining

Data mining is the quest to discover some sort of insight from the data. This involves a hypothesis of some sort and querying the data to discover complex associations given the hypothesis. Data mining is completely data-driven in that there are no preset queries as previously described. Looking at the number of sales of large noodle boxes that sold on a weekend in the southern region would be a normal query. Asking what and where the products most likely to be purchased with it are, or the characteristics of the customers that buy them, would be a data mining effort. It could be the start of a customer profiling effort, which could lead to customer-centric and profitability insights for the organization. Unless a specific data mart was created for this type of query or exists with all the dimensions and measures required for this query, it will require looking at the data at its lowest level of atomic detail.

Data mining is typically done on normalized data structures, as shown in Figure 7-7, which can be a specific data mart or the data warehouse repository. Data mining can require lots of data and can span many data components. In many instances, data

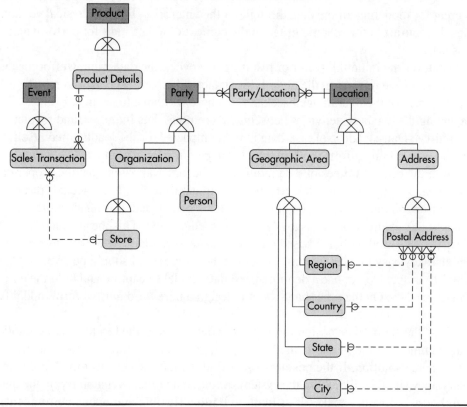

Figure 7-7 *Third Normal Form data model*

mining efforts consist of numerous queries by statisticians, actuaries, and so forth, all pertaining to a specific hunch or gut feel. At other times, it may be a precisely calculated effort in looking at how one aspect may relate to past events, specific patterns, or possibly the combination of data components given specific parameters. Such findings can lead to the foundation of specific business rules or refined theories influencing the next hypothesis or query.

If the possible requests can span all or any piece of data, then without knowing specific scenarios, the data should be modeled in its most granular form. This allows the broadest potential for any association between data components as desired. This sort of data model is called *normalized*, aka the "pizza" model. Think of rolling out the pizza dough, making it bigger and bigger to hold more and more toppings. Normalizing the data is to refine the model into an atomic model typically in a third normal form. Data warehouse repositories are typically third normal form (3NF), as are some data marts.

This type of data model can support any type of query as all the data has a specific home in one and only one spot. There is no duplication of data other than in aggregate form. This allows planning for any business scenario possibility. A design of this type is great for modeling all the data throughout the enterprise, but the physical version must be optimized for specific usage in the context of a data mart for performance reasons.

Whatever the initiating factor or resulting discovery, the data mining effort usually has an extensive impact on the underlying database performance. If data mining is a major aspect of the overall database queries, there will have to be an effort in balancing the database activities between data mining, data inquiries, and regular operations. Daily loading of new data may be impacted, or the loading may itself impact data mining efforts, both of which can be quite long-running.

From the different types of data inquiries, it becomes apparent that the proper data model can greatly influence the effectiveness of a business intelligence effort. For this reason, no matter what type of data model is being used, it is an absolute necessity to ensure that it is usable for the desired context. This means that it is clearly understood by being based on a solid data vocabulary. The structures should be relatively easy to use (database views can help here), and should be designed to simplify usage. Do not use a denormalized data model to capture and hold the entire enterprise data. On the other hand, do not design a pure third normal form model for all end-user data queries.

Using the appropriate design for the appropriate usage is the key to creating a solid data warehouse system and is the key to building a usable and accepted business intelligence solution. If the business users find the data structures too complex to query, they simply will not use the system. At the same time, oversimplifying the data warehouse repository makes it difficult to build a flexible and open environment. Hence these two areas should be separated for distinct purposes. Design the data warehouse repository in the data's simplest form in a normalized fashion so that the data warehouse repository can capture and hold deep historical data. And design the business access area for efficient and effective data retrieval, remembering that it is a subset of the data warehouse repository but in an optimized design for high-performance retrieval.

Fact Tables

A fact table is the central table in a star schema and contains business measures qualified by dimensions. Typically a star schema data mart contains one central fact table and a number of dimensions. It's best if the measures are numeric and additive across all dimensions. Measures are at the granularity of the primary dimensions.

Figure 7-8 shows a simple fact table example for daily sales. The granularity is at the day level for the time dimension and at the individual product level for the product dimension. Each row in the Daily Sales fact table has a foreign key (association) to each dimension. Row 1 in the fact table is composed of two foreign keys: Date_Id = 1

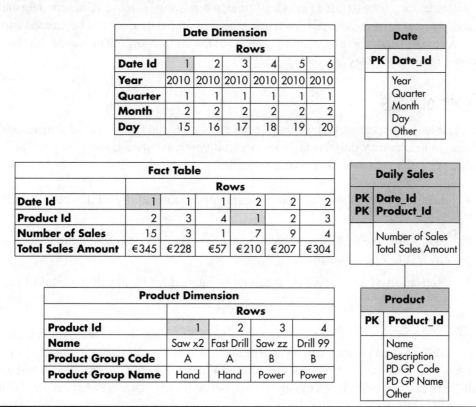

Figure 7-8   *Simple fact table example*

and Product_Id = 2. In the Date dimension, row Date_Id = 1 relates to Feb 15, 2010. In the Product dimension, row Product_Id = 2 refers to a product with the name = "Fast Drill." For each Daily Sales fact there are two measures: Number of Sales and Total Sales Amount, both for a specific day and specific product occurrence. In the example, the first row in the fact table has Number of Sales = 15 and Total Sales Amount = 345 Euros. The fact table could be more appropriately named Daily Product Sales to represent the underlying granularity.

Retail stores sell items at a point-of-sale transaction level. The Daily Sales fact table contains all sales summed up per day by individual product items. If a transaction sale fact table were required, then a different fact table would be created at the individual transaction granularity level.

With a fact table at the lowest level of granularity, any usage or aggregation is possible, but once a higher level of granularity is created, only queries at this level or higher can be satisfied. To create the measures in Figure 7-8, the lowest granularity of data, which is the individual sale transaction, would have to be kept somewhere, which is usually in an atomic data warehouse repository or staging area depending on the data warehouse architecture. Since operational systems usually do not retain the atomic data for extended periods of time, a repository is required where data can be kept for as long as desired. From this repository the data mart can be created and re-created as needed at any point in time since the atomic level data is available and stored in the repository.

Types of Facts

Fact tables have measures and, ideally, each measure is additive across all dimensions. Some measures may only be additive by certain dimensions and some may not be additive at all in the data mart. These are called, respectively,

▶ **Additive**   Measures that can be aggregated (summed) by all dimensions of the fact table

▶ **Semi-additive**   Measures that can be aggregated by only some dimensions of the fact table but not all

▶ **Non-additive**   Measures that cannot be aggregated by any dimensions of the fact table

From the example in Figure 7-8, the Number of Sales and Total Sales Amount are both additive because they can be aggregated individually for each dimension. For instance, to calculate how many products were sold in the month of June, simply add up all the Number of Sales in the month of June. Secondly, to determine what was the Total

Sales Amount for the year, simply add up all Total Sales Amount for all rows that are at the day granularity for all products in the desired year. It's the same idea for the product dimension: to determine what is the total revenue for each product, add up all Total Sales Amount by product. Mind you, without the time dimension, the aggregation would be for the entire duration of the Daily Sales retained history. If the table held three years of daily sales, the total revenue for all products without qualifying the time period would then default to the three-year period.

For the new Daily Sales fact table, as shown in Figure 7-9, the new measure called Inventory Count would be semi-additive, as it would not make sense to add it up by all individual days, but the measure could be aggregated for all stores on a specific day. The latter portion of Figure 7-9 shows six rows in the new fact table. Each day Product 1 (Saw x2) is sold, which reduces the inventory level. Adding up all the Inventory Counts for the six days would give 724 units, which is incorrect. Adding up the Inventory Count for all stores for a single day would make sense; therefore, the measure is called a semi-additive measure.

Figure 7-10 shows an example of a non-additive measure. The new Percent of Total Sales measure cannot be added up by days, or by store, or by product. This measure is simply an added descriptive element to the fact or row's existence and only good for the combination of fundamental dimensions for this fact table. Typical non-additive measures are ratios, percentages, variances, and averages.

	Daily Sales
PK	Date_Id
PK	Store_Id
PK	Product_Id
	Number of Sales
	Total Sales Amount
	Inventory Count

Fact Table						
	Rows					
Date Id	1	2	3	4	5	6
Store Id	57	57	57	57	57	57
Product Id	1	1	1	1	1	1
Number of Sales	3	1	2	3	7	2
Total Sales Amount	€90	€30	€60	€90	€210	€60
Inventory Count	127	126	124	121	114	112

Figure 7-9   *Semi-additive measure example*

Daily Sales	
PK	Date_Id
PK	Store_Id
PK	Product_Id
	Number of Sales
	Total Sales Amount
	Inventory Count
	Percent of Total Sales

Fact Table						
	Rows					
Date Id	1	2	3	4	5	6
Store Id	57	57	57	57	57	57
Product Id	1	1	1	1	1	1
Number of Sales	3	1	2	3	7	2
Total Sales Amount	€90	€30	€60	€90	€210	€60
Inventory Count	127	126	124	121	114	112
Percent of Total Sales	12%	2%	8%	10%	21%	3%

Figure 7-10   *Non-additive measure example*

Types of Fact Tables

There can be different types of fact tables:

▶ Transactional

▶ Snapshot

▶ Accumulating snapshot

A transactional fact table, shown in Figure 7-11, holds the measures at their finest level of granularity, which is the point at which the measure was created. For a retailer the transactional level is each point-of-sale transaction. For a telecommunications organization, the transactional level for phone calls is the call display record, or each individual call. Notice that in Figure 7-11, the fact table is similar to the one in Figure 7-12 with the added exception of a differentiating "POS Transaction No" column as part of the primary key. This column is the actual transaction number from the point-of-sale source system, which differentiates each individual transaction.

A snapshot fact table is created at whatever period in time is desired. For instance, inventory measures can be captured at any point in time or at specific repeating points in time. Figures 7-8 and 7-12 are snapshot fact tables as they take a pictures of sales by product by day.

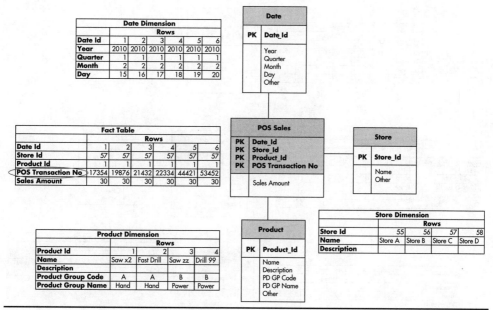

Figure 7-11   *Transactional fact table*

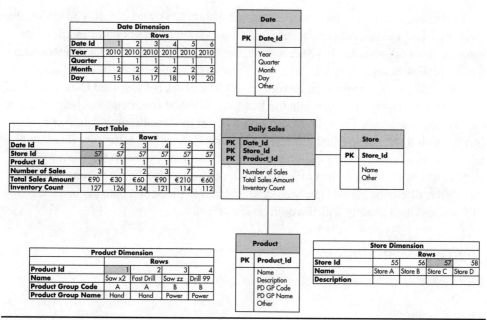

Figure 7-12   *Snapshot fact table*

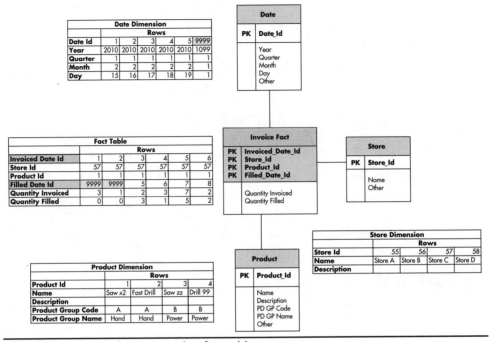

Figure 7-13 *Accumulating snapshot fact table*

A common variation is the accumulating snapshot fact table, which is an updateable fact table. This means that certain rows may be updated to reflect latest metrics. For instance, after adjustments have been done, the fact row could be updated rather than a new fact row being created. Figure 7-13 shows a fact table called Invoice Fact. This table tracks invoices from initial invoice to fulfillment via the Invoiced Date and Filled Date. Initially a row is inserted into the fact table with the Invoiced Date being the date the invoice is sent out. The Filled Date would be set to some dummy date row as the invoice would not yet be filled. Figure 7-13 shows a Date dimension row ID of 9999 representing a dummy date of January 01, 1099. For fact rows with this dummy date, such as fact rows 1 and 2, the Quantity Filled measure would be set to zero. As the measure is filled, the Filled Date would be updated to the actual date the invoice is fulfilled and the Quantity Filled would be set as well.

Source of Measures

Fact table measures can originate in one of two manners:

▶ Acquired

▶ Derived

Acquired measures are those which are accepted from a source outside the data warehouse system, which can be a source system, an operational data store, or a data warehouse repository. These are taken as is; for instance; the sales price of a POS item is $2.12 for a particular transaction. This is a fundamental measure acquired from an operational source system.

A derived measure is something that has been created within the data warehouse system. For instance, in Figure 7-8, the Daily Sales fact table contains two measures: Number of Sales and Total Sales Amount. If the data warehouse repository holds the atomic-level data that is each sale transaction, then the measures in the fact table would be created from this atomic-level data. All sales for each product would be added up per day and stored as a row in the fact table.

It is possible to have an acquired fact and a derived fact both representing the same measure, and they can have different values. The measures in Figure 7-8, for example, could be derived from the underlying atomic-level data in the data warehouse repository. A nice thing about this sort of derivation is that the measures are auditable within the data warehouse. In other words, the measures can be traced back to their origins, which are also in the data warehouse repository as just mentioned. On the other hand, the same two measures could be derived in an outside system and fed to the data warehouse system. In this case the measures are acquired from a source system and taken as is. If an audit exercise were performed between these measures, it is possible that they could have different values. The reason is that the source system that generated the acquired measures may have performed certain calculations or included or excluded certain atomic-level numbers. Of course, the derived measures are easily traceable to their atomic origins.

Fact Table Key

As seen in Figure 7-8, each row in the Daily Sales fact table is uniquely identified by its primary key. The primary key of the fact table is composed of primary keys from each associated dimension. Each dimension's primary key is a *surrogate key*, meaning that it has no value and is simply assigned a random number or the next number in the sequence.

The fact table primary key may have additional columns other than the dimension primary keys, such as a sequence key or transaction number, as in Figure 7-13. When a measure may occur more than once in the underlying granularity, then there must be a secondary differentiator such as a sequence key. Or for a transactional fact table to identify the exact atomic level, a transaction number can be used.

Grain of Fact Table

The grain of the fact table is dependent on the fact table primary key. In Figure 7-8 the granularity of the fact table is day and product. In Figure 7-12, because of the added POS Transaction No, the granularity becomes the absolute lowest level from the store's point-of-sale system, which is each and every sales transaction from the cash register. Aggregation on measures for Figure 7-8, Daily Sales, which are already summed up to a day level, can only be performed to higher aggregations. There can be no insights from time-of-day or other sub-day level granularities, such as sales at noon or end of business day. Since Figure 7-12 is at the lowest possible level, many types of aggregation can be performed below the day grain.

Fact Table Density

Fact tables should not hold all possible combinations of their dimensions but only those which occurred. For instance, if a store was closed due to water damage for a day, then do not enter a row in the fact table for each product in the store with Number of Sales and Total Sales Amount equal to zero. There is no need for these rows, and this sort of row population will add much volume to the table, which will degrade performance because database rows will be created, which means added CPU consumption and I/O occurrences. Keep the table as sparse as possible.

For instance, there are 200 stores and a total of 10,000 products for all stores. Not all stores sell all 10,000 products. For a daily snapshot fact table, the total number of all possible rows would be 200 * 10,000 = 2,000,000 per day. If the fact table is to hold five years' worth of measures, this would amount to 200 * 10,000 * 365 * 5 = 3,650,000,000 possible rows. In most situations, it is best to limit the fact rows to only those which occurred.

Factless Fact Table

A factless fact table is a fact table with no measures. This happens when the fact table is an association between the dimensions and the existence of a row in the fact table represents an occurrence of the dimensions. Such a fact table is created to track events. While there is no need for a measure, a simple measure can be added and will always contain the value of 1. For instance, a factless fact table could be used to track new enrollments in a store's discount clubs. Figure 7-14 shows the Membership Monthly Enrollment fact table having one measure called Enrollment Count. Since a member can only enroll once for a plan in a month, the measure will always be 1. The only reasons why the measure would be realized in the table would be for communicative purposes and so that business intelligence tools will be able to add up the rows more easily. The latter could, however, be circumvented with SQL.

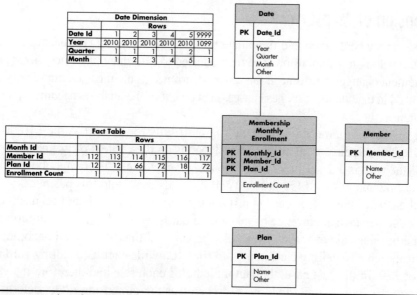

Date Dimension

						Rows	
Date Id	1	2	3	4	5	9999
Year	2010	2010	2010	2010	2010	1099
Quarter	1	1	1	1	2	1
Month	1	2	3	4	5	1

Date

PK	Date_Id
	Year
	Quarter
	Month
	Other

Fact Table

				Rows		
Month Id	1	1	1	1	1	1
Member Id	112	113	114	115	116	117
Plan Id	12	12	66	72	18	72
Enrollment Count	1	1	1	1	1	1

Membership Monthly Enrollment

PK	Monthly_Id
PK	Member_Id
PK	Plan_Id
	Enrollment Count

Member

PK	Member_Id
	Name
	Other

Plan

PK	Plan_Id
	Name
	Other

Figure 7-14   *Factless fact table*

Dimensions

A dimension is a table that qualifies measures in a fact table. Star schemas (Figure 7-3) and snowflakes (Figure 7-4) both have a fact table with measures qualified by several dimensions. Dimensions create the granularity of the fact table. Typically a star schema data mart contains one central fact table and a number of dimensions, but it is not unusual to have more than one fact table in a data mart.

When a fact table is queried, the query is filtered by the dimensions. Not all dimensions need to be used in the filter, but the more dimensions used, the more precise the end result will be.

Dimension tables contain columns in the physical database sense. In design mode, tables are called *entities* and columns are called *attributes*. Both terms are used interchangeably, but entities and attributes pertain to logical models, while tables and columns pertain to physical data models.

Dimension entities hold attributes, which qualify and describe the dimension. A Person dimension would hold attributes about the person, such as first name, last name, birth date, and so forth. Attributes are typically textual rather than abbreviated, so rather than "M" or "F" for Gender, the values would be "Male" and "Female." There should be no confusion as to the name of the attribute, either. Attributes may change over time, but generally their values are fairly constant.

Dimension or Measure

At times it may be difficult to differentiate between whether a data element is a measure or should belong to a dimension. The method used to determine placement is to ask if the data element changes over time at the same occurrence as the measure granularity and/or if it is used in calculations. In these cases, the context of the analysis becomes quite important.

For instance, if a mobile phone calling card sells for £10.00, is the £10.00 a measure or a dimension qualifier? That depends on the context of its analysis! The cost of the card is a descriptive aspect of the product itself. There may be queries to find out how many £10, £15, and £20 calling cards were sold this past week; in this case, the cost of the calling card is just another dimension attribute because it does not change for each occurrence of the sale of cards. However, if you want to analyze revenue by each sale over the past week, the value of the calling card becomes a measure; each £10 calling card item sold for £10, while each £20 calling card item sold for £20. In this last case, the fact table holds each sale and therefore the value of the product is indeed a metric to be aggregated as the dimension filters determine. Another consideration could be if a £20 card, the product, was sold at a discount, for example, £18, in which case the retail price and sales price would both be represented as measures on the fact table.

It is possible for a data element to be either a measure or dimension attribute at the same time. Figure 7-15 shows Sales Amount on the fact table and Value on the Product dimension. In these cases the placement is at the data modeler's discretion.

History and Dates

An important aspect of a dimension table is the way it holds history. Ideally all dimensions hold all values through the history of the organization simply because the measures in the fact table are over specific periods of time. There are three types of history (as per Ralph Kimball):

► **Type I**   No history required
► **Type II**   Full history required
► **Type III** Current and first or previous historical value

When designing a dimension, it is important to tag each attribute with one of these types of temporal aspects to ensure a full understanding of the data that will be populating the dimension table. Just as each attribute must be named, described, and a data type determined (integer, text, numeric…), each attribute must also be tagged with its temporal aspect. This gives an understanding of how to design the table, how

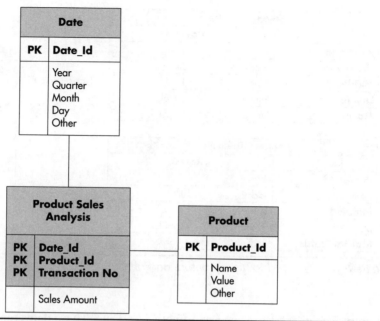

Figure 7-15   *Measure or dimension*

the table will be used, and how to architect the data flow, all with the resulting data mart solution in mind.

If all attributes on a dimension do not require any history, then the entire dimension is said to be of Type I. If any attribute requires full history tracking, the entire dimension is considered of Type II. Another name for Type II is the slowly changing dimension, SCD. Type III refers only to attributes. If a dimension has all Type I attributes and one Type III, the dimension can be considered Type I with a Type III attribute.

Type I refers to an attribute whereby no history is required. For instance, "marital status" is an attribute that changes only rarely for most people. It may be decided that if marital status is not something worth keeping track of for the business, then whenever it changes, it will be overridden. Figure 7-16 shows the Person dimension with Jill (row 2) having a previous marital status of Single. The change is made to Married on the same row. No new rows are added and all history is lost.

Type II refers to tracking all historical changes for an attribute. If marital status is important to the organization and each change must be maintained, then marital status becomes a Type II requirement. Figure 7-17 shows that a new third row has been added when Jill's marital status changed from Single to Married. To track when the change occurred, two new columns have been added to the table

Person Dimension		
	Rows	
Person Id	1	2
First Name	Jack	Jill
Middle Name	B	T
Last Name	Runner	Tumbler
Marital Status	Single	Single

Type I – Before

Person	
PK	**Person_Id**
	First Name
	Middle Name
	Last Name
	Marital Status
	Other

Person Dimension		
	Rows	
Person Id	1	2
First Name	Jack	Jill
Middle Name	B	T
Last Name	Runner	Tumbler
Marital Status	Single	Married

Type I – After

Figure 7-16   *Type I—No history before and after*

design: Effective From Date and Effective To Date. These dates represent when the change actually occurred in the real world and the time when it is no longer effective. Marital Status, for example, is effective on the date the marriage certificate is created.

Person Dimension		
	Rows	
Person Id	1	2
First Name	Jack	Jill
Middle Name	B	T
Last Name	Runner	Tumbler
Marital Status	Single	Single
Effective From Date	01/01/1990	01/01/1990
Effective To Date	12/31/2999	12/31/2999

Type II – Full History – Before

Person	
PK	**Person_Id**
	First Name
	Middle Name
	Last Name
	Marital Status
	Effective From Date
	Effective To Date
	Other

Person Dimension			
	Rows		
Person Id	1	2	3
First Name	Jack	Jill	Jill
Middle Name	B	T	T
Last Name	Runner	Tumbler	Tumbler
Marital Status	Single	Single	Married
Effective From Date	01/01/1990	01/01/1990	06/10/2010
Effective To Date	12/31/2999	06/09/2010	12/31/2999

Type II – Full History – After

Figure 7-17   *Type II—Full history before and after*

Other dates used are

▶ The business date, which is when the change was made or is valid in the operational system feeding the data warehouse system.

▶ The population date, which is the date the data was loaded into the data warehouse system. This date is usually a timestamp.

Best practice is to set a standard across the entire data warehouse system and design all tables with the same date terminology. The attribute definitions should explain the exact nature of the dates and how they are used.

In many projects, all three types of dates are used:

▶ Population Timestamp for the point in time when the data is loaded into the data warehouse system. If a data warehouse repository is used, this is the date the data warehouse repository is loaded, not the date the data mart is loaded. The data mart is a subset of the repository and as such uses all values from the repository.

▶ Valid From Date and Valid To Date, which represent the dates the data is valid in the operational system, A person may have changed their marital status last November 3, but the business only found out yesterday, meaning that all reports created between November 3 and yesterday may have been reporting incorrect results if based on the Marital Status of that person. Using Valid From/To Dates allows reporting to view data based on actual effective dates and the date the change was valid for business usage.

▶ Effective From Date and Effective To Date, representing the dates the data is realized in the real world.

Another design standard that must be chosen and adhered to is the value to use for the previous and current row changes. Figure 7-17 shows the initial, "before," row as having an Effective From Date = January 01, 1990. This is usually the date the row was initially added to the database if there is no other influencing factor. The Effective To Date is initially a standard high value used throughout the data warehouse system as desired. When a change to be tracked occurs, a new row is added to the database with the new columns and values; in this case Married for Marital Status, an Effective From Date set to the appropriate value, and the standard high value for the Effective To Date. In the design method shown in Figure 7-17, the previous row occurrence is updated with its Effective To Date set to a day before the value in the new row's Effective From Date. This allows for proper history ending and continuation between the two rows.

Another design method might be to not use the Effective To Date at all. This would simplify the loading of the table, but it adds complexity to the usage of the table in trying to determine which row to utilize for the query. The first method of adding the Effective To Date is the reverse—it complicates the loading process because an update of the previous row must occur, but it simplifies the usage of the table, as a query can easily determine if each row instance fits the query by using a "between" SQL filter.

```
Select First_Name, Last_Name, Marital_Status
From Person
Where input-date is between Effective_From_Date and
Effective_To_Date;
```

Type III, Figure 7-18, refers to keeping the most current version and either the first or previous value, depending on how it is used. An insurance company may want to know the current marital status of a policyholder as well as that person's initial marriage status when he or she first became a customer of the organization. This could reduce or increase coverage potential and therefore revenue and costs. Plus, this may influence the overall actuarial statistics calculations for the organization as well.

Person Dimension		
	Rows	
Person Id	1	2
First Name	Jack	Jill
Middle Name	B	T
Last Name	Runner	Tumbler
Marital Status	Single	Single
Marital Status Date	01/01/1990	01/01/1990
Initial Marital Status	Single	Single
Initial Marital Status Date	01/01/1990	01/01/1990

Type III – Current and Previous – Before

Person	
PK	**Person_Id**
	First Name
	Middle Name
	Last Name
	Marital Status
	Marital Status Date
	Initial Marital Status
	Initial Marital Status Date
	Other

Person Dimension		
	Rows	
Person Id	1	2
First Name	Jack	Jill
Middle Name	B	T
Last Name	Runner	Tumbler
Marital Status	Single	Married
Marital Status Date	01/01/1990	06/10/2010
Initial Marital Status	Single	Single
Initial Marital Status Date	01/01/1990	01/01/1990

Type III – Current and Previous History – After

Figure 7-18 *Type III—Current and previous history before and after*

The idea is that only two values are kept; the current and first or previous value. To keep things simple, both values are on the same row and therefore the row may be updated rather than a new row being added.

Dimension Table Key

As seen in Figure 7-8, each row in the Daily Sales fact table is uniquely identified by its primary key. The primary key of the fact table is composed of primary keys from each associated dimension. A dimension's primary key is a surrogate key, meaning that it has no value and is simply assigned a random or next-in-sequence number. This non-business key gives the dimension the ability to be completely independent of any source system.

If a business natural key were used rather than a surrogate key, the key would be dependent on the source system's operations, which created the key. If the source system changed the value of the key, then the data warehouse dimension key would have to change, which would cause much disruption and confusion in the data warehouse. Figure 7-19 shows the same person in a Human Resource System and a Billing System. The primary keys for these systems become simple descriptive attributes to the dimension in the data warehouse.

Every dimension that can "spin over time" (change over time) needs to have some sort of anchor or unique identifier. If the person dimension has a Person_Id of 2 and the name of Jill, if another Jill is added to the table with Person_Id of 10, how do you know which Jill is being discussed? As seen in Figure 7-19, a source system or natural key is required. When HR is discussing Jill, they are talking about HR System Id 354, but when Billing is discussing Jill, they are talking about Billing System Id 38976, and both are talking about Jill in the data warehouse with Person Id of 2. When a change occurs, such as Jill gets married, the data warehouse will add

HR System	
Employee Number	354
First Name	Jill
Middle Name	T
Last Name	Tumbler
Sex	F

Billing System	
Customer Id	38976
First Name	Jill
Middle Name	
Surname	Tumbler
Gender	1

Person Dimension	
Person Id	2
HR System Id	354
Billing System Id	38976
First Name	Jill
Middle Name	T
Last Name	Tumbler
Marital Status	Single
Effective From Date	01/01/1990
Effective To Date	12/31/2999

Figure 7-19   *Key example*

another row to the Person dimension with a new Person Id, as seen in Figure 7-17. Later when Jill is inquired upon, the only method of determining between this Jill and any other Jills is by the source system keys, which are HR System Id and Billing System Id.

Dummy Key

Since there is a possibility that no values in a dimension are associated to a fact table in which the dimension exists, then to keep up proper data integrity rules, whereby each foreign key in the fact table's primary key must have a value from its dimension, a dummy dimension row may be necessary.

For instance, a person enters a retail store and is offered the opportunity to register and obtain the store's credit card in return for 10 percent off any and all products in the store that day. All sales for that person will enter the store's POS system with the new credit card number, which is issued immediately on-site. That night the data warehouse system pulls from the POS system and creates a row in the Sales fact table for each item sold in the store that day for each customer. But the individual's personal details will most likely not filter through to the data warehouse system for several more days. To keep the fact table primary key's integrity with the Person dimension even though the individual is not yet entered into the system, the fact table Person primary key will point to a dummy Person row with value Unknown, as shown in Figure 7-20. In several days, when the Person row is entered into the data warehouse system, the fact row can be updated to point to the proper Person row.

Grain of Dimension

The grain of the dimension is the atomic level of the dimension itself. For the Person dimension, the grain is at the individual person itself. When used in a fact table, the fact table measures would pertain to an individual person.

Person Dimension				
	Rows			
Person Id	1	2	3	4
First Name	Jack	Jill	Unknown	Johnny
Middle Name	B	T		
Last Name	Runner	Tumbler	Unknown	Uphill
Marital Status	Single	Single	Unknown	Married
Effective From Date	01/01/1990	01/01/1990	01/01/1990	08/12/2010
Effective To Date	12/31/2999	12/31/2999	12/31/2999	12/31/2999

Fact Table				
Date Id	5	5	5	Before
Store Id	57	57	57	
Product Id	1	1	1	
Person Id	2	3	3	
POS Transaction No	22334	44421	53452	
Sales Amount	30	30	30	

Fact Table				
Date Id	5	5	5	After
Store Id	57	57	57	
Product Id	1	1	1	
Person Id	2	4	3	
POS Transaction No	22334	44421	53452	
Sales Amount	30	30	30	

Figure 7-20 *Unknown Person row*

All the primary dimensions associated to a fact table form the basis for that fact table's granularity. For instance if the Date (day grain), Person (individual grain), and Product (item grain) dimensions are associated to a sales fact table, then that fact table granularity is at the sale of a product item per individual person by day.

Source and Value of Dimension Attributes

A dimension can be composed of attributes from a number of external systems. Figure 7-19 shows two operational systems feeding into one dimension. One primary concern of designing a dimension is to ensure a common vocabulary. In Figure 7-19 the HR system has a column called "Last Name," while the Billing system contains "Surname." Both have the identical meaning, but only one can be used. The Person dimension settled on "Last Name" but could have used whatever nomenclature it wanted. The point is that attributes in a dimension can come from different sources. The "HR System Id" and the "Billing System Id" are obviously from different systems.

A second design concern is conforming the attribute data values from differing sources. For instance, in Figure 7-21 the HR system table uses a column called "Sex" and the Billing system uses a column called "Gender." Both represent the same concept; however, the data values are different even though they have the same meaning according to their respective code tables.

When designing the Person dimension, what column name should be used, Sex or Gender? In this case Gender is selected. Secondly, what data values should be used? If the two code tables represent all the possible values, we are halfway to a solution.

Ideally, when the business uses the dimension to query the fact table, if filtering on the Gender column, the Gender description would be used. In this scenario it is fairly simple to see that the code values from either system or a general code value would be useless as the description is available and universally understood. However, two

HR System	
Employee Number	354
First Name	Jill
Middle Name	T
Last Name	Tumbler
Sex	F

HR System Codes			
Code Name	Sex	Sex	Sex
Code Value	Female	Male	Unknown
Code Abbreviation	F	M	U

Billing System	
Customer Id	38976
First Name	Jill
Middle Name	
Surname	Tumbler
Gender	1

Billing System Codes		
Code Name	Gender	Gender
Code Value	Female	Male
Code Abbreviation	1	2

Figure 7-21   *Data value differences*

systems could be using their own accounting codes, which have the same meaning. The business users are used to code 5702, for instance, in HR and 1388 in Billing. In many cases, the business users do not know what the code refers to, just that the code number is used for this or that in their system. One school of thought is to not include the code so that the business users must become familiar with using the description. The other is to retain the individual source system code values as well as a universal description. The resulting Person dimension could look like Figure 7-22 with the corresponding Gender Code table used in the enterprise data warehouse (EDW) to conform all sources into one common understanding. A universal Gender Code could also be used but is not necessary for reporting purposes. A generic Gender Code might be useful in processing efforts. The Gender Code table is not complete and is only for communicative purposes in this example.

Usually business intelligence data marts are sourced from a central repository, which may be physicalized or in a staging environment. Either way, each attribute must have a set vocabulary throughout the enterprise and a base universal value set. Whether this is done in the repository or in the data mart does not matter as long as some standard is used throughout the enterprise.

Types of Dimensions

A dimension table represents a business data concept to be used as a filter in the analysis of measures within the specific context of a fact table and/or data mart. Organizations are made up of fundamental dimensions, which follows the pillar diagram concept explained in Chapter 2. These fundamental dimensions are key to the enterprise as they can be reused again and again in many different analysis scenarios.

Person	
PK	**Person_Id**
	First Name
	Middle Name
	Last Name
	Marital Status
	Marital Status Date
	Initial Marital Status
	Initial Marital Status Date
	Gender Description
	HR Gender Code
	Billing Gender Code
	Other

Gender Code			
Gender Code	10	20	30
Gender Description	Female	Male	Unknown
HR Gender Code	F	M	U
Billing Gender Code	1	2	0

Figure 7-22   *Multiple source codes*

Dimensions can be designed in a specific manner and physicalized in another but must keep the initial concept intact. Much depends on specific and general usage. Store, for example, is a fundamental dimension in a retail business. The store concept can have many attributes logically, but when physicalized or used in a specific data mart, only the name and location may be of relevance, while in another usage the number of employees, department hierarchies, and organization structure are required. As such, dimensions can be subdivided, merged, partially duplicated, and optimized, based on their roles and usage.

The following is a list of useful dimension types, which is by no means exhaustive.

Conformed Dimension

These dimensions are as described previously; they are fundamental concept dimensions that represent the informational pillars of the organization. Conformed dimensions are reusable throughout data marts, which can span the enterprise. Employee, Store, Product, Customer, and so forth are classic conformed dimensions. These are usually all Type II slowly changing dimensions, as history is typically required to be tracked as it happens.

Date Dimension

The number one fundamental dimension each organization must have is the Date dimension, also known as the Time dimension. Business happens at specific time intervals: an item was sold at 16:01 on June 3, 1998; a telephone call was made at 14:02 EST for 18 minutes on December 25, 2006; a claim was logged on March 5, 2009; a stock was purchased at 09:58 October 12, 2010, and so on. Dates can be based on the Gregorian calendar, an organization's predetermined fiscal calendar, and/or in whatever manner desired. All dates boil down to a day interval. Time can also be introduced, but since this drastically increases the number of rows in a Date dimension, this concept is left to its own dimension, as seen in the next section.

The Date dimension is fairly basic to begin with: calendar year, quarter, month, week, and day, as shown in Figure 7-23. Figure 7-24 shows typical data values for the simple Date dimension.

Adding to this is the organization's own internal fiscal calendar if it's different than the calendar year. For instance, the fiscal year might be from February 1 to January 31, as shown in Figure 7-25. This allows finance to avoid the busy Christmas season. Employees can return to work after the holidays and then begin with closing the year. Figure 7-26 show how both calendar and fiscal year are connected in the Date dimension.

The Date dimension in Figure 7-26 would be at the calendar day granularity level. Each of the other entities could also be their own dimensions: Calendar Year, Calendar Quarter, Calendar Month, Calendar Week, Fiscal Year, Fiscal Quarter, Fiscal Month,

Date Dimension

Date Id (PK)
Date
Day of Week
Day in Calendar Week
Day in Calendar Month
Day in Calendar Quarter
Day in Calendar Year
Calendar Week
Calendar Month
Calendar Quarter
Calendar Year

Figure 7-23 *Simple date dimension*

and Fiscal Week. Each of these dimensions would have its own attributes including all the attributes from the levels above it.

Several data warehouse projects have combined all the date entities into one Date dimension. In this scenario there would be all-day granularity rows, plus 52 Calendar Week rows (possibly 53 depending on the fiscal year) where all day-level attributes would be null. Then there would be 12 Calendar Month rows with all day and week attributes null, and so forth. This effectively merges all different date granularities in the same table, allowing all date usages to be from the same source. When you are using this collapsed hierarchy dimension in the presentation layer of the data warehouse architecture, views could be created called Calendar Year, Calendar Quarter, and so forth. While this usage is feasible, it does require administration to ensure that grains are not used incorrectly. However, creating multiple date dimensions at the desired granularity is not a major effort; therefore, having a Calendar Year dimension, Calendar Quarter dimension, and so forth is still the best practice. Usually most fact tables will use the day-level granularity, and as such the basic Date dimension from Figure 7-26 will do.

Date Dimension									
Date Id (PK)	1	2	3	4	5	6	7	8	9
Date	Jan 1, 2007	Jan 2, 2007	Jan 3, 2007	Jan 4, 2007	Jan 5, 2007	Jan 6, 2007	Jan 7, 2007	Jan 8, 2007	Jan 9, 2007
Day of Week	Monday	Tuesday	Wednesday	Thursday	Friday	Saturday	Sunday	Monday	Tuesday
Day in Calendar Week	1	2	3	4	5	6	7	1	2
Day in Calendar Month	1	2	3	4	5	6	7	8	9
Day in Calendar Quarter	1	2	3	4	5	6	7	8	9
Day in Calendar Year	1	2	3	4	5	6	7	8	9
Calendar Week	1	1	1	1	1	1	1	2	2
Calendar Month	1	1	1	1	1	1	1	1	1
Calendar Quarter	1	1	1	1	1	1	1	1	1
Calendar Year	2007	2007	2007	2007	2007	2007	2007	2007	2007

Figure 7-24 *Simple date dimension rows*

Calendar 2010

Calendar Year	Calendar Quarter	Calendar Month	Calendar Week	Month	Fiscal Week	Fiscal Month	Fiscal Quarter	Fiscal Year
2010	1	1	1	January	47	12	4	2009
2010	1	1	2		49	12	4	2009
2010	1	1	3		50	12	4	2009
2010	1	1	4		51	12	4	2009
2010	1	1	5		52	12	4	2009
2010	1	2	6	February	1	1	1	2010
2010	1	2	7		2	1	1	2010
2010	1	2	8		3	1	1	2010
2010	1	2	9		4	1	1	2010
2010	1	3	10	March	5	2	1	2010
2010	1	3	11		6	2	1	2010
2010	1	3	12		7	2	1	2010
2010	1	3	13		8	2	1	2010
2010	1	3	14		9	2	1	2010
2010	1	3	14	April	9	2	1	2010
2010	2	4	15		10	3	1	2010
2010	2	4	16		11	3	1	2010
2010	2	4	17		12	3	1	2010
2010	2	4	18		13	3	1	2010

Calendar contents:

January: M T W T F S S — 1 2 3 / 4 5 6 7 8 9 10 / 11 12 13 14 15 16 17 / 18 19 20 21 **22** 23 24 / **25** 26 27 28 29 30 31

February: M T W T F S S — 1 2 3 4 5 6 7 / **8** 9 10 11 12 13 14 / 15 16 17 18 **19** 20 21 / **22** 23 24 25 26 27 28

March: M T W T F S S — 1 2 3 4 5 6 7 / **8** 9 10 11 12 13 14 / 15 16 17 18 19 20 21 / 22 23 24 25 **26** 27 28 / 29 30 31

April: M T W T F S S — 1 2 3 4 / **5** 6 7 8 9 10 11 / 12 13 14 15 16 17 18 / 19 20 21 22 23 24 25 / 26 27 28 29 30

Figure 7-25 *Calendar and Fiscal dates*

In one particular project there were fact tables at the month granularity and others at the day granularity. There was an issue of aggregating the day rows in one fact table to the month rows in another fact table. This was satisfied by using the "Calendar Month" attribute from the Date dimension and comparing to the Calendar Month dimension.

Time-of-Day Dimension

If a lower granularity other than day is required for measure analysis, such as minute or seconds, then a new Time-of-Day dimension is required. This should not be within the Date dimension as the volume would grow from 365 rows per year to 365 days * 24 hours * 60 minutes = 525,600 rows for minutes. And if you were maintaining the table at the seconds level, this would be another factor of 60, resulting in 31,536,000 rows per year.

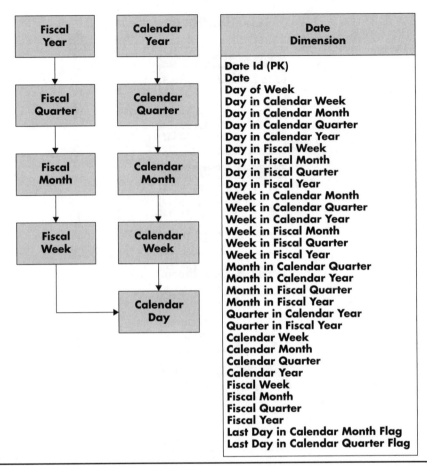

Figure 7-26 *Calendar and Fiscal date dimension*

A better strategy would be to keep the Date dimension at the day granularity and create a new table called Time-of-Day dimension, Figure 7-27, which would hold 1440 rows at the minute granularity or 86,400 rows at the seconds granularity.

When using multiple Time-of-Day dimension foreign keys to a fact table, simply give the fact table attributes different names. This method can be used for any dimension where more than one foreign key is used in another table.

Degenerate Dimension

When dimensions occur at the same granularity as the fact table row, then chances are the dimension can be collapsed into the fact table. For instance, as in the example for point-of-sale retail transactions, the transaction number belongs to a dimension possibly called POS Transaction Dimension. This dimension would only have a

Time-of-Day Dimension	
Time of Day Id (PK)	934
Time	15:34
Minute	34
Hour	15

Time-of-Day Dimension	
Time of Day Id (PK)	2943
Time	15:34:03
Second	03
Minute	34
Hour	15

Figure 7-27   *Time-of-Day dimension for minutes and seconds*

limited number of attributes if more than one, such as the transaction number of the point-of-sale transaction. Rather than retain this dimension, it could be collapsed into the fact table as part of the primary key. Figure 7-28 demonstrates the degeneration.

Band Dimension

Band dimensions are essentially dimension holding ranges. An example is the Age Range dimension:

▶ Band 01: 00–10 years of age

▶ Band 02: 11–20 years of age

▶ Band 03: 21–30 years of age

▶ Band 04: 31–40 years of age

▶ Band 05: 41–50 years of age

▶ Band 06: 51+ years of age

Junk Dimension

Junk dimensions are to consolidate many odds-and-ends types of dimensions into one Junk dimension table rather than having many small dimensions. Good usage of a Junk dimension would be for indicators, or flags. Combining many flags together in the same dimension gives a good binary style result set for the dimension.

Mini-Dimension

A mini-dimension is created from a Type II slowly changing dimension. Using Person dimension as an example, the idea behind a Type II SCD is that when one

POS Transaction Dimension			
	Rows		
PK **POS Transaction Id**	22334	44421	53452
POS Transaction No	22334	44421	53452

Fact Table			
	Rows		
PK **Date Id**	5	5	5
PK **Store Id**	57	57	57
PK **Product Id**	1	1	1
PK **Person Id**	2	4	3
PK **POS Transaction Id**	22334	44421	53452
Sales Amount	30	30	30

With Dimension FK

Fact Table			
	Rows		
PK **Date Id**	5	5	5
PK **Store Id**	57	57	57
PK **Product Id**	1	1	1
PK **Person Id**	2	4	3
PK **POS Transaction No**	22334	44421	53452
Sales Amount	30	30	30

Degenerate Dimension

Figure 7-28   *Degenerate dimension*

attribute changes for a person, an entire new row is created in the database. If the dimension has a good number of rows, it is possible that many new rows will be created for each change of Type II attributes, causing the slowly changing dimension to seem like a fast-changing dimension. When the person is married, a new row is created; when the person has another child, a new row may be created; if the person moves, a new home address may be created, and so forth. These attributes are more dynamic than other more stable or static attributes such as birth date, which does not change unless it is a correction; gender, which is static; eye color, which is static; and so forth.

For these types of dynamic dimension attributes, and depending on volumetrics and overall row size, one or more mini-dimension(s) may be useful to limit volume and rows size. The idea is to separate the static and more dynamic attributes into their own tables. For the static attributes, usually Type I and Type III, the master Person dimension entity, for this example, works well. For the other more dynamic attributes, Type II, one or more mini-dimension(s) can be quite useful. The thought is that the static portion or base table will not spin over time as much as the mini-dimension table. This of course presumes that the original table has quite a large number of rows and creating mini-dimensions will reduce the addition of many more rows.

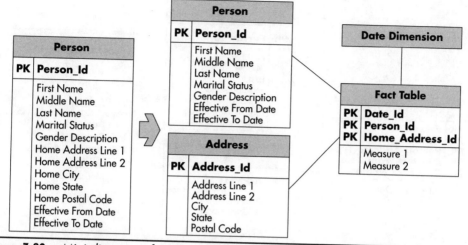

Figure 7-29   *Mini-dimension for Type II SCD*

Figure 7-29 shows the Home Address attributes from the Person dimension being extracted from the design and placed in a new Address mini-dimension. Now both the new Person and Address dimensions would relate individually to the fact table. Notice that on the fact table, the Address dimension foreign key has a role name called Home_Address_Id. In this special case the Address dimension can hold many addresses, which can be used for many purposes. An address may be a home address in one instance, a delivery address in another context, and a communication address in yet another usage. Therefore its usage can be represented by a role key where it is used.

In certain instances the business user may want to associate the Address dimension directly to the Person dimension without a fact table context. In these cases, an associative table or bridge table could be used. Figure 7-30 shows a "Person X Address" table relating each to the other. This special table holds the primary keys for each dimension as well as the reason for the association being held in Person_Address_Type, which in this case would have the value Home Address. Having this usage type column allows any address association as mentioned earlier, which could include home address, billing address, communication address, and so forth. Since the association may change as a person moves from one home to another, an Effective_From_Date is also included along with its Effective_To_Date. Sequence Number can also be added for cases where there can be more than one address effective at the same time for the same purpose. This method uses the normalization approach discussed in Chapter 8.

A more tuned version of the associative table is seen in Figure 7-31. The Person_Address_Type from Figure 7-30 describing the usage is removed and a table

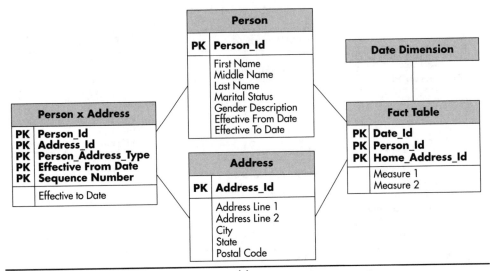

Figure 7-30 *Mini-dimension association table*

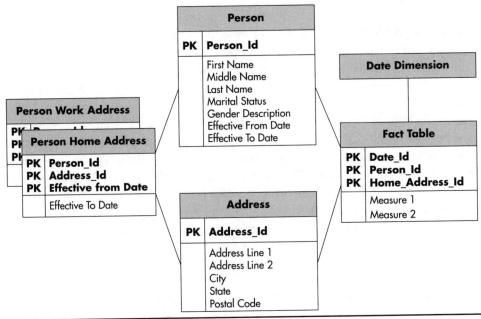

Figure 7-31 *Mini-dimension with tuned association table*

representing each data value is realized. If another address were to be associated to the Person dimension, another associative table would be realized. This, of course, is a simple and easier-to-use method from a user's perspective. The sequence number could also be removed, but then there would be only one possible home address in this example for a person per effective date.

To keep the design leaning more toward a denormalized "Kimball" style model, when you are relating the Address to the Person dimension, the primary key of the Address dimension could be placed in the Person dimension row directly. A role would be used on the Person address attribute, as shown in Figure 7-32. For this scenario to function properly, the Home_Address_Id would have to be Type I. If a change occurs in the address, the value or key would be changed without maintaining history, or else the Person dimension would incur a new row for each address change—which is what was being avoided in the first place. The address in Figure 7-32 is also known as an Outrigger dimension.

Mini-dimensions are also used for demographics. Gathering several Type II attributes under one dimension allows the primary dimension to spin less often over time. Demographics can include age, income level, marital status, city, and so forth.

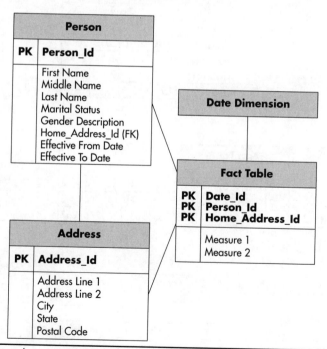

Figure 7-32   *Mini-dimension Type I*

Hierarchies and Helper Tables

Hierarchies are constantly used in organizations. Figure 7-26 shows how year, quarter, month, and week are all hierarchies to the Date dimension. Other typical hierarchies within organization are

► Report-To hierarchies (management-style reporting chains)

► Geographic hierarchies

► Product hierarchies

Hierarchies can be collapsed into a flat dimension such as seen with the Date dimension, or they can be designed in a helper-style table.

As with Year, Quarter, Month and Day, going up the hierarchy from Day to Year is called "drilling up." Going down or to a finer level of granularity from Year down to Day is called "drilling down." Figure 7-33 shows a fact table that has Date and Geography dimensions. Both have flattened hierarchies. Notice that all rows in the

Date Dimension

	Rows			
Date Id	1	2	3	4
Year	2010	2010	2010	2010
Quarter	1	1	1	1
Month	2	2	2	2
Day	15	16	17	18

Date

PK	Date_Id
	Year
	Quarter
	Month
	Day
	Other

Fact Table

	Rows									
Date_Id	2	2	3	3	3	3	4	4	4	4	4
Geography_Id	1	2	2	4	3	1	4	2	4	4	3
Sales Amount	$50	$12	$75	$12	$14	$88	$55	$23	$26	$76	£67

Daily Sales

PK	Date_Id
PK	Geography_Id
	Sales Amount

Geography Dimension

	Rows			
Geography Id	1	2	3	4
Country	Canada	Canada	Canada	Canada
Province	Quebec	Quebec	Ontario	Ontario
City	Montreal	Quebec City	Ottawa	Toronto

Geography

PK	Geography_Id
	Country
	Province
	City

Figure 7-33   *Hierarchy example*

fact table are at the lowest level of each dimension's granularity. The first row in the fact table is Date_Id = 2 (Feb 16, 2010) and Geography_Id = 1 (Montreal, Quebec, Canada). If you want to count all Sales Amount for Toronto for February 2010, then simply add all rows with Geography_Id = 4 and Date_Id = 1, 2, 3, or 4. The result will be $12+$55+$26+$76 = $169. In this case, the same result would apply to all Toronto rows in the first quarter of the year, and in the current year since the Date dimension only has four rows. The point is that the fact table granularity is at the Day and City level. To "drill up" to month or quarter or year, simply aggregate the fact rows to the desired level. Use the same idea for the Geography dimension if you want to "drill up" from City to Province or Country.

Helper Table

A helper table aids in querying hierarchies by including every single possible hierarchy relationship combination: parent/child, parent/grandchild, parent/great-grandchild, and so on. Figure 7-34 shows a number of countries each with a number of differing levels: "country, province, city," or "country, province, county, city" (county would have to be added as a column in the Geography dimension in Figure 7-33). If the query were to add up all sales by whatever geographic area desired, it would be complicated. A method to help these sorts of queries is to create a table with all the possible combinations. For this example the combinations are

- ▶ All/All
- ▶ All/Country
- ▶ All/Province
- ▶ All/County
- ▶ All/City
- ▶ Country/Country
- ▶ Country/Province
- ▶ Country/County
- ▶ Country/City
- ▶ Province/Province
- ▶ Province/County
- ▶ Province/City
- ▶ County/County
- ▶ County/City
- ▶ City/City

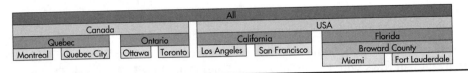

Figure 7-34   *Geography Helper table data example*

Figure 7-35 shows the helper table values. Notice it has an added column called "Bottom Flag" to indicate the lowest level of granularity.

To find all Sales Amount, Figure 7-33, for any combination of geographic areas, simply select all rows in the fact table joining the Geography dimension to the result list of all Geography_Helper table rows that have the required Parent with a Bottom_Flag = "Y."

For example, to obtain all Sales Amounts in Ontario, simply select all rows in the Geography_Helper table where Parent = "Ontario" and Bottom_Flag = "Y." Then join these rows to the Geography dimension, Geography.City = Geography_Helper.Child, and use all these Geography rows to obtain their associated fact table rows via the Geography_Ids. Of course, other dimension filters may also be used.

To determine how many rows will be in a helper table, use this formula: Sum the number of rows per level multiplied by the level number. Looking at Figure 7-34, we would calculate as follows:

Level 1 * 1 = 01	All
Level 2 * 2 = 04	Canada, USA
Level 3 * 4 = 12	Quebec, Ontario, California, Florida
Level 4 * 7 = 28	Montreal, Quebec City, Ottawa, Toronto, Los Angeles, San Francisco, Broward County
Level 5 * 2 = 10	Miami, Fort Lauderdale
Sum:	55 data values as seen as the number of rows in Figure 7-35.

Profile Tables

Profile tables are similar in concept to mini-dimensions. The idea is to extract a number of Type II attributes and group them together into a table, which can then be associated to the fact table. This concept can remove volume (rows) from the fact table. For instance, if a fact table uses the Person dimension and it is replaced with a Person profile table, the granularity of the fact table may change from the individual to the profile level. This means fewer rows. This scenario is useful if the Person granularity is not necessary, but Person details such as marital status, income level,

| Geography Helper | | | |
Geo Helper Id	Parent	Child	Bottom Flag
1	All	All	
2	All	Canada	
3	All	USA	
4	All	Quebec	
5	All	Ontario	
6	All	California	
7	All	Florida	
8	All	Broward County	
9	All	Montreal	Y
10	All	Quebec City	Y
11	All	Ottawa	Y
12	All	Toronto	Y
13	All	Los Angeles	Y
14	All	San Francisco	Y
15	All	Miami	Y
16	All	Fort Lauderdale	Y
17	Canada	Canada	
18	Canada	Quebec	
19	Canada	Ontario	
20	Canada	Montreal	Y
21	Canada	Quebec City	Y
22	Canada	Ottawa	Y
23	Canada	Toronto	Y
24	Quebec	Quebec	
25	Quebec	Montreal	Y
26	Quebec	Quebec City	Y
27	Ontario	Ontario	
28	Ontario	Ottawa	Y
29	Ontario	Toronto	Y
30	Montreal	Montreal	Y
31	Quebec City	Quebec City	Y
32	Ottawa	Ottawa	Y
33	Toronto	Toronto	Y
34	USA	USA	
35	USA	California	
36	USA	Florida	
37	USA	Broward County	
38	USA	Los Angeles	Y
39	USA	San Francisco	Y
40	USA	Miami	Y
41	USA	Fort Lauderdale	Y
42	California	California	
43	California	Los Angeles	Y
44	California	San Francisco	Y
45	Los Angeles	Los Angeles	Y
46	San Francisco	San Francisco	Y
47	Florida	Florida	
48	Florida	Broward County	
49	Florida	Miami	Y
50	Florida	Fort Lauderdale	Y
51	Broward County	Broward County	
52	Broward County	Miami	Y
53	Broward County	Fort Lauderdale	Y
54	Miami	Miami	Y
55	Fort Lauderdale	Fort Lauderdale	Y

Figure 7-35   *Geography Helper table data*

age range, and other statuses are. This allows the grouping of descriptive attributes rather than the individual Person level.

Figure 7-14 shows a fact table associated to a Member dimension. The fact table represents monthly plan enrollments per member with one enrollment per plan per month if any. If Member dimension were replaced with a Member Profile table, the fact table could change to a member monthly enrollment profile analysis fact table. This granularity would no longer be at the member level but at the member profile level.

Number of Dimensions

There is always a question about how many dimensions are too many and how many are too few. A rule-of-thumb guideline is four to ten dimension tables, which include profile tables as well. Typically when many dimensions are used, the fact table usually tries to cover many analysis areas rather than just one or two. With too few dimensions, the effort seems too restrictive. *Centipede fact tables* are so named because they have a very large number of dimension associations. For these types of designs, it might be worthwhile to rethink the primary usage of the data mart and merging some dimensions into profiles or junk dimensions.

Sizing

The size of a fact table and dimensions is twofold as it can refer to the number of columns and/or the number of rows. While fact tables have a large number of rows, dimension tables can have a large number of columns.

Fact tables can hold millions and billions of rows depending on the type of fact table. For instance, a telephone company tracks each and every telephone call, which can amount to a huge number of calls per day and even at the hour level. Dimension tables contain descriptive elements of the dimension itself. Since dimensions are interested in textual descriptions rather than codes as in transactional systems, dimension size can add up quickly. A customer dimension can easily add up to 500 bytes with all the descriptions. But this is small in comparison to the overall fact table size. A large telephone company can have 10 million customers each making on average 10 telephone calls per day, which is the industry norm for calculation purposes. This means 100 million fact table rows per day. Keeping history for three years can really add up. To calculate the size of a fact table, multiply each associated dimension's cardinality:

Date dimension	1,095 = 3 years * 365 days
Time-of-Day dimension	86,400 = 24 hours * 60 minutes * 60 seconds
Product dimension	20,000
Person dimension	500,000
1095 * 86400 * 20000 * 500000 =	946,080,000,000,000,000

Obviously this is a high-end calculation. To be realistic, think of how many fact rows are feasible at the granularity chosen. Many times this is based on pre-existing estimates from past sales, or calls: 10 million telephone customers making on average 10 calls per day is 100,000,000 fact rows, considerably fewer than initially calculated. Calculations can now be made at this level and extrapolated for planning purposes.

It's always a good idea to discuss sizing estimates with the database administrator initially to ensure system capacity. Based on usage and expected performance, the DBA can estimate I/O consumption and CPU processing power required. The number of rows being retrieved from the database impacts performance because they require CPU power to process. I/O is the actual reading, or fetching, of database pages from storage (disk) to memory.

Many databases have restrictions on the number of rows per block or database page, such as 255 rows per page, which is dependent on row size. These restrictions also add to estimates, and the database administrator takes all of this into consideration when performing sizing calculations.

Remember, designing and building data marts is for business usage and therefore each table must be carefully planned especially for ease of communication and understanding by the business user. Hand in hand with usage considerations is performance. Business users must be able to easily use the data marts and response time, or performance, must be acceptable for the entire solution to be considered a success.

CHAPTER

8

Enterprise Data Models

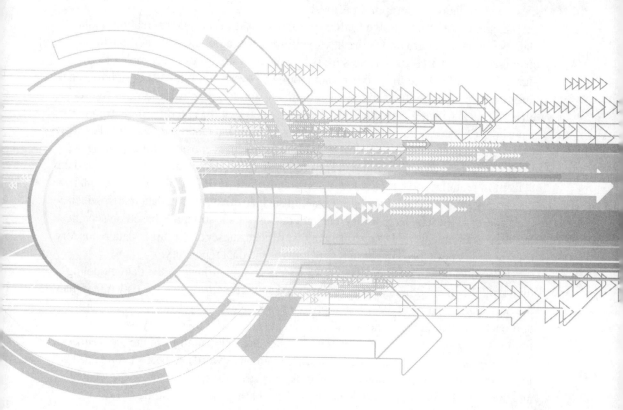

T his chapter discusses the different types of data models in a data warehouse and their uses. Chapter 7 focused on data models within the performance and user presentation layers while this chapter discusses overall data modeling with a focus on the centralized data layer. The goal for this chapter is towards an enterprise repository perspective of data modeling from conceptual to physical along with insights of each.

Data Models Overview

The architecture of a data warehouse solution must allow for the effective capture and retention of the underlying data and therefore must be organized in a fashion conducive to this purpose. It then becomes apparent that the proper data model can greatly influence the effectiveness of a data warehouse effort. For this reason, no matter which data model is being used, it is an absolute necessity to ensure that the data model has a clearly understood and consistent data vocabulary. The structures should be relatively easy to use and should be designed for specific usage, in this case to hold data over temporal periods.

Using the appropriate design for the appropriate usage is critical in creating a solid data warehouse system and is the key to building a usable and accepted business intelligence solution. If the business users find the data structures too complex to query, they simply will not use the delivered solution. And oversimplifying the design makes it difficult to build a flexible and open environment and to grow the design for future efforts. This is why it is important to differentiate between the enterprise data warehouse repository of historical data versus the business focused data marts. Design the data marts for specific business usage, and design the data warehouse repository for capturing and holding historical data. Designing the repository in a normalized manner allows for data at its most granular and simplest level, allowing for full flexibility of the fundamental data components and how they inter-relate. In such an environment, data marts, which are a subset of the larger repository, can pull data into their structures based on specific business requirements and usage. Data marts, while a subset of the larger data repository, usually do not have the same design structures as the data repository.

The architecture of the data warehouse system greatly influences the data modeling direction. When the primary focus of the data warehouse effort is on the data rather than the business questions, a data-first approach is taken, aka a repository architecture approach. This approach is not to initially create an environment to answer specific business questions but to create a data foundation environment to facilitate the business analysis efforts for the organization as a whole—in other words, a means to an end. The idea is to create a commonality of data items, data structures, data definitions/vocabulary, and thus limit business unit and department data-sharing incompatibilities.

Organizations are realizing that data is the key to understanding the operations and competitive environment of their business. Without data integrity and data quality, a business may be functioning under false or misleading parameters and limiting or overemphasizing its growth potential. There must be a single enterprise definition of data and it must be organized as a single contextual version of the truth. This means central common structures with a single definition, for its impact to be truly controlled and effective. After all, data within context is information, and organizations need quality information to guide decision making and strategize based on facts.

An enterprise data model (EDM) for the central repository is the result of a conscious and deliberate effort to understand and represent business foundation data. An EDM is useful in a number of ways. It facilitates communication between IT and the business, and modeling standards allow data to have a consistent representation across the enterprise in every application. Also, EDM reduces data redundancy and complexity through an understanding of how the data components inter-relate across the many uses within the enterprise.

The goal of an EDM is to analyze and model as much data as possible to create an enterprise vocabulary and conformed data structures. In the process of doing this, the business of the organization will be categorized in great detail, which will support future enterprise and focused business intelligence efforts. The approach is to identify and analyze the organization's core business areas and then divide these further into components. Continue dividing these into subcomponents for a more refined or forensic insight as to what makes the business function.

When beginning this effort, the terminology is very business-oriented. As the business is decomposed, its components become more data-oriented. Eventually the business terminology maps to pure data components, thus allowing a transparent relationship between the business vocabulary and its underlying data foundation.

An enterprise data model is a mammoth undertaking, and given such a large endeavor, rather than the big-bang approach, the strategy should be to phase the efforts. Figure 8-1 is an example of how this can be done within the development cycle.

The first level, in Figure 8-1, is called the *subject area model* or SAM. This is the initial breakdown of an organization's business into 10 to 25 chunks. The second level is the *conceptual model*, which is to further divide the subject area model into more notable components. The third level is to continue subdividing the conceptual model into a model usable for the data modelers, which is called a *conceptual entity model*, aka an entity relationship (ER) data model.

Each level is intrinsically related to the others and all contribute to the overall enterprise data model. All three levels in total are known as the *logical enterprise data model*.

This phased approach to the EDM development allows for a controlled level of focus, facilitates resource scheduling, and allows cost budgeting according to boundaries of

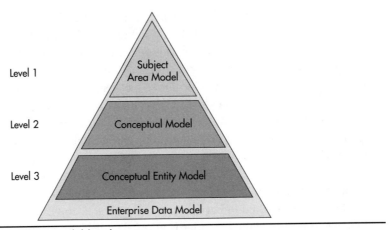

Figure 8-1   *Enterprise data model levels*

each phase expectations. This methodology drives the development in a controlled manner that is more practical to manage and allows for achievable deliverables. A phased approach allows for the re-evaluation of direction and feasibility at major milestones: after Level 1 and after Level 2.

Consider these levels as a horizontal method of analyzing, designing, and building for each vertical project. The first level is lengthier as a common development method takes root. Subsequent projects should become shorter as each project's business scope adds to the fundamental data models. As more projects are developed, concepts, entities, and attributes are reused and the models grow into a very usable and flexible enterprise data model.

Therefore, in order to create a data warehouse system, the data must be organized. Organizing the data is done with a data model. As mentioned in Chapter 7, data models can be logical, which is similar to blueprints for a house, or physical, which represents the optimized logical data model tuned for creating database tables for specific databases. High-level logical data models are called *subject data models*, which come in many flavors but essentially are first attempts to set a vocabulary and understand the business at a high level. Subject and conceptual data models are communicative tools to help with an understanding of the business elements.

As seen in Figure 8-2, the focus within this simple data warehouse architecture is on the centralized data layer. The idea is that data is to be centralized in terminology, definition, structure, and values to allow for a common enterprise-wide understanding of the data. Since the data is an enterprise-wide asset, setting a common understanding of the asset is critical to the business for sharing across the organization now and in future ways not yet known.

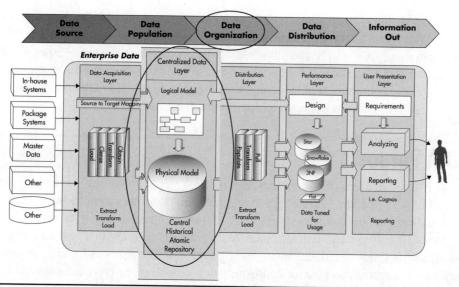

Figure 8-2   *Date warehouse architecture: data flow*

While Chapter 7 focused on data models specifically for business intelligence solutions, data models in this chapter's context are primarily for a data warehouse repository but can also be used for other applications, as mentioned at the end of this chapter.

In the data warehouse context, the enterprise data models are designed to capture and hold data over extended periods of time. The focus is not on retrieving or querying the data but on capturing and holding the data, which are two completely different perspectives. A data mart is focused on optimizing and presenting the data for the sole purpose of business usage. A data warehouse repository is focused on identifying and defining the data as well as holding the data values which will be extracted at a later time into structures more appropriate for specific business usage.

Inmon and Kimball

Bill Inmon and Ralph Kimball are both major contributors to data warehousing with their own differing perspectives on data modeling and data architecture. At a very simplistic level, the Inmon view is to organize all enterprise data for later business usage, while the Kimball view is to organize parts of the enterprise data for current specific business usage. Chapter 7 was generally geared more toward the Kimball usage perspective, and this chapter leans more toward the Inmon enterprise data organization view. The Kimball methodology, however, still requires a method of holding historical data, which will also be discussed as the chapter progresses.

Both methodologies require a high-level business data model for the data warehouse and consideration of the data as an enterprise asset. The non-application-specific enterprise data model can be the glue holding the corporate data asset together. In other words, an EDM organizes all the corporate data in one central design. Each application wanting to use components of this corporate asset can do so, and each application would design its data environment as appropriate for its own usage.

EDM Purpose

As with all other areas of data processing, the first step is to determine the purpose or goal of the impending efforts. Each organization is different, and as such, each has its own directives for business intelligence, data warehousing, and data management.

One organization may wish to minimize the time to market with a new business intelligence solution to aid and enhance the decision-making process, while another may wish to organize its data for conformity throughout the enterprise for several types of downstream applications. And yet another organization may wish to approach a specific application such as a data warehouse system from a data perspective rather than from an analysis or data-mining starting point. Perhaps your strategy is twofold; beginning with a reporting solution while ensuring enterprise data conformity at the terminology, definition, and values levels and later building an enterprise data model to which the reporting data model conforms, thus organizing the overall data asset into a usable master data management solution. Or maybe the reverse: the effort is to create a structured and organized master data environment partly funded by a business-analysis reporting solution. Either way, understanding the appropriate data model, its usage, and how it relates to other data models is the secret to modeling the corporate data asset.

This chapter assumes that a data warehouse system is the purpose of the effort, and as such, it is important to understand the organization's data management strategy and the data warehouse project strategy. Every corporation can benefit from a central data management solution, and the key is planning in focused stages given the timeline, budget, and resources.

EDM Benefit

The many benefits of data modeling have been detailed throughout the book so far, but just to be sure the basic points are understood, the following lists pinpoint the benefits. The main data modeling benefits include the following types of consistency

- ▶ Consistent enterprise vocabulary
- ▶ Consistent data component definitions
- ▶ Consistent representation of the data asset throughout the organization

In addition, data modeling benefits the organization by

▶ Functioning as a communication tool in business and data terminology

▶ Providing a foundation for the enterprise data asset

▶ Describing fundamental, descriptive, and associative aspects of the data components

▶ Reducing data redundancy via centralized design

▶ Facilitating data sharing

▶ Reducing development time and costs by eliminating redundant designing efforts

Different data models have different benefits. A conceptual model is primarily for understanding and communicating its components. A logical data mart model typically communicates an analysis focus and a physical data model represents tables and columns for a specific DBMS.

Data Model: Where to Start

Efforts to create an enterprise data model can begin in several areas depending on the data modeling expertise and insights within the internal data modeling team and given the goal or purpose of the overall effort. A full top-down initiative would be required if modeling an organization's entire data asset, which is no simple task. To model the data asset based on a specific source system is another top-down effort but with a limited view. A data warehouse centralization effort is yet again another top-down project. Data mart consolidation can also be an interesting enterprise data model initiative. Depending on whether the data marts are conformed to a central vocabulary, this last effort can be quite consuming.

Top-down efforts are difficult if you are starting from scratch. Modeling only on current views of the data tends to limit the flexibility of the design and usually results in much rework. For example, if only a small handful of data elements are known for the product, the design will reflect this limitation. Later, when another source or deeper insights are known about the product, it is very possible that the current design will have to be reworked to accommodate the new developments. Using a prebuilt data model geared toward your particular line of business can be beneficial because the designs can not only hold what is currently known within your scope, but can also include future data components not yet locally understood. This obviously adds tremendous benefit because it allows for flexibility and insight, and potentially reduces future efforts, which directly translate to lower costs.

Full Top-Down Data Model

As mentioned previously, one method of creating a data model is to scope all the data within the entire organization. Obviously this is an impossible task to accomplish in one sitting and can take years. The idea then is to look at the business of the organization from a very high level and break it down to lower levels until an entity relationship model can be created. An entity relationship data model is a data model in which data is represented as abstract designs defining, describing, and associating the data components. From such a logical data model, a focused physical data model can be created, allowing the building of database objects that can be populated with data for business consumption.

In modeling a process or an entire enterprise, there must be a focus or the task will never complete. In our case the context is to model a data warehouse system from a nonanalytical perspective. The idea is to model the data asset well enough for the entire organization to have a foundation of understanding and commonality. As each new project develops, some data components will be reused and others will be newly added to the "big" ever-growing enterprise data model. To allow the ongoing addition or extension of the data model, the design must be in as flexible a manner as possible to minimize any rework, which can have a large impact on usages that have already been built.

The approach to modeling the organization is by analyzing the main value chains of the business. Value chains are the main processes the organization performs, which form the core of the business. From these views, the essence of the business can be captured within the data model. A method of full top-down data modeling using the value chains consists of data model components, as seen previously in Figure 8-1:

- ▶ Subject area modeling
- ▶ Concept modeling
- ▶ Conceptual entity model, aka entity relationship (ER) data model

However, it is important to stick to business value chains, or the overall exercise can become quite overwhelming without boundaries. The project has to have some strong parameters that control the depth of the project scope, else the effort may never end.

Subject Area Model

The idea of a subject area model is to define the business information at its core. Figure 8-3 shows a slice of a simple investment fund subject area model used for financial reporting purposes. The Level 1 focus is to determine what the business is and to organize it into high-level business subjects. This allows an organized starting point to further break down the subjects within the next level. This model is used to get a very high view of the business as a whole.

Affinity Meeting

One method of creating a business subject model is by using the affinity process. *Affinity meetings* are essentially brainstorming sessions with the main business people within the organization. The point is to determine what the business does from their perspectives, since they run the business. Therefore the people involved are upper management. The largest hurdle for an affinity approach to modeling the organization is in obtaining the proper people and having them participate in such meetings. Unless sponsored and driven by upper management, this method is quite difficult to accomplish.

Gather four to six key business people per session. It's best if they represent different areas of the organization: finance, network, purchasing, and so forth. People from different ends of the business will add unique insights as to how the business operates. Having a crowd from the same business unit will produce a very detailed insight in only one business area. Adding variety to the meeting will hopefully produce an enterprise representation of how the business operates. These people are the business-savvy people in the organization, not supporting staff or IT resources. These are department heads, business mentors, administrative leads, specialists, and so forth. It is not unusual for this group to have members that are quite active in seeking out information across business

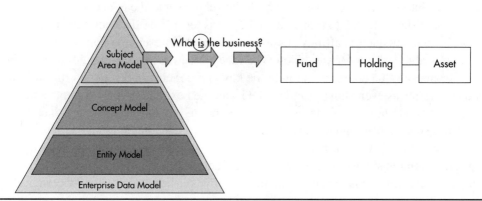

Figure 8-3   *Level 1 Enterprise data model breakdown*

silos for ad-hoc or project-specific reports. This can be invaluable not only in seeing the business needs but also in addressing its frustrations.

Within a given time period of 30 minutes, each person creates as many one- or two-word topics representing their area of the organization. It's best if they think about their own value chains to focus on their main business events and how they come to be. Think of the data currently being used, the processes currently running, and what will be happening in the future. Think of the organization as a whole and how your area of the business fits into the overall corporate structure. Think of the business and not necessarily the current system limitations.

It's best to write each of these topics on individual sticky notes so they can be posted on a wall. This exercise usually produces approximately 200 to 300 (possibly more) sticky notes per session. There are no discussions, no mingling—at this point, everything is an independent exercise. After the 30 minutes are up, the group as a team will organize each sticky note into associated topics as they see fit. Then determine a name for the grouping, which becomes business subjects. Have the participants discuss why the individual stickies should be grouped in the way they have chosen.

Notice how each sticky note can only be placed into one grouping, but the underlying concept can be used in several groupings. The subject areas will contain a mix between business concepts and data fundamentals. Some may seem to span both. For instance, demographics is easily identified as a business term since it can be subdivided into its underlying data components, but an individual or person can be a business concept and a data component. This happens often when, for instance, a person can play different roles within the organization's business. A single person can be an employee, a patient, a customer, a vendor, and so forth. When this type of confusion arises, try to use the role rather than the data component.

The group headings are an initial attempt at a subject area model. The sticky notes are the first attempt at a conceptual business model. Once all sessions consisting of all key business people within in the organization are complete, IT will merge all groupings into one central design for both the subjects and the concepts.

The next step is for IT to translate the business terms into data components. This effort is done outside the affinity sessions and must be presented in an easily communicable fashion for validation. The idea is that the process should identify the main business value chains along with the key components in business terms at first and data terms as everything progresses. IT can then expand on the concepts and subconcepts. Do not get too descriptive at this point, but adding some key data attributes such as person name and birth date is quite acceptable as side notes.

Figure 8-4 shows one of many representations of a subject area model. This particular version shows the business subjects across rings of underlying data subjects. This version is purely for communicative purposes to show how certain business topics can be grouped into data subjects.

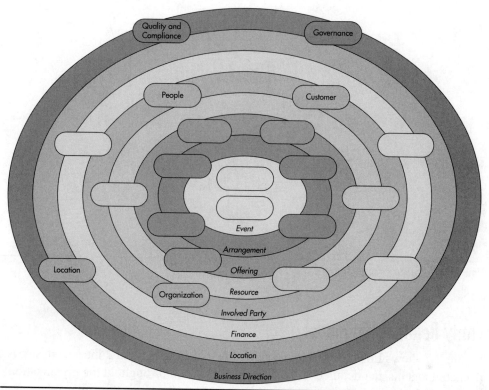

Figure 8-4 *Subject area model*

Figure 8-5 shows another high-level subject area model. There are several ways to model an organization; pick the best representation for your audience.

Concept Model

Level 2, shown in Figure 8-6, is to break down the business subject model into more comprehensive components. This model is used to communicate the business fundamentals and how the business operates from a business and data perspective within the organization. The idea is to break down the business subjects into more understandable components with a data flavor. Since the goal is to build an enterprise data model, the business must be broken down into its fundamental data components so it can be communicated at a pure data level. A concept data model is a good middle tier showing what is in the business subjects.

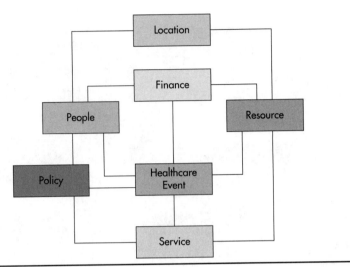

Figure 8-5   *Subject area model*

Entity Relationship Model

Figure 8-7 shows Level 3, which is a breakdown of Levels 1 and 2 into the business data components at a detailed level. This model is used throughout the organization to capture the individual data components, data items, and how they inter-relate in the most granular form.

This level of data modeling consists of entities, attributes, and associative relationships. This model is the most detailed level of business data modeling and is

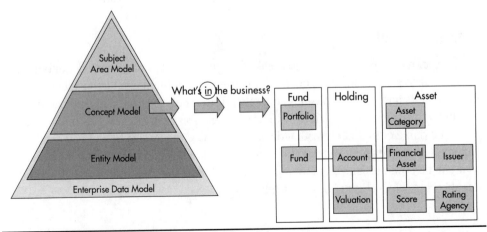

Figure 8-6   *Level 2 Enterprise data model breakdown*

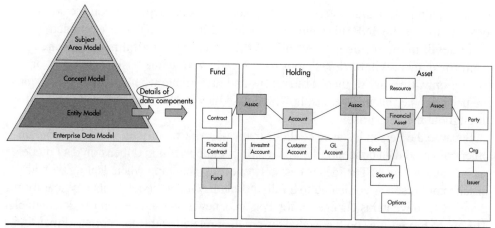

Figure 8-7   *Level 3 enterprise data model breakdown*

represented in a normalized fashion. The Model Insights section of this chapter discusses this type of ER enterprise data model.

Figure 7-2 in Chapter 7 shows a number of data models. The top portion refers to this Level 3 data model. This type of ER data model represents the business's data without the influence of any application. Since a data warehouse system spans much of the enterprise, the majority of this Level 3 entity data model will be used in the creation of the data warehouse repository. A data warehouse repository model could differ slightly from this business data model design, such as with normalizing classifying attributes or simply excluding certain subjects due to scope limitations. A business data model is exclusive of temporal details while a data warehouse application would require history attributes.

Bus Architecture

The bus architecture is a component of the Kimball methodology used in creating an enterprise data design for a specific application. The application is a business intelligence analytical environment. The idea is focused on a master gathering of dimensions that can be used and reused throughout the organization to analyze the business data. Dimension tables and fact tables are brought together in a data mart. The tables that are shared across data marts are called *conformed*. Data marts are created based on specific business analysis areas. These conformed dimensions together form the bus architecture.

Conformed dimensions are denormalized second normal form entities based on a particular concept. For instance, a Person entity would contain person data and may contain address and address type. Note: Since address is dependent on the address type, it violates the 3NF rules and remains in a 2NF format. This is explained in more detail in the following sections of this chapter. Not all dimensions are conformed; there will be dimensions used locally within one business process or project only. Be wary of these dimensions and investigate whether these dimensions are used in other business areas, in which case they could be centralized and used throughout the enterprise.

Because the Person instance contains many descriptive attributes and may contain other collapsed data concepts, the dimension is quite useful in dimension data models such as star schemas. The idea is basically one-stop shopping when dealing with an instance of Person as compared to a fully normalized data model. In its physical form, if any descriptive items change for the Person, a new row is created in the Person table. The analysis measures on the fact tables are then related to the appropriate dimension instance. On the downside, there can be much redundancy as new rows are added when only a single attribute may have changed. On the optimistic side, since the volume of dimensions is not drastic, having such redundancy is in theory (and in most practical implementations) negligible from a disk space perspective.

As different business processes are analyzed, data marts are created. These data mart dimensions take from the enterprise bus architecture, thus reinforcing the reusability of the conformed dimensions as seen in Figure 8-8. All the data marts, including the conformed tables, together form the business aspect of the enterprise data warehouse.

In the bus architecture the data warehouse repository consists of the conformed dimensions and fact tables. All processing and intermediate data is within a staging environment. In the normalized data warehouse repository architecture, the staging environment is a normalized repository similar to the bus architecture staging environment, but a normalized repository is maintained. From this repository, data marts consisting of conformed dimensions or 3NF submodels are created. More importantly, the data marts are created to conform to the data warehouse normalized repository. If the

Business Process	Business Priority	Conformed Dimensions						
		Date (Order, Start, Ship)	Product	Promotion	Customer	Employee	Part	Shipper
Orders Forecasting	2	x	x	x	x	x		
Orders Forecasting	1	x	x	x	x	x		
Purchasing		x	x		x	x	x	x
Parts Inventory		x	x	x			x	
Manufacturing	6	x	x				x	
Finished Goods		x	x					

Figure 8-8 *Bus architecture*

repository is not physicalized, then the data marts conform to the logical normalized business data model.

From an enterprise data asset perspective, the normalized enterprise data model is required because it relates all the data components at an atomic level. From a business analysis perspective, it is usually more effective to represent the data in a star schema with conformed dimensions. Most business intelligence tools such as Cognos, Business Objects, and Microstrategy work best with star schemas. Plus these designs are simple to understand and therefore very usable to the business community. Design based on the usage perspective and the audience. Does the organization want a simple reporting environment, or do they want to understand their data at the finest level of granularity as it pertains to any application throughout the enterprise? Design accordingly.

Purchased Data Model

A purchased data model must be specific for your line of business and the application project at hand. Do not purchase an operational billing data model to create a data warehouse, as these are completely different types of applications. Purchase a data model that is relevant to the application efforts, which in this case is a data warehouse repository.

A data model that is purchased has its own pros and cons. The main positive point is that the data model should represent your business area and have some form of organized structure. Of course, each entity and attribute must be defined, or else there will be some sort of guessing as to its meaning and purpose. If guessing is okay in your organization, please let us know, as we can develop undocumented data models quite quickly and still charge a high price for our efforts!!

Some data models are data-focused; others are data- and business-focused. Either way, the business data must be represented and a common vocabulary must be used throughout the organization. Having a repository of synonyms is not the goal—it can be useful in requirements gathering, yet it is not the goal at this level.

The great part about purchasing a data model is that it is already created. The downside of purchasing a data model is that it is already created. If it suits your needs, a purchased data model is great. If it is poorly understood, difficult to interpret, or too abstract, or high level, for your efforts, then it may not satisfy its purpose. That said, it could still be used as a reference model or guide to base development efforts. Be sure your primary business can be represented in at least the early stages of the project or in the preliminary gathering of requirements. If the attributes and dimensions that arise from those processes do not have some match to the existing model, then there has to be further consideration either of other models or one started from scratch. The latter, of course, represents additional costs and resources which must be taken into account when costing project efforts.

All data models should have a high-level conceptual data model representing the key points within the model and how this relates to the business. This facilitates mapping the prebuilt model to your own business, which can be quite an exercise depending on resource data modeling experience. Concept models as described earlier are high level, have no or little descriptive attributes, and have few associative entities. For example, Figure 8-9 shows a simplistic securities fund concept model from a financial reporting perspective. The subjects are: Fund, Holding, and Asset. The concepts further break down the subject, that is, Fund has Portfolio and Fund.

Build Estimate

From this concept model, further breakdown into an enterprise data model can be achieved. A purchased data model, as with a built-from-scratch data model, should have a further breakdown of these concepts into entities, attributes, and associations. A purchased data model will save lots of effort since the model is already thought out, designed, built, and tested on many customer projects.

To build your own enterprise data warehouse model from scratch, the industry standard effort level is 20 minutes for each and every attribute. This rule of thumb usually applies to add-on efforts for existing data models. In other words, to add 20 entities with an average of 10 attributes per entity is 200 * 20 = 4000 minutes, or 33 weeks. This time includes analysis of the business context, determination of definition, validation and design of the data item itself in context to the entity, and the business and data concepts. This rule of thumb is not linear in that it is not true that if 33 data modelers were to tackle the requirement, the data model would be completed in one week as opposed to 33 weeks. There is a saturation level, which is difficult to determine. Typically, two individuals commence the overall data modeling efforts focused on a specific business subject or project boundaries. A third would validate the efforts with a view of ensuring a unified enterprise focus as well as a flexible, or open, architecture to allow for future enhancements with minimum

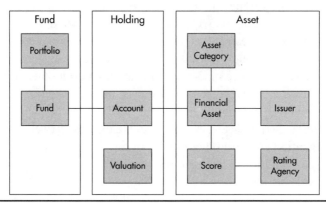

Figure 8-9 *Concept model*

rework. If the two modelers are working independently, then the third will coordinate and integrate as well as perform some modeling. If both primary modelers are working together, the third modeler is not as important depending on their experience level. Remember, an enterprise data warehouse design is usually quite a larger undertaking than a transactional or operational system data model.

To build an enterprise data warehouse data model consisting of a business data model, a data warehouse repository model, and a number of data marts could very well take years. Purchasing a ready-made model that contains your business focus and has been tried and tested in the industry can save an enormous amount of effort and advance the project significantly. Doing the math for a large industry data warehouse model package (repository, data marts, possibly a business data model), if the data models combined hold 10,000 attributes, roughly speaking, this could easily take two full years of development effort.

Model Insights

The following topics have been mentioned previously in the book but I thought it might be good to centralize them in one spot for easy reference.

Data Components

The Data Components section in Chapter 2 describes the basic building blocks to data modeling, which are: Fundamental, Descriptive, and Associative data components. These form the foundation of data modeling. The following list recaps what these are:

- ▶ **Fundamental**   Pertains to fundamental concepts
  - ▶ Person, Address, Product, and so on.
  - ▶ These are usually entities in a normalized data model.
- ▶ **Descriptive**   Pertains to giving color or flavor to the concepts
  - ▶ Name, Eye Color, Birth Date, and so on.
  - ▶ These are normally attributes of entities but can themselves be entities. For instance, if Name is normalized from the person entity, it would become its own concept and therefore its own entity rather than just an attribute. Of course, it would require an association to the Person entity.
- ▶ **Associative**   Pertains to relating one concept to another
  - ▶ Person Home Address entity: This relates person to an address under a specific context.

▶ These are entities with their own descriptive attributes but could be collapsed in a denormalized dimension model. In a normalized data model, associations are entities.

The first portion of Figure 8-10 shows the fundamental data components of a data model as represented by Location, Address, and Postal Address. The middle portion shows how certain fundamental entities have descriptive attributes. The bottom portion is focused on the associative entities, which are associating one entity to another.

Both normalized and denormalized data models can be created using these basic data components. Denormalizing a data model is the process of collapsing, or merging, one or more fundamental and associative data components into one fundamental entity called a *dimension* in a star schema representation.

Normalizing a Data Model

The purpose of creating a normalized data model is to ensure that the data will not be duplicated within the database and to ensure data consistency in its simplest form. This means designing a data model in which the design is flexible, meaning that the data components can be associated in different contexts without redundancy. For instance, Figure 8-11 shows a table called Person, which has two columns, Person Name and Company Name. Putting these two together in the same table means that if Company Name is to be used in another context other than in the Person table, then there will be redundancy. Therefore, isolating these two contexts would be more appropriate if you ever want the concepts to be used independently. Figure 8-12 shows Person and Company tables along with an associative table. The associative table, in this design, shows the context of the Person and Company relationship. From the person's perspective, the Person is an Employee of the Company and from the company's perspective; the Company has a Person as an Employee.

The first three types of normalized forms that are typically followed (used as a guideline) in data modeling are unimaginatively called *first normal form* (1NF), *second normal form* (2NF), and *third normal form* (3NF).

▶ **1NF**   First normal form eliminates repeating groups and requires each row to have its own unique identifier, or key.

▶ **2NF**   Second normal form requires the satisfaction of first normal form and the elimination of dependencies on a partial key by putting the fields in a separate table from those that are dependent on the whole key.

▶ **3NF**   Third normal form requires the satisfaction of both the first and second normal forms and the elimination of dependencies on non-key fields by putting them in a separate table. At this stage, all non-key fields are dependent on the key, the whole key, and nothing but the key.

There are other levels of normalization, but typically only these first three are used.

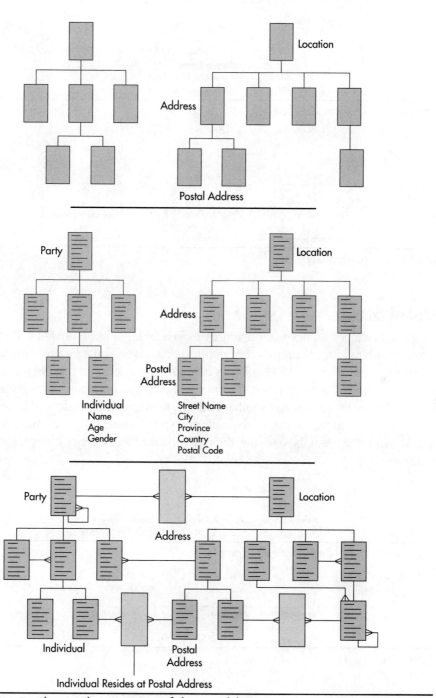

Figure 8-10 *Fundamental components of data modeling*

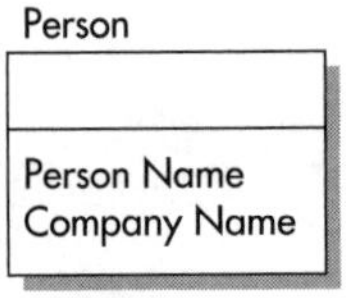

Figure 8-11   *Unnormalized design*

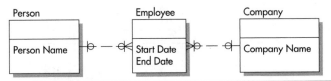

Figure 8-12   *Normalized design*

Worked Example

Suppose that a person has several addresses in a table, as in Figure 8-13. First normal form requires the removal of duplicate data items (aka groups); in our case, this is the removal of duplicate address columns. This does not refer to the data values themselves, just the items. The reason behind this normalization effort is that, if in the future the person has another address, then the entire table will have to be changed. To avoid this scenario, the table shown in Figure 8-14 is created, which means that rather than the one row, the new structure will have two rows, for our example.

Person Name	Home Address	Work Address
Bob	Miami, Florida, 12345	Dallas, Texas, 44432

Figure 8-13   *Initial denormalized example*

Person Name	Address	Address Type
Bob	Miami, Florida, 12345	Home
Bob	Dallas, Texas, 44432	Work

Figure 8-14   *First normal form step 1*

Although the main reason for normalizing a table is to remove duplication, to satisfy the first normal form there will be duplication of data, as with Person Name. But there will be a singularity of data concepts within the table design for 1NF.

The second part of the first normal form is to ensure that each row in the table has its own unique identifier. Figure 8-15 shows that the table now has a unique key made of two rows: Person Id and Address Id. These attributes were added to differentiate between the two types of addresses on the table as they pertained to the same Person within a unique row instance. We could have added one primary key column and the design would have passed the 1NF test, but the later 3NF would have divided up the table based on non-key fields being dependent on other non-key fields; Address would have been dependent on each occurrence of Person.

Having more than one column in a primary key is called a *concatenated* or composite key.

The second requirement for first normal form is now completed and the table is now in first normal form as it does not have recurring data groups and each row has a unique row identifier with the composite keys being: row 1 is Person Id = 1 and Address Id = 1, while row 2 is Person Id = 1 and Address Id = 2. Figure 8-16 shows an entity relationship (ER) model representation of Figure 8-15.

Second normal form requires no partial dependencies on a concatenated primary key. This means that each column in the table must be completely dependent on the entire primary key, or else the table is not in second normal form. If one column fails the test, then the entire table fails the 2NF test.

2NF test: Is the Person Name from Figure 8-16 completely dependent on the Person Id and the Address Id columns that form the composite primary key? No, a person's name is only dependent on the Person Id; therefore, the table is not in second normal form and a new table must be created to resolve this normalization issue. Figure 8-17 shows two tables; one representing the Person and the next the Person Address information association.

An entity relationship model view, Figure 8-18, is much more easily understood as it communicates the solution quite well. It shows the one-to-many Person to Person Address association.

Since Person now has a single column as the primary key, it passes the second normal form. However, "Person Address" does not pass the 2NF test as the Address column is not dependent on the Person Id portion of the primary key. This means that another table must be created, as shown in Figure 8-19.

The ER diagram in Figure 8-20 shows that the Person and Address tables are fundamental entities as they are stand-alone tables in their own right and can be reused in different contexts. This means that these two tables form part of a flexible design that allows for growth within an enterprise environment. The "Person Address" table is now an associative table between the Person and Address. It can be used in any number of instances, which is represented by the Address Type value.

Person Id	Person Name	Address Id	Address	Address Type
1	Bob	1	Miami, Florida, 12345	Home
1	Bob	2	Dallas, Texas, 44432	Work

Figure 8-15   *First normal form step 2*

Figure 8-16   *First normal form: ER model*

Person Id	Person Name
1	Bob

Person Id	Address Id	Address	Address Type
1	1	Miami, Florida, 12345	Home
1	2	Dallas, Texas, 44432	Work

Figure 8-17   *Second normal form step 1*

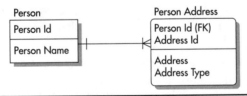

Figure 8-18   *Second normal form step 1: ER model*

Person Id	Person Name
1	Bob

Person Id	Address Id	Address Type
1	1	Home
1	2	Work

Address Id	Address
1	Miami, Florida, 12345
2	Dallas, Texas, 44432

Figure 8-19   *Second normal form step 2: data*

Figure 8-20   *Second normal form step 2: ER model*

Address Type now seems poorly named as it represents the Person Address context. An address can be used for many purposes; therefore, Address Type becomes Person Address Type for clear communicative purposes. At this point Person Address Type seems to be dependent on both the primary key attributes as well as further clarifying the association, so it should be part of the primary key itself as in Figure 8-21. To clarify the type, a description is required and therefore a new entity called Person Address Type.

It would seem from this result that a Person could have a number of Addresses or a number of address rows. If a person relocates to a new home, their home address would change. This means a new start and end date per person and address association. Adding these new temporal columns to the Person/Address table means that the end date is dependent on the start date. The third normal form states that no non-key fields should be dependent on other non-key fields. This means that something must be done with the new start and end date columns. After analysis, it is apparent that the Start Date should be part of the Person/Address identifying key, which means that the End Date now satisfies the third normal form, and the relationships shown in Figure 8-22 are created.

The initial design of a person with multiple addresses on the same table is now fully normalized to the third level. This design is now fully flexible in that it holds distinct fundamental entities with descriptive elements along with an independent

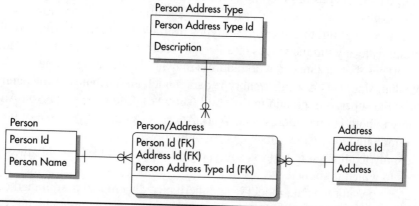

Figure 8-21   *Second normal form step 2: ER model*

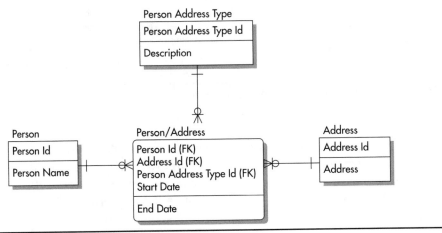

Figure 8-22 *Third normal form: ER model*

associative relationship. Each of the fundamental entities can be reused in other contexts. And the Person Address can accommodate any number of current and unforeseen associations such as: mailing address, communication address, delivery address, service address, and so forth.

Supertype/Subtype Models

The previous section discussed the design representation in physical terms such as table and columns. In a design mode, in this case a logical data model, tables are entities and columns are attributes. A method of representing the list of possible address types could be communicated as in Figure 8-23. This figure shows both Home Address and Work Address as subtypes of the association. Of course, if there were dozens and dozens of potential Person Address Types, it would suffice to show only the most popular for brevity's sake, show specific subtypes, or show none at all. One reason for highlighting specific subtypes over another in this fashion would be to communicate any unique values of a Person Address subtype not used in any other subtypes. For instance, a work address may hold a Building Name.

Note that, since this is a super/subtype data model, all attributes of the parent, also known as the supertype, pertain to the child (subtype). End Date on Person Address will apply to both Home Address and Work Address. Again for the sake of brevity and to eliminate redundancy, attributes are only shown once as needed. If End Date did not apply to all Person Address subtypes, it would be placed on only those subtypes to which it applied.

A supertype/subtype data model is an inheritance data model design method. Inheritance is from the top level of the supertype/subtype structure, which is called

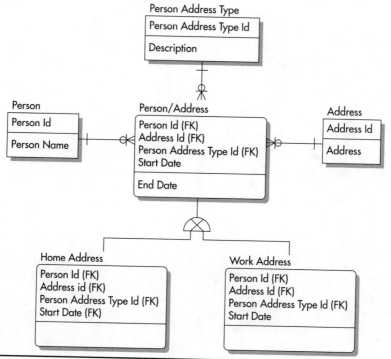

Figure 8-23   *Third normal form: ER model*

an *anchor*, downward. Anchors are data subjects, which are primary fundamental concepts. As each anchor is analyzed, its context can change, which creates more subconcepts. Then each subconcept can have its own context, creating another level of subconcepts. This continues until the desired level of detail is determined. For instance, a data subject can be Party. This anchor can be broken down into subconcepts as its context is determined. Party can be in one instance a Person and in another usage an Organization. Organization can further be subtyped into types of organization such as internal and external organizations. Internal organization could be units of the organization such as regional units, branches, and so forth. External organization can be companies, government, trusts and so forth.

It is the "type" of concept that is the key to a supertype/subtype data model. Applying the question "what type of" to the concept allows walking from parent to child. What type of Party? Organization, what type of Organization? Internal Unit, what type of internal unit? Branch 57. Each table having subtypes will have its own "type" attribute. The "type" values will be the subtype entity names themselves.

The lowest level in the anchor/subtype chain is called a *leaf node*. Pillar diagrams, as shown in Chapter 2 Figure 2-11, are based on supertype/subtype data models (Figure 8-24) with anchors and leaf levels only (usually). Dimensions in star

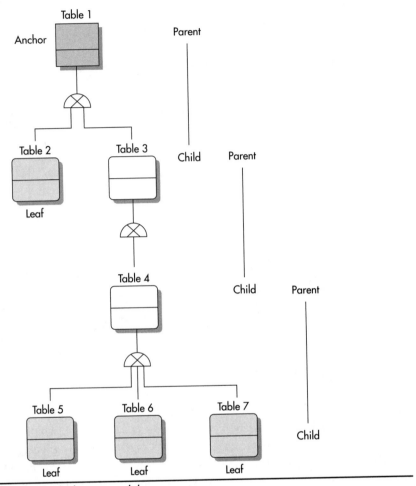

Figure 8-24 *Supertype/subtype model*

schemas are also typically derived from leaf levels from an enterprise inheritance data model. Of course, this is not a rule but a guideline, but essentially, since the leaf level is the most granular of any anchor chain, it makes sense that it could be used directly as a dimension. In many cases the leaf level nodes are collapsed upward (rolled up) to their common parent and the parent could then be a dimension in a star schema.

Chapter 2, Figures 2-3, 2-4, and 2-5, show the three main concepts behind a data model: fundamental, descriptive, and associative data components. Typically, in a supertype/subtype data model structure, all the subtypes are redefinitions of the parent entity with its own child-specific attributes, if any. These then are fundamental entities.

Each entity has descriptive attributes: a person has a name, birth date, eye color, and so forth. Fundamental entities are then associated to other fundamental entities either in their own anchor subtype structure, meaning other instances of the same anchor, or to other anchors and their subtype structure.

With an understanding of how to normalize data and with these three types of data model components, large enterprise data models can be created in a flexible manner allowing for future growth without having to redesign each time additions are required. In many instances, fully normalized data models are used as business data models, meaning that their design represents how the data is defined and associated. These models are not normally used one-to-one in the creation of database tables, as their purpose is not optimized for usage of any sort other than for defining data structures and their associations. These designs are excellent for an enterprise business data model, which is the first step in designing a data warehouse repository model.

Capturing History in a Normalized Data Model

Capturing history is the process of ensuring that the data model can hold the data as it changes over time. The manner in which the historical data item is recorded depends on the design of the data item. Only associative and descriptive data elements will change. Fundamental data items will not change, but their descriptive aspects may. The following sections describe methods of designing history into a fully normalized data model.

History via Associations

Referring to the design in Figure 8-23, if a person's home address changes, the associative table can easily handle temporal changes. Figure 8-25 shows the Person Address table with two rows. Initially there would only be one row with an End Date of Dec 31, 2999, which represents a high date, meaning that the value is active until some point of time in the future. When the address changes, a new row is placed in the Address table if not already there, and another row is added to the Person Address table with the Address Id of the new address row. As well, the new row in Person Address will have a Start Date of the active date and an End Date set to Dec 31, 2999. At this point the previous row's End Date will be modified to the active date minus one, as seen in Figure 8-25.

History Types and Designs

Descriptive data items are attributes that describe the data, for instance; marital status, gender, eye color, and name. Step one in defining how data is to be retained over time is to identify the temporal aspect of a data item. The Kimball method is quite good as it categorizes temporal changes in three levels:

▶ **Type I**   No history is required.

▶ **Type II**   Full history is required.

▶ **Type III**   First or previous and current versions are required.

Person

Person Id	Person Name
1	Bob

Address

Address Id	Address
1	Miami, Florida, 12345
2	Dallas, Texas, 44432

Person Address Type

Type Id	Description
44	Home Address
55	Work Address

Person Address

Person Id	Address Id	Type Id	Start Date	End Date
1	1	44	Jan 01, 2010	Jun 12, 2010
1	2	44	Jun 13, 2010	Dec 31, 2999

Figure 8-25   *History via associative table*

Typically, if an attribute is tagged as a Type I, then no history is captured. These types of changes are typically corrections without retaining the previous version. A Type III history change usually involves a design where an entity has two attributes to record the change and two to record the date it changes: Person Name, Person Name Effective Date, Previous Person Name, and Previous Person Name Effective Date. A Type II change requires more effort. In a fully normalized data model, Inmon flavor, the attribute is removed from the entity it is based on, and a new entity is created to hold all the possible values, each having its own unique identifier. The new entity is then associated back to the original base entity and history is kept via occurrences of the associative table. The exact history is traced via the Start Date and End Date attributes on the associative table, as shown in Figure 8-26. This Inmon flavor is called "spinning at the columns or attribute level" because the design is to manage history at the column level.

Type II design reflects a change at the attribute level. For each Type II attribute change, a similar design will be created. If an entity has ten Type II attributes, then ten individual designs will be required. Some data modelers like to see each and every distinct Type II design. Others prefer fewer entities and merge all into one central design, as seen in Figure 8-27. This can be further refined by using anchor tables rather than subtype tables on the left side of the relationship in Figure 8-27. Remember, this model is a supertype/subtype data model, as in Figure 8-24, meaning that an instance of Person is the same instance of Party (if party is the anchor). In other words, the value of the primary key for Person will be the same primary key for the anchor since the subtype is a redefinition of the same row.

Figure 8-28 shows sample data as would be used in the central code table design from Figure 8-27. If the association were to be at the anchor level, Party, the Party Id

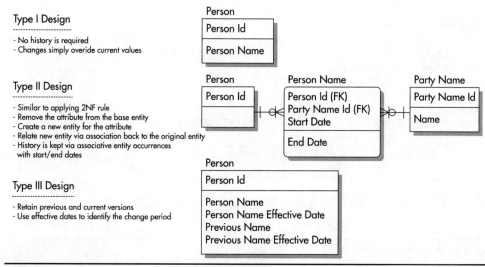

Type I Design

- No history is required
- Changes simply overide current values

Type II Design

- Similar to applying 2NF rule
- Remove the attribute from the base entity
- Create a new entity for the attribute
- Relate new entity via association back to the original entity
- History is kept via associative entity occurrences
  with start/end dates

Type III Design

- Retain previous and current versions
- Use effective dates to identify the change period

Figure 8-26 *History types*

would be the same as the Person Id. This type of design is called a Type A, or repository history at the attribute type level since the code table represents the type or name of the attribute.

The issue with this design, although it is used throughout the data warehouse industry, is that once physicalized, the tables will not show all its columns. To find the columns, a view is required to join the table and all related code table entries. In other words, Marital Status and Gender columns would not show up in the Person table in the physical representation, and therefore the physical implementation can be very taxing when trying to retrieve data.

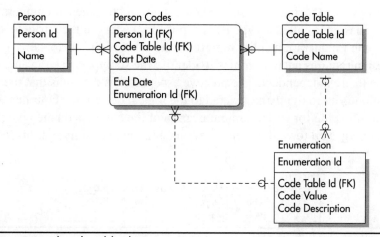

Figure 8-27 *Central code table design*

Person

Person Id	Name
1	Bob

Code Table

Code Table Id	Code Name
77	Marital Status
78	Gender

Enumeration

Enumeration Id	Code Table Id	Code Value	Code Description
3	77	S	Single
4	77	M	Married
5	77	D	Divorced
6	78	M	Male
7	78	F	Female

Person Codes

Person Id	Code Table Id	Start Date	End Date	Enumeration Id	
1	77	Jan 01, 2010	Jul 11, 2010	3	was single
1	77	Jul 12, 2010	Dec 31, 2999	4	was married on Jul 12, 2010

Figure 8-28   *Central code table*

History in a Denormalized Design

History in a data model with a Kimball design flavor is said to "spin at the row level," while a design with an Inmon flavor would "spin at the column level." In the Kimball flavor design, for any given change being tracked over time, the entire row is replicated, as seen in Figure 8-29. Of course, a natural key column would be a necessity, or how would a new "Bob" be differentiated from the existing "Bob"?

This type of design is great for dimensional data models such as star and snowflake schemas.

This design is also useful for a data repository as well. In a repository with data spinning at the row level, this means that each row will have all attributes, but each change will be a new row hence spinning at the row level. Figure 8-30 shows the Person entity with associations (foreign keys) to the code values or enumerations. This type of design is called a Type B, or repository history at the attribute value level, since the Enumeration entity represents the value of the attribute.

This design requires anchor entities to identify the subtype since the anchor Id and the subtype Id are independent. The positive aspect of this design is that the physical representation is more tightly associated to the logical design; the columns will be visible, thus allowing for easier communication of the columns on the table; and the design is more geared toward dimensional modeling but not fully optimized for

Person

Person Id	Name	Marital Status	Effective Date
1	Bob	Single	Jan 01, 2010
2	Bob	Married	Jul 12, 2010

Figure 8-29   *History ala Kimball for dimensions*

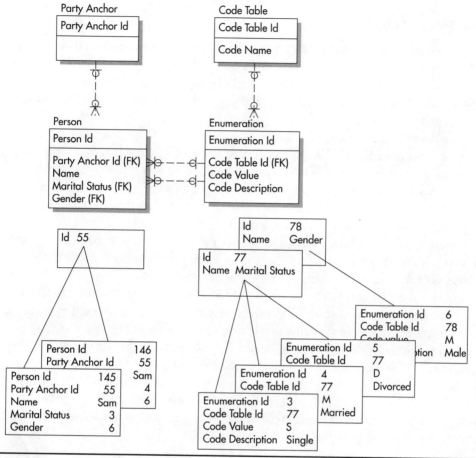

Figure 8-30   *History à la Kimball for repository*

dimensional modeling. Dimensional modeling can collapse, for instance, a person's address onto the person dimension or can represent fundamental person and fundamental address dimensions independently with the relationship via an association. For a repository, associations are still required to bridge the anchors.

History Summary

In short, capturing history can be done in a number of fashions. The previous section described two methods of designing the capture of history in a repository:

▶ **Type A**   Spinning at the attribute level which involves associative entities representing the changes in values.

▶ **Type B**   Spinning at the row level which involves a new row occurrence for each new attribute design. This method is used quite often in dimensional modeling but can also be used in a normalized repository design.

Surrogate Keys

A *surrogate key* is the primary key design of all entities in a normalized data model. The surrogate key has no business meaning.

If a Marital Status has four codes (S = single, M = married, S = separated, and D = divorced) with the abbreviation as the key to the table, how could both S for single and S for separated be in the same table if the key to the table is always unique? And if the value of the key changes, how would this be tracked? For instance, suppose S = single, M = married, and D = divorced. If S's definition changes to another value such as separated, again, how will it be tracked? To resolve these types of issues, the primary key is always set to a meaningless value and a natural key is maintained, which in this case is the code value: S, M, E, D: 01: S = single, 02: M = married, 03: E = separated, 04: D = divorced.

Figure 8-29 shows two rows in a table using a surrogate key, Person Id = 1 and 2. Tables with surrogate keys need some sort of anchor to uniquely identify the contents of the row. If another row is to be added to the Person table in Figure 8-29 with the name Bob, a new row would be added, but there would be no distinction between the currently existing Bob and the new entry. Hence a natural key must be used. Typically, a source system value is propagated through the data warehouse system to uniquely identify the row occurrence. So Person table now contains, for example, HR Number with a possible unique value of 345234 for this Bob person. Figure 8-31 shows three rows, two Bobs as defined by two distinct HR Numbers.

If no source system natural key is available, the anchor key would be used in the subtype, while the subtype would have its own surrogate key as shown in Figure 8-32 and the ER diagram in Figure 8-33.

Logical vs. Physical Data Model

The main difference between logical and physical data models is that a logical data model is created to communicate a design, and a physical data model is created for optimized usage via technology.

Party

Party Id
98
99

Person

Person Id	Party Id	Name	Marital Status	Effective Date
1	98	Bob	Single	Jan 01, 2010
2	98	Bob	Married	Jul 12, 2010
3	99	Bob	Married	May, 2006

Figure 8-31   *Natural key*

Party

Party Id
98

Person

Person Id	Party Id	Name	Marital Status	Effective Date
1	98	Bob	Single	Jan 01, 2010
2	98	Bob	Married	Jul 12, 2010
3	98	Bob	Married	May, 2006

Figure 8-32   *Anchor natural key*

A normalized logical business data model is created to show data components and how they inter-relate at the finest level of granularity appropriate. An enterprise version takes into account the data components within a larger corporate context with a design geared toward being flexible enough to minimize rework. A star schema logical data model is designed for ease of understanding with dimensions defined typically in business or obvious terminology. The usage of the logical data model is its transformation into a physical data model. The physical data model is geared toward an optimized specific usage. Of course, the logical business data model and data warehouse data model differ from data marts in that they are intended for broader use within the enterprise, whereas the data mart tends to have a more narrow business support mission.

For instance, a data warehouse repository physical model is designed based on volumetrics, the underlying DBMS, and for capturing and holding data. A physical data mart model, on the other hand, while also taking into account volumetrics with all its dependencies along with the underlying DBMS, is designed for data extraction by end users. The data mart design is usually denormalized to "squish" data together.

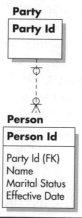

Figure 8-33   *ER diagram anchor natural key*

For instance, a person's address may be denormalized onto the person table, therefore allowing all data to be retrieved in one SQL statement. A normalized data model would normalize, or isolate, the two concepts and then relate them together via an associative entity. Both are good designs based on their practical usage.

The physical data model may be one-to-one with the logical data model or it may be collapsed; it all depends on the usage.

Referential Integrity or Not

Referential integrity (RI) is a database term referring to a foreign key in a child table always having a supporting row in the parent table. For instance, the Person table has a Marital Status column, which is a foreign key to the Marital Status code table. Having referential integrity between the two tables means that for every row in the Person table, the Marital Status column must have a value in the Marital Status code table. No row could be added to the Person table if there is no value in the Marital Status column, which is mandatory data (and therefore the foreign key is not nullable within the database).

Suppose a person enters a retail store and is offered a one-day-only 10 percent discount on all items in the store if they subscribe then and there to the store's credit card. All purchases by that person would typically flow into the data warehouse system that evening, but the person details may only enter the data warehouse a day or two later. Since all sale transactions have referential integrity to the person who made the purchase, what should happen in the database? Should the sale transactions not be added to the database until the person details are available, thereby possibly missing out on daily sales or inventory analysis? The answer is no because the sales data is quite valuable, and re-adding it may be a massive exercise in some organizations. Therefore while the design says every Person row must have a valid Marital Status value, in reality there may be discrepancies due to load timings. The method to resolve this issue and keep referential integrity is to add a row in the Marital Status table having a value of "dummy." When a Person row is added and there is no Marital Status value available, then simply use the Marital Status code table row with the "dummy" value. The proper value can be added to the Person row at a later time for proper business integrity.

The issue becomes quite visible in star schema dimensional modeling. Every dimension should typically have a dummy value row specifically for these type of issues. Best practice dictates that every fact table row must have a dimension value. If no proper dimension value exists, then a dummy dimension row can be used.

If this issue is not resolved at design spec time, the ETL job will certainly encounter such issues during testing. In actuality, since data mart ETL jobs should always ensure that all fact table primary keys have integrity with their dimensions, there should be no need for DBMS enforced RI. Normalized repository databases on the other hand typically do have DBMS referential integrity turned on. But again if the ETL process ensures that all integrity is proper, then enforcing RI is not required within the DBMS.

Other Data Models

There are a number of other types of data models, both logical and physical. For a data warehouse system, the enterprise data model can include input source system models as well as intermediate staging data models.

Since an enterprise data model represents the organization's data asset, all data components should be based on, or mapped to, this data model.

Input Data Model

In lieu of absolute source system data models, the physical data can be reverse-engineered and then mapped to the enterprise business data model. Since the enterprise business data model represents all data within the organization irrespective of any application, then all data assets should be mapped to this normalized data model. A further effort can also be made to map the source data model to the data warehouse repository data model to show data flow.

If the source systems are not available or unknown at the time of data model analysis and design, then an intermediate source system can be built. This is usually the design of expected input data layouts and typically called *structure input files*. Think of a software package that has a distinct input interface that identifies the data required by the application.

Staging Data Model

Another typical data model included in the enterprise data model is the staging data model. A staging environment is used as a working area to get the data ready from source input for the next holding area, which is the data warehouse repository in this context.

If the source data does not have change timestamps that pinpoint when a change is made to the data, then delta processing must be determined in the staging environment. Failing to identify input changes means that each load of the data repository will either replace or add to what is already there. Either way, it adds an unnecessary complication and therefore must be performed in the staging area.

Another use of the staging area is to maintain data when multiple sources must be merged. This usually happens due to timing issues. Data may be captured from system A on Fridays and from system B nightly at 3:00 A.M. Data must be retained in the staging area all week long waiting for Friday morning for the final merge before entering the data warehouse repository.

Final Thoughts

It may not be necessary to materialize the logical business data model, otherwise known as the EDM, into a normalized data warehouse repository. The data architecture should decide the data requirements from a holding perspective. If only a reporting environment is required, then perhaps only a data mart is required without physically implementing a data repository. The enterprise data model can still be created logically to understand the data fundamentals and associations since the data is an asset to the organization and should be understood.

If possible, this author much prefers purchasing a prebuilt data model rather than going through the process of creating a subject area model, deriving a concept model, and developing an enterprise data model from scratch. This whole process is time-consuming and involves lots of questions regarding how best to organize and structure the data. Usually the subject area model is foregone and the concept data model is created in passing. The main focus is on a normalized business data model to understand and capture the business at a fundamental data layer. Once the data is understood, a data warehouse repository and/or data marts are physicalized.

Data Warehouse Architecture: Components

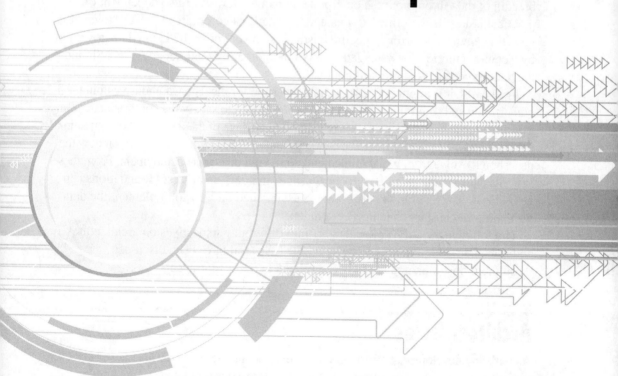

Trial his chapter presents different data warehouse system architectures and common issues typically discussed these days. The term "architecture" can refer to a number of perspectives, components, and how they inter-relate. In short, architecture refers to the manner in which a system's solution is planned and organized with emphasis on the design of its components and their associations based on the governing environment and predetermined usage. The best method of communicating the architecture initially is by the use of simple diagrams as shown in this chapter's figures. As a project progresses, details are added to the diagrams, such as hardware, capacity, volumetrics, backups, and so forth.

We begin with an overview, insights into roles, followed by architecture tiers, types, and components. The discussion concludes with a view toward implementation approaches and insights into accelerators that can help with development efforts.

Architecture Overview

Data warehouse architecture is dependent on a number of factors such as time to market, strategic vision, data architecture awareness, governance policies, and breadth of data throughout the enterprise, to name a few. It is also dependent on practical issues: Is the effort "to manage the data as a corporate asset" or "to create a reporting environment for a specific business sponsor" or both? Is the data governed by a central authority or managed locally among the regional departments? Should the data be centralized or distributed?

In all cases, it is important to set a strategic vision for the data warehouse within the organization and determine how it should be developed to satisfy the corporate direction. The next step is to determine the current and future usage of the data warehouse within a data management perspective and develop an appropriate architecture based on how the data should evolve from initial implementation to full enterprise deployment. From these insights data architecture, governance, usage, and data-as-an-asset foundations can be realized. Then a plan of action can be established on how to implement the data warehouse and business intelligence solution.

The following sections give insights into different perspectives on architectures and how their components can be assembled. Several have been discussed throughout this book and are now centralized here for reference.

Architect Roles

As with any development effort, and as a fundamental element of a data governance initiative, a vocabulary or terminology must be set to ensure that everyone understands what is being discussed. In the context of a data warehouse, it is quite common to encounter many individuals with the term "architect" in their job title. Recently a new employee joined a project and introduced himself as the solution architect. When I asked why the project required two solution architects since one already existed, he quickly replied that he was the ETL solution architect, not the overall data warehouse solution architect.

This section gives a brief insight into the potential architect tiles/roles in a data warehouse project. The term "architect" can be used in a number of scenarios in regard to a data warehouse and business intelligence solution. There are solution architects, data warehouse architects, technical architects, data architects, ETL architects, BI architects, and probably a number of others as well. The most used and misused term is the solution architect, as this title is quite generic and can be used for any subrole within a project.

As with any data warehouse system, the first step is to set a foundation of vocabulary or terminology to be sure that everyone is talking about the same subject. The following sections set the vocabulary by defining the architect roles and titles.

Solution Architect

The solution architect role is responsible for coordinating overall design for a data warehouse or business intelligence system. This role works hand in hand with the project manager in delivering the overall solution from requirements to output usage. This role is sometimes referred to as the *information architect* or *data warehouse architect*. The tasks include all technical areas with a goal of making the solution come to life. While a project manager is responsible for ensuring that the political path is cleared, resources are available, and the project plan is adhered to, the solution architect is responsible for ensuring a clear vision and focus, and ensuring that the project plan is feasible and maintained. If the project manager has expectations that the solution architect is not aware of, then chances are the expectations will go unrealized. If the solution architect is not fully aware of the project direction or has an unclear vision of the solution, then efforts will lag the project plan. Both must work together, both determining what is required and both overseeing the design and building of the product.

Data Warehouse Architect

As mentioned in the preceding section, the data warehouse architect role is similar to the solution architect role. If the project is quite large with multiple streams that may include re-platforming efforts, there would be a distinction between these two roles in that the solution architect is responsible for the overall solution of all streams, while the data warehouse architect is focused only on the data warehouse or business intelligence system deliverables.

Technical Architect

The technical architect is responsible for the physical environment, ensuring that appropriate servers (machines), storage disk, middleware, file systems, software, and such are available and operational. This role takes into account data volumetrics and usage requirements for a specific system lifecycle of typically three to five years to determine the appropriate physical environment capacity requirements for an appropriate responsive system, as defined in the project requirement specifications.

Data Architect

The data architect is responsible for data modeling, possibly oversees database administration, and is tasked with fully understanding the data flow within the data warehouse system, as well as being tasked with leading the data governance if no data governance lead role exists independently. The data architect oversees all data modeling aspects and typically guides the ETL and BI architectures. If data architects are responsible for overseeing the physical data models, then the role also coordinates the physical design with the database administrators. The data architect role has evolved from both the data modeler and the database designer roles.

ETL Architect

The ETL architect is responsible for all aspects of planning and designing the ETL, which involves source capture, source data transformation, and loading into the database. Source capture typically involves the source system transferring or *pushing the data* files to the data warehouse project environment to isolate the source system from third-party access. The reason is that the source systems are typically the business operational systems. If a source system should fail, it is possible the business could suffer; therefore, it's best if the source system generates the required data files and transmits them to the data warehouse system itself, rather than the data warehouse ETL routines accessing the operational systems. If the data warehouse system extracts data directly from the source system, it is called *pulling the data*.

The ETL architect tasks also include the extraction from the repository and distribution to the data marts if the architecture holds a realized data repository. ETL programmer efforts are guided by the designs of the ETL architect, which are directly associated to the data architect source-to-target mapping document.

BI Architect

The Business Intelligence architect is responsible for all aspects of planning and designing the end-user reporting and usage environment. This role obviously does not exist if a pure top-down approach is used for the purpose of designing the data asset without any reporting or informational perspective to the solution.

The BI architect is familiar with data modeling and understands what data is required and how it should best be structured for the specific BI tool in use. This role works closely with the data architect and in many instances creates reporting data marts, which are later synchronized with or become the data warehouse's data mart designs.

In many cases, the BI architect takes on a technical architect role but focuses only on the BI tool being used. Insights include all aspects of the setup and administration of the BI tools itself.

Overall

In a data warehouse or business intelligence project, the roles described so far are sometimes collapsed upward into the solution architect role, otherwise known as the data warehouse architect. Or the parent role can be implied in its underlying lead role, such as a lead data modeler who takes on the many tasks of a data architect. Or the lead BI programmer takes on the BI architect duties, and the lead ETL programmer takes on the ETL architecture tasks.

Typically a data warehouse project has one data warehouse architect role initially, which can evolve to a solution architect role when the project increases in resources and scope. Figure 9-1 illustrates where architects are positioned within a simple data flow design of a data warehouse system.

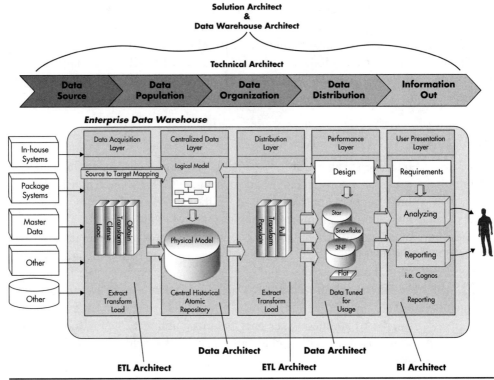

Figure 9-1   *Data warehouse architects*

Architecture Tiers

A data warehouse system can be formed from a number of inter-related systems, each called a *tier*. The following section describes the most common data warehouse tiers. Isolating these tiers and showing how they inter-relate allows for a focus on the individual systems rather than an all-at-once perspective.

Single-Tier Architecture

The first efforts in creating a data warehouse were geared more toward a pure reporting environment, which consisted of the source and user presentation layers. The only things between these two layers were views of the operational system.

The single-tier architecture, Figure 9-2, is so named because there is no distinction between source and data warehouse systems. This type of architecture is rarely seen any more under the data warehouse umbrella, as it was quite intrusive to the operational system. But of course it is still used where a large number of

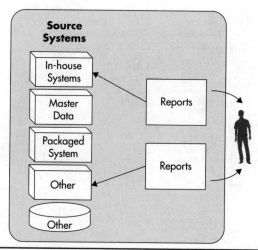

Figure 9-2   *Single-tier architecture*

variables have to be re-evaluated and incorporated into an extremely dynamic reporting environment, typically with little or no historical information. Most often this trades off with a far slower retrieval of information in return for very tight relations to highly variable source data.

For every analytical query or report routine, the source system would be directly accessed and would take on the extra CPU and I/O burden. This meant an impact to the business operations, which could take away from the core business; therefore, it was dropped back in the late 1980s for the most part. Long-running analytical queries were at the mercy of the operational system, nightly loads, backups, and batch processing and were limited to data from only one operational system at a time. The other side of the coin for this architecture is that no data would be duplicated onto other systems. This meant no redundancies and no ETL overhead.

In effect, this single-tier data warehouse architecture is not really a data warehouse but more of a reporting system as it does not meet the basic architecture requirements of distinguishing between the transactional and analytical areas, as stated later in this chapter.

Classic Two-Tier Architecture

Figure 9-1 represents the central repository architecture, which is the classic two-tier data warehouse architecture consisting of source systems and a data warehouse system as simplistically represented in Figure 9-3. The emphasis is on the differentiation between the source and data warehouse systems from an operational perspective.

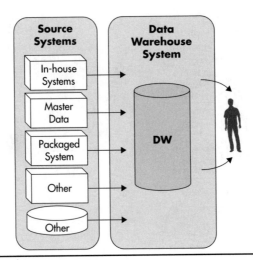

Figure 9-3   *Two-tier architecture*

Separating the system's various components allows for a focus on the data warehouse system independently from the operational source systems. This leads to a further realization of the fundamental subcomponents, as seen in the central repository data warehouse system in Figure 9-1:

- ▶ Data acquisition layer
- ▶ Centralized data layer
- ▶ Distribution layer
- ▶ Performance layer
- ▶ User presentation layer

Now with a clear focus solely on the data warehouse system, we can develop an appreciation of the components required to identify the data flow and lineage of the data, giving rise to an understanding of project scope and to position efforts during development. Once the data warehouse architecture is decided based on the strategic vision of the organization and the implementation method is determined based on the goals of the data warehouse project, efforts can begin to identify the actual business usage requirements at a high level and to determine the required source systems. This in essence is the connecting point between the source system and the data warehouse system. Resources can now be placed based on expectations of the user presentation layer without worry as to how the performance layer will be created, with source data profiling efforts shortly lagging behind.

Depending on the implementation approach, efforts will be either to identify source system data and design the central repository layer or to identify the business reporting requirements and design the performance layer conforming to a logical business data model. Breaking the two-tier architecture into components allows for easy access to whichever layer is in focus while understanding how and why they all interconnect to form a data warehouse system that is independent of the source systems. The two-tier architecture allows the creation of an independent data warehouse, which can then be designed for optimized usage, given a focus of the individual layers within. It also forces a central or conformed data model design apart from the original data sources and identifies whether the data is acquired or derived within the data warehouse.

This then brings to light data governance and data quality aspects, since there is a data acquisition layer apart from the performance layer. The acquisition layer can focus on issues such as delta processing, timing, and change management. This independent system perspective allows for the operational or transactional systems to operate without dependence on the other system and vice versa for the data warehouse system. Isolating the systems also allows the integration of additional systems into the data warehouse via new additions to the acquisition layer while conforming to a set enterprise vocabulary.

Advanced Three-Tier Architecture

The three-tier architecture, shown in Figure 9-4, involves the inclusion of another system, typically an operational data store (ODS). An ODS is fed from the source systems and is typically the "current" view of customer information. Data quality and governance are also applied to this tier, allowing a simpler integration into the data warehouse system. Typically, no history is kept in an ODS other than a profile-type table with historical scores and such. The main point is that an ODS is its own system feeding from the source systems and in turn used to feed the data warehouse system; hence the three-tier architecture. The data warehouse system is typically also fed from other source systems as well, but the ODS would be the primary source for most customer type data. An ODS can also be used independently of a data warehouse system but is usually created in conjunction with a data warehouse using data warehouse structures and definitions.

It is tempting to think of the three-tier solution as the best of both the highly reactive but very limited one-tier architecture and the two-tier isolation of the data warehouse as an accessible asset. The reality is somewhat more complex given the need in the three-tier architecture to align the ODS to the DW via data governance and overall performance structures.

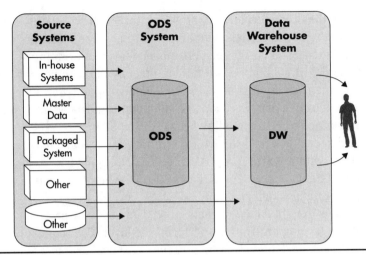

Figure 9-4   *Three-tier architecture*

Data Warehouse Architectures

Data warehouse architectures can be seen as four primary designs ranging from departmental to enterprise data-sharing solutions. The following sections describe solo data marts, bus architecture, corporate repository architecture, and a federated architecture solution. It is up to the solution architect to determine the appropriate architecture to support the current requirements while ensuring a flexible design that allows for unknown future requirements.

Solo Data Mart Architecture

The simplest form of a data warehouse is the solo data mart, or better stated, the independent data marts, as there can be many data marts that are just not connected in any way. The creation of this data mart architecture typically starts as a business departmental effort to centralize data into one database for reporting purposes. The first data marts, without going back too far, were primarily in Microsoft Access and Excel. The department—typically finance, sales, or marketing—would hire their own mini-IT staff or designate someone as the IT expert, and pull data from one or a number of source systems into a central area within their department boundaries and manage the data as they saw fit. As this progressed into more and more physical data marts, the effort in identifying, pulling, and managing the data became overly complicated or cumbersome for the limited staff and IT would typically be called in to manage the growing effort. IT would normally optimize (redesign) the many

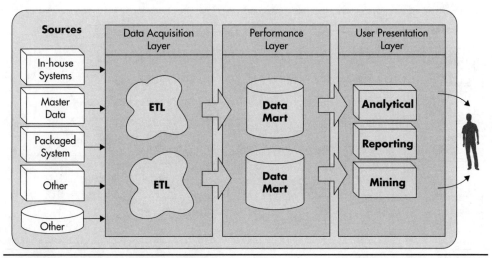

Figure 9-5   *Data mart architecture*

departmental data marts and reduce the loading routines to a minimum to optimize the delivery to the business.

Figure 9-5 shows a typical data mart architecture flow where the flow would be from source systems into solo data marts. While Figure 9-5 shows a data acquisition layer, in many instances the data is directly pulled into the data marts and managed thereafter. Reporting would be directly against the data mart using whatever tools were at hand.

Bus Architecture

The architecture shown in Figure 9-6, developed by Ralph Kimball, is a slight twist on the solo data mart architecture and is called the *conformed dimension* or *bus architecture*. As mentioned in the bottom-up approach (described later in this chapter), this design is based on synchronizing the dimensions across the enterprise; in other words, reusable dimensions within the organization. Data marts are designed primarily in star schemas and can normalize out to snowflake designs, as discussed in Chapter 7.

Unlike the solo data mart architecture, the bus architecture requires central management of the data models to ensure that the dimensions are indeed conformed. A staging area is typically required to prepare the data for distribution, as shown in Figure 9-7.

The staging area is purely to prepare the data and is not meant as a repository in the central repository architecture sense (which will be explained in the next section).

The bus architecture resides in the performance layer and contains the conformed dimensions as an enterprise shared data resource. The dimensions themselves hold all data over extended periods of time, while the fact tables are used to associate the dimensions for specific analytical contexts.

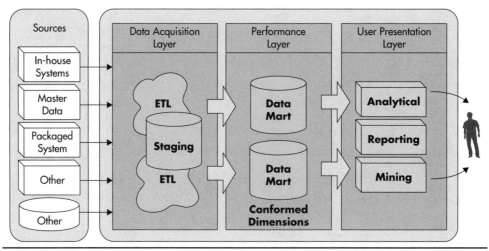

Figure 9-6   *Bus architecture*

Central Repository Architecture

Figure 9-8 represents the central repository architecture, which parallels the top-down implementation approach by Bill Inmon. This architecture specifically emphasizes the repository aspect to hold enterprise atomic data in a normalized fashion with full history over time. The data marts are a subset of the repository but are not necessarily designed in the same manner and can be either 3NF, star, or snowflaked.

The repository is at the heart of this architecture and emphasizes flexibility and scalability of design. The repository by its nature is the central source of conformed data.

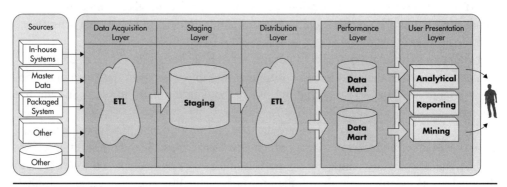

Figure 9-7   *Full bus architecture*

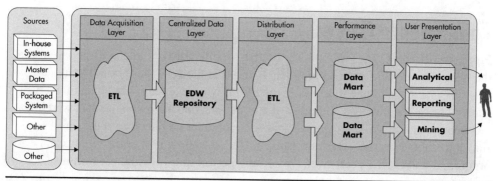

Figure 9-8   *Central repository architecture*

Federated Architecture

Figure 9-9 represents a federated architecture. The main emphasis is on the user presentation layer, which is sourced from a number of pre-existing data marts and/or data warehouses. Figure 9-9 only shows the data acquisition and performance layers but could very well have included a centralized data and the distribution layer as well.

This architecture usually arises from an immediate usage of distinct systems, usually when two departments wish to integrate or upon a merging of organizations. Operating multiple distinct data warehouses can be costly, and therefore this design is eventually merged into one central repository architecture once a data policy has been developed to suit the strategic direction of the organization.

The merging of multiple data marts is usually done via logical federated views, thus resulting in usage with minimum redesigning of existing systems. Maintaining a federated architecture of the multiple systems can be difficult to manage and quite costly.

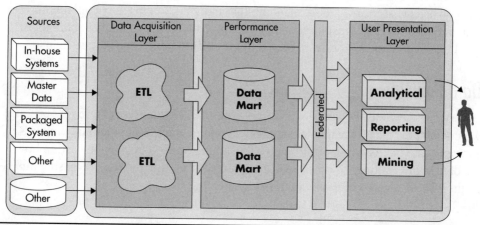

Figure 9-9   *Federated architecture*

Components (Layers)

From the different types of data warehouse architectures, it becomes apparent that there are commonalities of components, and it is the way these components are assembled and positioned that creates the resulting architecture. Implementing a data warehouse can be done via a number of approaches, depending on the data warehouse architecture chosen. A strategy may follow a particular architecture at the onset and flow into another as successes are realized. Understanding how components can be organized and their usage gives way to understanding how data warehouse architectures function and how they best fit the overall strategic vision of the organization.

The components of Figure 9-1 have been discussed previously in this book, but an architecture perspective may be beneficial at this point. A simple data warehouse system has certain fundamental components, which are viewed from a top-down data flow architecture. A bottom-up or hybrid approach may be used in designing the system, but the data flow is always from a top-down perspective.

Data Sources

Data sources may involve source systems directly or a structure interface file if the source systems are not fully known. For instance, purchased products have interface files simply because the developers cannot possibly know about all potential source systems their clients may be using. In other words, if you do not know what the customer may have, then tell them what you need.

As mentioned earlier, while data sources are not part of the data warehouse system, they do form the input aspect of a data warehouse system and are therefore mentioned here.

Of course, data sources may be *structured*, meaning that the fields are identifiable and consistent, or *unstructured*, meaning that individual fields may contain more than one data item. For instance, an unstructured address field may contain house number, street name, and city all in one field rather than in three unique fields.

Data Population

Otherwise known as the data acquisition layer, data population is the ETL portion which captures data from the data sources in one manner or another and prepares it for input into the data organization area. A staging repository may be used to hold the data while waiting for other source captures for merging, delta processing and so forth. ETL is covered in more depth in Chapter 10.

Data Organization

The data organization layer is essentially the data repository, also known as an enterprise data warehouse (EDW) repository according to the Inmon methodology. This is the centralized data layer, which involves holding lots of data for long periods of time, which is why a data warehouse repository can grow to tremendous sizes. The EDW is modeled in a normalized fashion to ensure that the business data is fully understood fundamentally, descriptively, and associatively. There is much design around this area depending on the master data management or data-as-a-fundamental-asset strategy within the organization. This involves logical and physical data models from subject to concept to entity relationship models, as described previously in this book.

Data Distribution

Data distribution is another ETL area within the data warehouse system. It involves pulling the data from the data organization area and distributing it to the various data marts environments. The data mart environments may be normalized (3NF) or denormalized (2NF, star, or snowflaked) as required by the "information out" requirements. There can be a big difference between the normalized data organization repository and the "information out" data marts, which may require a considerable mapping exercise between these two layers. The result being this data distribution layer.

Information Out

Getting the information out involves two layers: performance and user presentation layers. Since the information out area deals with the actual usage of the data from the business users' perspective, it must be designed for communicative purposes, which means it is easy to understand and use. And it must perform appropriately. In other words, when the user clicks the button to perform a database query to obtain a chart, graph, or output report of some sort, the system should respond within an appropriate amount of time and not take an hour before a result is returned. Therefore there is a design aspect called the performance layer, which is the underlying database structures, otherwise known as data marts. There is also a user presentation layer, which contains the reporting programs. Typically the programs are in the form of a BI tool such as Cognos, Business Objects, Microstrategy, and so forth. These tools require programming efforts to create the final report, which is what the business user sees and uses.

Implementation Approaches

A data warehouse solution can be based on pure analytical requirements, data as an enterprise asset, or both. When a solution is based on data completely derived from specific business reports, the data is viewed from only those report perspectives. As more reports or analytical requirements emerge, the focus widens and the underlying fundamental data with all descriptive and associative aspects tends to reveal itself in a wider sense. The issue then becomes how many analytical requirements are necessary until a proper view of the data is possible and how will this impact the data architecture of the data warehouse.

Consider a project to create an enterprise data warehouse based on a good number of regulatory reports with little help from a business subject matter expert (worst possible scenario!). Regulatory reports are usually based on aggregations of atomic data. The idea would be to analyze all the reports and determine common dimensions and measures to formulate a data model that could be reused as other requirements surface. If the underlying atomic data and its data structures are not accessible, there will be confusion about how the data should aggregate, and assumptions will have to be made.

In this scenario dimensions can be created, but there will be duplication, as it is unknown how the data truly associates at a fundamental level. For example, suppose there are two reports, one based on aggregations of financial assets within portfolios, and another on specific types of financial assets within funds that have reference to portfolios. For example, should all financial assets belong to one and only one fund and each fund to a specific portfolio? Or can some financial assets belong directly to a portfolio? The answer is not certain because the definitions of financial assets, funds, and portfolio are not properly understood, nor are the underlying business rules. It would be quite possible to create one dimension with individual financial assets along with the fund and portfolio hierarchy for one report and another dimension with financial assets and portfolio without the fund information. If there were many financial assets, this would be inefficient.

Without further details of these concepts and their business associations, perhaps three fundamental concepts would be appropriate: portfolio, funds, and financial assets all merging together at a fact table usage. If only a reporting application is required in the final solution, then this is fine. But if the data is to be modeled as an enterprise asset reusable in other applications or in other facets within a data warehouse, then there must be an understanding of the atomic data associations in order to properly model the enterprise data in a fully flexible manner. If the data is to represent all possible aspects within the organization, including applications other than business intelligence analytical applications, then a normalized view of the fundamental data components and how they inter-relate must be realized. Based on this premise, modeling the data within an organization must be seen as more than just at the analytical level, and therefore the transactional and analytical aspects of the data should be separated, and this then greatly influences the basic data architecture.

As the scope within the enterprise expands, the data model and the data architecture designs should facilitate additions without having to completely redesign what has been previously created. And since an enterprise data warehouse system is bound to grow, its creation must be scalable as volume and requirements themselves extend.

In short, the basic architecture of an enterprise data warehouse should have the following fundamental characteristics:

▶ **Distinct layers**   Allowing analytical usage and fundamental business data differentiation

▶ **Flexible design**   Allowing the fundamental base designs to remain constant as the scope expands over time

▶ **Scalable**   Allowing what has been built to be extended rather than being completely rebuilt for each extension phase

▶ **Usable**   Must be communicable to those using it while being simple enough in design to understand and administer

Data Design and Data Flow

With these fundamental data architecture characteristics in mind, the data warehouse architecture should be approached from both a data design perspective and a data flow perspective. In a BI and combined enterprise perspective, the purpose is to grant an analytical environment as well as to ensure that the enterprise data asset is maintained and usable now and positioned in a manner allowing for future unforeseen scenarios.

Given these baselines, the data should be modeled at the corporate level in a normalized manner, allowing for all possible data associations. A good representation of such a modeling technique is the supertype/subtype design, as discussed in Chapter 8. The business usage of the data can be in a distinct denormalized environment to facilitate reporting and analytics in a fashion communicable and usable to the business user. The data flow from an architecture blueprint perspective can be as represented in Figure 9-10.

Figure 9-10 shows how the different types of data models fit together along a simple data warehouse architecture flow. The designs in this example show a central normalized repository approach.

Logical vs. Physical Models

Since data architecture forms a large aspect of the data warehouse, the following discussion has been included.

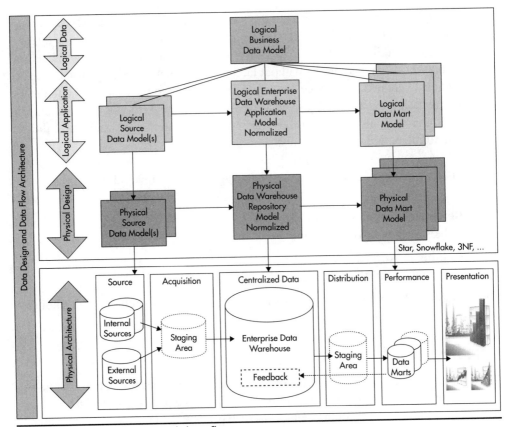

Figure 9-10   *Data design and data flow*

Figure 9-10 shows a distinction between logical and physical data models. The top logical business data model is a representation of the data components and how they inter-relate without any particular application focus. This data model is highly normalized. The second level is an abstraction from the logical business data model for specific applications: source applications, EDW, and data marts. The design of each of these is completely different, yet they can represent the same data items, but in a manner conducive to their usage within that particular application. The third level is the translation from logical to physical design.

In the case of the source system applications, the difference between the logical and physical may be negligible since typically the source systems are reverse-engineered from the physical database to map into the enterprise logical business data model. Only the names usually differ; for example, Person in the logical business data model and Individual in the physical source data model version. The reason for the difference is that the enterprise settled on the term Person while the source system may have been purchased or acquired and is using the term Individual, which is beyond the control of your organization. The important point from a data governance perspective is that the application terms have a home in and map to the governing business data model.

The logical Enterprise Data Model (EDM) can be quite normalized, which is great for identifying the data components and how they relate, but implementing such a design may be quite difficult to navigate with SQL. In this case the physical version can take certain liberties in denormalizing the abstractness. In essence, the idea is to optimize the physical design for usage. This is not to say that Address, for example, would denormalize into Person, but a new table could be created for "current person address." The effect would be a simple table and simple SQL to obtain the current address for a person, but it would add to the ETL loading routines, which would have to determine the current address per person and most probably reload the table on each run. Since end users typically access their respective data marts rather than the EDW, the point in doing this in the EDW would be to reduce the data distribution ETL routine at run time. Many would say this optimization of the EDW should actually be done at the logical EDM level rather than at the physical level, which is absolutely fine. In this case the physical version would be identical to the logical version other than index creation, data partitioning, and so forth.

Specific ETL columns could be added to the physical level or designed into the logical level, both of which are fine. These additions include population dates and other control elements. Not shown in Figure 9-10 is the staging design, which can also be derived from the logical business data model, as will be seen in Chapter 10.

In many products using this overall methodology, the data marts are extractions from the logical EDM, which means they are not optimized for usage. In these cases a new logical data model should be created. Typically data marts would be highly snowflaked if designed directly upon the logical EDM normalized data model rather than designed in a pure star, which is more desired by most BI tools. For instance, in a normalized data model, the Person entity is associated to the Address entity via an association as per Chapter 8, Figure 8-23. There is no denormalization consisting of the combination of Person and Address on the same entity, and therefore a new entity design would be required. In the new design, as in Chapter 7, Figure 7-29, the leftmost Person entity would then map to both Person and Address in the logical EDM and logical business data model. Again, this should be part of the logical design, but if for some reason this is not possible, the physical data mart model can be used to hold these new designs justified by an optimization for usage effort, which converts snowflake to star designs. In this case the data modeler would have to lead the physical data model development, leaving the DBMS physical additions (indexes, partitions if any) to the DBA.

Top-Down Approach

Otherwise known as the *centralized* or *corporate approach*, the top-down architecture and implementation methodology was popularized by Bill Inmon and has a large following. The idea is to build a central area where the data can be held over time with all its changes in its most granular form. The focus in this top-down data flow, as shown in Chapter 1, Figure 1-10, is on managing the corporate data. The trick is to structure the data in a format that will allow it to be flexible and grow as more projects add new data items to the data warehouse.

The overall concept is quite simple; data is acquired from source systems, transformed into the desired formats, and merged into the data warehouse repository. Once the data is in the data warehouse repository, any business user can have access to it by way of a data mart. Data marts in this approach are simply subsets of the overall data warehouse repository but may not necessarily be in the same structures. Because data marts are designed for business usage, they are optimized specifically for a particular usage, which may differ from the design of the repository.

The data flow in this architecture, as seen in Figure 9-11, is to capture from source systems or operational data stores, reconcile the data as needed by using the ETL routines in a staging environment, and populate a central data repository that is designed in a normalized fashion. Specific data is extracted and distributed to specific data marts for specific business usage. The data marts can be designed in a normalized or denormalized fashion, whichever is most effective for the business usage.

The difficulty with this approach is in ensuring a repository design that is flexible and scalable as each project adds to the previous design efforts. The worst case scenario is having to redesign the repository to satisfy previous requirements and a new requirement, as this activity would affect all previous designs, ETL routines, distribution routines and so forth, as seen in Chapter 2, Figure 2-14. Best practice for this method is to purchase a pre-existing data warehouse logical business data model and EDW application data model specifically developed for your line of business: retail, banking, insurance, healthcare, telecommunications, and so on.

Bottom-Up Approach

Otherwise known as the "data mart–oriented" approach, the bottom-up implementation approach is focused on business analytics or oriented toward end results. In the past departments would create their own data marts to satisfy their own reporting requirements. As more departments created their own data marts, the nightly or periodic feeds from source systems became repetitive and therefore inefficient. Eventually, a project would try to centralize the designs and have in essence one central loading effort. Obvious problems were the mismatches between table names, their descriptive

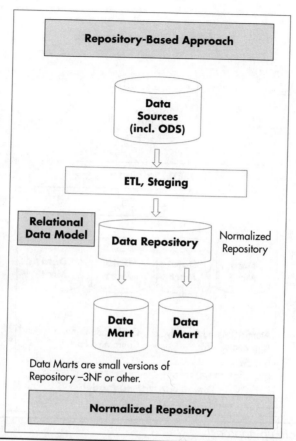

Figure 9-11   *Top-down approach*

elements, their definitions, and how the tables were created. In simple terms, there was no governance and therefore no ownership or commonality.

Ralph Kimball took this method and added a governance aspect, which was to preserve the definition and structures of specific tables across the enterprise. This meant conformed vocabulary, structure, name, and therefore data all reusable by the many departments throughout the organization. This also meant simplicity as everyone would now be using the same dimensions for their analytical efforts.

Essentially, conformed dimensions are the fundamental concepts of the business designed with specific denormalized guidelines. This makes the business usage of the data quite simple as the dimensions are in business terms, making them quite communicative and simple to use.

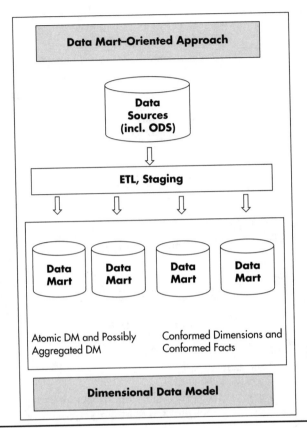

Figure 9-12 *Bottom-up approach*

Figure 9-12 shows a data mart–oriented approach, which has data sources and data marts with a staging intermediate level used to prepare the data for distribution to the data marts.

A negative aspect of this approach is that data is typically based on reporting requirements. If only the reports are used to determine the data fundamentals, an overall associative aspect will be lacking. Reports are a view of the data, possibly based on some aggregation, and may not present a complete picture of how the data inter-relates, which is fundamental to a master data management perspective of the enterprise data asset. A simple solution is to identify the analytical or reporting data requirements and have a business subject matter expert determine their associations. This will give insights allowing for a more stable data model and architecture design. However, the overall data architecture is still only leaning toward an analytical usage.

Hybrid Approach

A hybrid methodology that is a mixture of both the top-town and bottom-up approaches, as shown in Figure 9-13, is the best of both worlds. It involves a bottom-up perspective as a target with the governance of a top-down data-as-an-asset perspective.

This architecture is best guided by a prebuilt business data model to set an enterprise data structure and associative foundation. The idea is to scope and extend a pre-existing data model to understand how all the data fits together, and to design a business solution in a manner optimized for specific usage. This means conformed dimensions for the data marts for analytical purposes as well as normalized data marts if needed; basically, whatever best suits the business usage scenario. All data structures, conformed dimensions or not, would map to a data warehouse repository design, and all would be governed by an enterprise business data model. A staging environment would also be used in this architecture as a holding area to reconcile the captured source data.

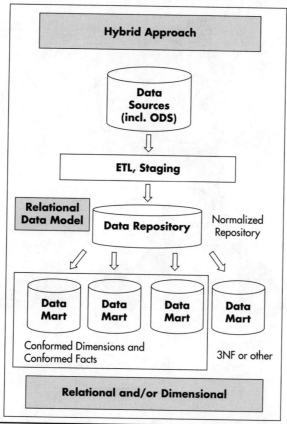

Figure 9-13   *Hybrid approach*

As a side note: the initial implementation of this architecture, depending on time to market, might be to not realize the repository and simply govern the data marts with the corporate repository data model and the business data model for a quick tangible solution. Later efforts would physicalize and populate the corporate repository for the first phase and subsequent efforts.

Accelerators

Given the many possible areas of failure in developing a data warehouse, insights from Chapter 3, along with insights into the implications of rebuilding or reverse-engineering, and views on how to approach the building of a data warehouse, it should be determined whether certain components are to be built in-house or purchased. The idea behind purchasing components would be to accelerate the time to develop a data warehouse system and to reduce the risk of failure. Beware, however, of purchasing the wrong data model as there can be pitfalls.

Looking at each layer within the central repository data warehouse architecture, an evaluation should be done as to whether or not a component should be purchased. A deciding factor is whether your resources are experts in one tool or another. If you have ETL experts using a specific ETL tool, do not purchase another ETL tool just because the primary vendor sells it. The same idea applies to the business reporting tools, databases, and servers—unless there is a really good reason for doing so. When it comes to designs, this is a different story. A data model is definitely something to consider purchasing. Ensure that the model covers your business areas, has support, and is open and flexible. All data models expect some sort of extensions by the customer, so the question is how scalable, open, and flexible is the data model? Typically, individuals only see two to four different data warehouse systems in their career, and as such are not aware of the many data modeling techniques and abilities. Hence introducing a new data model can be quite a difficult task even for the most senior data modeler. Ensure that the vendor leads the modeling efforts at first to ensure direction and knowledge transfer.

Data Acquisition Layer

The data acquisition layer, also known as the data population layer, usually is a mixture of a purchased tool such as DataStage and in-house written programs such as Unix scripts or Cobol programs. This layer can also include messaging tools such as MQ Series, now part of the IBM WebSphere family, known as WebSphere MQ. Much depends on the knowledge and abilities of the current staff. If your resources are expert DataStage programmers, it's probably a good idea to use this tool going forward.

Centralized Data Layer

The data organization or centralized data layer consists of the central data warehouse repository, which holds all the enterprise data. In the Inmon methodology, this layer consists of an enterprise data model that organizes all the data components. A staging area is used in the transformation of the captured source data for such purposes as determining deltas, sorting the data, merging disparate data, and so on. The staging area for both Inmon and Kimball methodology is for holding the data while it is in transition; for Inmon to the central data warehouse repository and for Kimball to the conformed dimensions and fact tables.

From a Kimball approach, creating a dimension/measure cross-reference matrix will give insight into building data marts. If a model is prebuilt specifically for your organization's line of business, this would be an excellent starting point from a business perspective.

From an Inmon approach, creating what is called a *corporate information factory* means breaking the business into chunks and further into concepts before arriving at a normalized data model. This is quite difficult, and I personally believe in purchasing a model if one exists for the line of business rather than starting at the high data subject areas and working down to a normalized data model.

In both cases, having a prebuilt model that was developed specifically for a data warehouse application is an excellent approach. The negative point for this direction is that this sort of model is typically rather large and takes time to understand enough to use properly. The positive side is that it exists. With a prebuilt enterprise data model, the top-down approach using the pillar diagram can be used along with a bottom-up dimension/measure cross-reference matrix. Using both greatly facilitates the development of an enterprise data warehouse solution.

Because a purchased model exists, it means that the data vocabulary exists and will be consistent and defined throughout the organization. Do not underestimate this point—having a predesigned data model with a complete vocabulary is truly one of the key points in development of an enterprise data warehouse and business intelligence solution. But again, prebuilt models are large and can consist of thousands and thousands of data objects constructed based on specific methodologies. Be sure the vendor has a services department that supplies courses on how to use the model. Hiring their consulting services is also a good idea to help not only with initial education but also with planning direction and to lead design development efforts.

Data Distribution Layer

The data distribution layer parallels the data population layer, with one exception. This layer coupled with the data mart performance layer can be virtualized. This means that views can be placed on the data warehouse repository to look as if the data mart is its own independent area. Be warned that if virtual data marts exist, meaning there is no data distribution layer, there may be contention between loading the data warehouse repository and usage of the virtual data mart. Plus there may be performance issues, as the underlying repository tables may not be optimized for the business usage.

Again, an accelerator for this layer is to purchase an ETL tool.

Performance Layer

The performance layer is a fancy way of describing the data mart areas. The reason it is called this is that the data marts are optimized areas for end-user usage. Hence the data marts are optimized for performance. Data marts can be built directly from the cross-reference matrix insights. Or the design can be purchased along with or independent of a data warehouse repository data model. If the design is purchased, the data marts should map to the data warehouse repository since data marts are subsets of a central data warehouse repository; therefore, the mapping must exist between the two. Data marts are rarely a direct one-to-one subset of the data warehouse repository, as the repository is optimized for capturing and holding data while the data marts are optimized for data extraction—two completely different uses and therefore two completely different representations. Also be aware that the central historical data warehouse repository can be a "logical design only" environment with the physicalization being the conformed dimensions and fact tables.

User Presentation Layer

The user presentation layer is the part the business users will see and use. This is where the business users will click buttons. This area is typically left to the Cognos, Crystal Reports, Microstrategy, and Business Objects type of tools. This is definitely an area where you could purchase a proven tool. Performance optimizations can be placed at this layer, the performance layer, the distribution layer, the repository layer, or the acquisition layer. Everything depends on the development strategy.

Another accelerator is to purchase prebuilt BI reports with underlying data mart designs. If the reports match your business requirements, then this direction is best and simply requires mapping to the underlying data repository and enterprise business data model.

Methodology

A methodology on how to develop a data warehouse and business intelligence solution is not something normally thought about, but it should be. Typically services are hired to lead the development efforts, which should parallel a specific methodology. The methodology can usually be represented by a template project plan, which of course must be tailored to the customers' environment and project. Understanding the many facets of a data warehouse system is a prerequisite to fully appreciate a vendor's methodology and how it applies to your environment.

Typically all methodologies consist of the following:

▶ Preliminary analysis: High-level perspective

▶ Business requirements phase: High-level business requirements

▶ Solution or architecture strategy: High-level solution outline

▶ Technical architecture: Technical solution

▶ Detailed solution: Solution with project plan including gap analysis

▶ Migration planning, if any

▶ Implementation planning

▶ Change management planning

Out-of-the-Box Solution

There is no complete out-of-the-box solution for a data warehouse system. No vendor knows exactly what your specific business requires to operate from a reporting or analytical perspectives, and no one can presume to know your source systems and all the data quality issues surrounding it. Therefore no out-of-the-box solution is possible. Whatever is purchased must be tailored in one fashion or another to properly fit your environment.

ETL and Data Quality

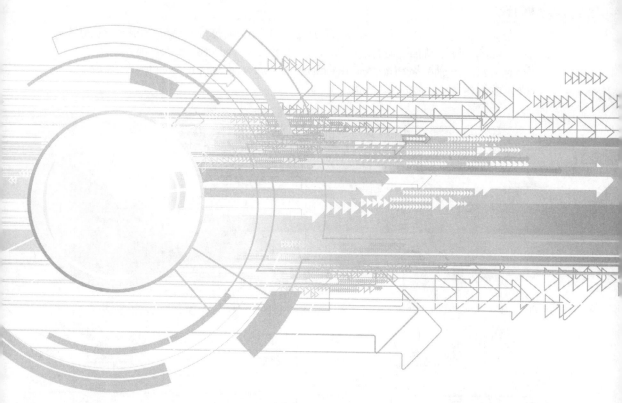

A data warehouse is a system with input, processing, and output. This chapter looks at the input aspect of the system, which is called extract, transform, and load (ETL), for a lack of better terminology within the industry. The first ETL process in a data warehouse is from source to a preparation and holding area, which is called *data population*, as shown in Figure 10-1. The second ETL portion in a data warehouse is from the holding area to the data marts, which is called *data distribution*, as shown in Figure 10-1. The holding area in this context can be the central repository or a staging environment depending on the architecture.

NOTE

It is possible for ETL from the data population to bypass the holding area and directly populate data marts, depending on the overall design and contributing factors.

The high-level ETL flow is one of the major determining factors of the overall data warehouse architecture. As with any architecture, the best method of communicating the ETL flow is via a number of simple diagrams.

NOTE

This chapter is not an ETL tool evaluation effort but a general discussion about ETL with practical insights. There is a wide range of ETL-related tools that perform all, parts of, or isolated actions that are described in this chapter. Practical insights shared here will be of higher use to the reader once a specific tool is selected and in determining how to strategize on its usage.

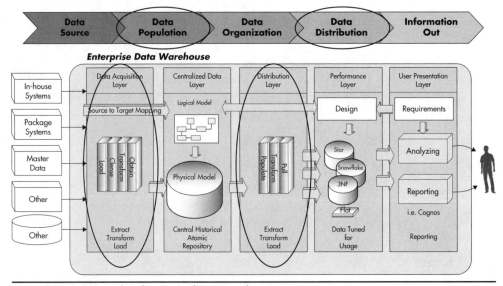

Figure 10-1   *ETL in the data warehouse architecture*

Since data is an asset to the organization, it is management's due diligence to ensure that the corporate asset is properly maintained. This means that the data has value to the organization and in many cases is fundamental to the operations of the organization. With poorly maintained or incorrect data, business decisions based on this information, which is data in context, will most likely be incorrect and misguide management, causing the organization to drift from its strategic course. Therefore it is vital that data is properly managed with a high degree of transparency, quality, and availability.

To facilitate this effort, organizations are creating data warehouse systems to support their business intelligence analysis. A fundamental aspect of a data warehouse strategy is to centralize corporate data, which initially is via logical data model designs. Typically the physicalization of a data warehouse is centralized as well but can be federated throughout the organization. In this case, the physical and logical designs must be managed centrally to ensure conformity to vocabulary and fundamental design structures throughout the organization.

It is this physicalization stage where ETL enters the picture. In the design stage, ETL represents data flow from source to target with some sort of transformation happening somewhere within. ETL then evolves to data mapping between source and target and later into actual program specifications to guide the ETL programmers in building the solution. The key to creating an ETL subsystem is in understanding the involved sources and targets and in how they inter-relate, as well as understanding the timing as to when data is available for processing.

The ETL portion of a data warehouse project is typically the most challenging part of the project and, as an old rule of thumb, takes approximately 70 percent of the overall effort. Over the past several years, however, a good portion has been absorbed by the data architecture role, primarily in the identification of and mapping between source and targets.

Architecture

In general terms, ETL is the extraction of data from the input source, transforming it into an appropriate format for loading and loading it into the target database—a fairly simple concept that can have enormous complications. Let us examine each of these phases from an architectural perspective and later in detail.

The term "transformation" involves many subprocesses and steps depending on the requirements of the transformation. These can include any of the following: cleansing, merging, sorting, defining unique identifiers, ensuring population timestamps, ensuring validity period date stamps, delta processing, creating data, validating data, ensuring referential integrity, aggregating, summarizing, and profiling data. Any number of these steps can be done within the ETL subsystem depending on the architecture and the requirements of the solution.

Transformations can be performed on data in flat files, in a DBMS, or partly in both. Much depends on the tools being used, the volume of data, the amount of time required for processing, the processing window (nightly batch window), and the dependencies of the data.

Data Population

Even though Figure 10-2 shows only one layer under the data population phase, it can really be split into two perspectives:

▶   The data acquisition aspect of source to staging

▶   The data population aspect involving the staging to the central data layer

From a high-level introduction, the data population involves much processing with an emphasis on understanding the required data, the technical landscape, the differences between the source, which is typically operational online transactional processing system (OLTP), and the data warehouse, which is an online analytical processing system (OLAP). OLTP is basically a static design that continues until a process changes. OLAP is much more dynamic, especially in

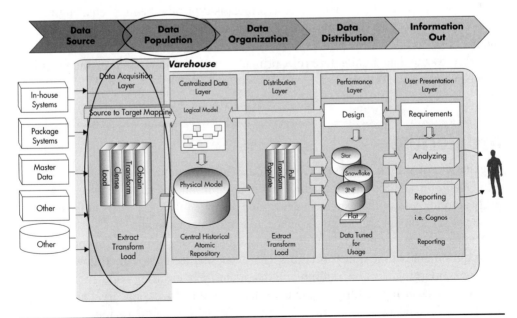

Figure 10-2   *ETL data population layer*

the ETL areas, as additional end-user analytical requirements may dictate additional feeds from source systems, source system changes themselves, optimization of processes' requirements, and feed volume increases on a regular basis. Hence an ETL architect's role is to ensure a flexible, scalable, and most importantly a documented environment in a controlled manner.

In simple terms, the data population environment is the input to the data warehouse and typically involves massive transformation from a number of source systems. The staging area within the data population environment can itself hold data for extended periods to facilitate proper preparation for loading into the central data repository.

Data Distribution

The data distribution layer, shown in Figure 10-3, is another ETL environment with focus on extracting from the holding area, whether staging or a central repository, converting to specific data mart formats, and loading one or many data marts with the data. In many instances the data mart designs are star schemas, while the central repository is in third normal form, meaning that the transformation has much to do with key generation, converting from history at the column level to history at the row level.

In theory data marts can be completely dropped and reconstructed from the data warehouse repository, but this rarely happens for larger data marts, as it would be too costly. Typically data is inserted into the data marts, and older rows, if no longer

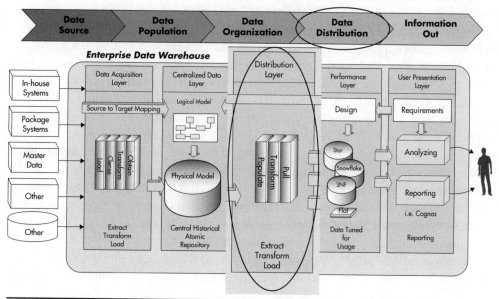

Figure 10-3 *ETL distribution layer*

required, would be deleted as necessary, based on the service agreement of the individual data marts with the business users.

Once data marts are delivered to the business user, they are used for a period until the business becomes comfortable with the details and, in many instances, are then enhanced with more details to satisfy more in-depth analysis. As the business user becomes more familiar with the data, more granularities are requested and more aggregations upon it are required as the users look at different ways to analyze the business. This means that the data distribution layer becomes quite dynamic, with changes happening much more often than in OLTP systems.

The ETL architect must be keenly aware of the business data requirements and must ensure a scalable environment from many perspectives including: data volumes, DBMS capabilities, ETL routine flexibilities, run-time durations, and tooling. The ETL architecture must be able to adapt to the changing data and technological requirements without requiring a complete redesign of the environment.

ETL Mapping

A critical tool used in data modeling for the ETL process specifications is the mapping document. Figure 10-4 shows a basic data mapping document. The idea is that the document should represent the data flow from source system (leftmost) all the way through to the final data mart and BI tool usage (rightmost), if different from the data mart.

Typical details include source system name, since there can be multiple source systems, and the source system fields, or table and column names, along with data types and universe of values (none of which are shown in Figure 10-4). Following are the repository environment, then the data mart, and BI tool environment. A descriptive mapping area is shown between each environment where rules and comments can be placed. As the mapping document progresses, the mapping area line item may also contain SQL specification or actual SQL statements if the source is known. This document then becomes the primary data lineage documentation between source to the repository and repository to the data marts. If bypassing the repository, it may also represent source to staging to data marts, again all depending on the chosen architecture.

The author recommends creating this document in a source-to-target format to parallel the data flow, as presented in Figure 10-4, as it becomes much more intuitive with the left-to-right mapping flow and allows any portion to be mapped without the other at any instance. Later additions can be incorporated as need be.

In many instances, however, a preliminary mapping is required if you are looking at the effort from a target perspective. In this case a high-level target-to-source mapping document can be used, but only for a high-level understanding of where

Initial Source	ATOMIC Repository								DATA MART								BI Tool			
Mapping	Mapping	Entity Name	Attribute Name	Data Type	Nulls	Value	Description		Mapping	Entity Name	Attribute Name	Data Type	Nulls	Value	Description		Mapping	Entity Name	Attribute Name	Description
Define as need be.																				

Figure 10-4   *Source-to-target mapping document*

DATA MART			Mapping	ATOMIC Repository		
Entity Name	Attribute Name	Description		Entity Name	Attribute Name	Description

Figure 10-5   *Target-to-source mapping document for data marts to repository*

ATOMIC Repository			Mapping	Source System					
Table or Entity Name	Column or Attribute Name	Description		Source System Name	File Name	Table Name	Column Name	Description	

Figure 10-6   *Target-to-source mapping document for repository to source*

Target			Mapping	Source System					
Table Name	Column Name	Description		Source System Name	File Name	Table Name	Column Name	Description	

Figure 10-7   *Generic target-to-source mapping document*

data is sourced. Figures 10-5, 10-6, and 10-7 show simple target-to-source data mapping documents: for data marts to repository, repository to source, and a generic target-to-source mapping respectively.

Initial and Incremental Loads

The first data warehouse project will require a special loading effort, which is called an *initial load*. The initial load process takes into account items that would normally pre-exist in the data warehouse system and therefore would not normally be considered in ongoing ETL designs. These are areas such as initial code tables and date and time data.

Special loading steps can be considered as well since the database is empty. Initial load strategy would include bulk loading; index creation after loading; referential integrity, if any, enforced after initial load; and all treated as Type I (no history). All "effective from dates" can be set to a specific date period and all "effective to dates" can be set to high values.

Once the data warehouse has the initial load completed, incremental loads take over. The difference is that data already exists in the data warehouse for the designed tables.

In this case delta processing must occur. *Delta processing* consists of routines to determine whether an input row is new or has changed since the previous load. If nothing has changed from the previous load, then its occurrence from the load file is removed. If something has changed, a process is run to determine the impact of the changed column. If the source system has a change timestamp indicator signifying that something has changed, then the delta processing within the ETL Data Acquisition phase must determine what exactly has changed.

Once the database is up and functioning, older rows must be removed as per the data warehouse strategy of each table. Some tables require no rows to ever be deleted, while other tables are only required to hold, for example, 36 months' worth of data and therefore on the 37th month, the oldest rows must be removed or archived.

ETL vs. ELT vs. ETTL

Usually the data acquisition layer is called the ETL area. This implies that data is extracted from the source system, transformed in some manner, and loaded into the central data layer or staging area. Use ETL as a general term, as there are a number of possible architectures, as seen in Figures 10-8 and 10-9, which the industry still refers to as ETL.

Figure 10-8 shows the difference between ETL and extract, load, and transform (ELT). In ETL the data is transformed at the operating system level, meaning in flat files of some sort, and then loaded into the database. ELT refers to loading the data into the database first, and then performing the transformation steps. Both of these show the extract step as part of the data warehouse system, which implies that the data is pulled from the source systems. Figure 10-9 depicts the extract step in the source system, which explicitly represents a pushing of the source data files to the data warehouse. The process shown in Figure 10-9 would be better described as ETTL, or extract, transfer, transform, and load.

It is best practice to have the source system push the required data to the data warehouse environment. This gives the source system, which may be a core operational system, the ability to plan, schedule, and manage the required data extractions. If a backup is running late, a special long-running batch job is taking longer than expected, or database administration is scheduled, the data extraction can be managed appropriately. Having the data warehouse pull from a source system means that the data warehouse system must access the source system directly as per the data warehouse schedule, irrespective of the source system events or status. If problems occur, the ongoing operations of the source system may be affected, which in turn affects the core business. This can create an overall negative impression of the data warehouse, which could influence the livelihood of the data warehouse project and efforts.

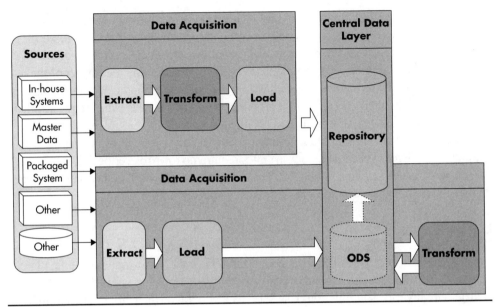

Figure 10-8 *ETL vs. ELT*

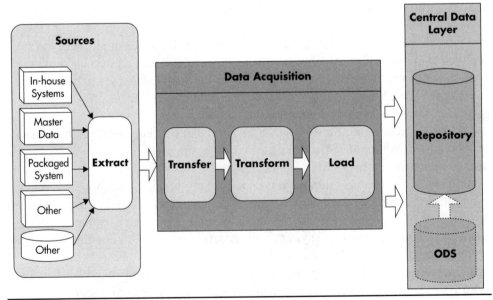

Figure 10-9 *ETTL (push method)*

In general, it's best to tell the source system what is required, when it is required, and have it generate the data sets, preferably into a predetermined file system in a structured and orderly manner.

Even though ETTL is the proper term representing how data is pushed from operational source systems, the industry still uses the term "ETL" in a generic sense.

Parallel Operations

As a quick note, this section is intended to state that ETL processing should be managed in a parallel fashion. Too many implementations create streams with pure waterfall dependencies, which are not necessary. "Have Y always run after X" means that the system will take X + Y duration. In many instances X and Y can run in parallel, so be sure to audit your ETL data flow streams ensuring that nondependent flows are run in parallel.

In one particular instance, a very large telephone company had difficulty in loading all the daily telephone calls into the database each night. It took 12 hours just to load all the call detail records (CDRs), which seemed rather long. After an audit of all processes and timings, it became apparent that many steps were unnecessarily waiting on a previous step. After replanning the data flow and mapping the source availabilities to data warehouse processing, we were able to reduce the load time by two-thirds, which is quite significant and translated to considerable cost savings.

ETL Roles

ETL is driven by an ETL architect guided by the data architecture. The ETL architect owns the ETL from physical design, extraction, operations, and technical environment, and has forward-thinking planning abilities to ensure that the daily operations continue in a well-oiled manner. The ETL architect has a team of ETL programmers who are responsible for creating the actual ETL routines to manage the captured data and load the central repository or staging environment as needed and depending on architecture. The roles also cover the data distribution layer, which delivers data marts for business consumption.

While the database modeling role is within the data architecture group, the physical database administration may fall under the ETL architect umbrella. The data architect creates source-to-target mapping documents, and the ETL architect uses these to develop the ETL routines to capture and load the data repository.

NOTE

In the early stages of a data warehouse project, while the data architects are determining what data is required and where it can be found, the ETL architect can help efforts by performing data profiling on the identified source systems. Data profiling greatly helps the data architect in identifying the universe of data values, which is important in order to ensure that designs and actual data are indeed in sync.

ETL Architect

The ETL architect oversees all aspects of the ETL environments and understands all technical aspects of the data warehouse data during the development phase. The ETL architect interacts with the source system technical owners, DBAs, and infrastructure architects to create an effective ETL solution for the data warehouse system. This is not a junior role and should be quite familiar with data warehouse and business intelligence systems.

The ETL architect works hand in hand with the overall data warehouse architect, who is ultimately responsible for ensuring that the data warehouse system is feasible and becomes tangible. If the project manager is responsible for ensuring a path to where a vehicle should be present on a specific day in a specific spot, the DW architect is responsible for ensuring that the vehicle exists and will be there, while the ETL architect is responsible for ensuring that the vehicle is operational and runs as expected.

All ETL technical documents for the data warehouse are initially created and maintained by the ETL architect. This role owns the data warehouse, non-BI aspects, from an operational perspective and creates documents describing the many real data aspects, run-time routines, operational dependencies, and schedules. The person in this role is responsible for attending and being aware of any change control issues in the operational source systems as well as any from the data warehouse environment.

The ETL architect will develop, with the data warehouse architect, a notification system and flow diagrams showing overall interdependencies.

Once the data warehouse system is put into production, operations takes over as the ETL architect's role converts to an ETL lead support role.

ETL Programmer

The ETL programmer reports to the ETL architect, who may also act as an ETL programmer. The programmer's role is to write the ETL program routines and ensure a seamless operational flow.

ETL programmers are focused on capturing the data from the source system, transforming it in whatever manner is necessary to load it into the database. This function in many organizations is outsourced. The technical architect, data architect, data modeler, and DBA are usually involved with the ETL programmers to ensure that they understand the requirements and that the programs deliver the required data components into the designed database. This role is also involved in delivering data from the data warehouse repository to the data marts.

In the data modeling phase of the data warehouse, ETL programmers are tasked with performing data profiling of the source systems. Data profiling is quite important to the data modeler, who must know if each table column holds the expected data or not. For instance, a product color in a source system may contain blue, red, and large black. The "large black" color is a data quality issue as it includes size with color. This data quality issue might not have been known if data profiling were not performed.

In many instances, the source system analyst is also the ETL lead and may be involved with the physical database design with the DBA, as the DBA's role is very aware of volumetrics.

Data Flow Diagrams

Overall a data warehouse system should have the following six operational data flow diagrams. These diagrams stem from the ETL operational area and are typically the responsibility of the ETL architect. It is recommended to create the diagrams first and follow up with written documents explaining the diagrams at a later time. This will allow the diagram to immediately communicate and define the data flow to management and developers.

While several of these diagrams can be superimposed, it is recommended to initially create them individually to enforce a focus on the specific area.

▶ **ETL data flow** Overall data flow processes

  ▶ All assumptions should be point form documented on this diagram. Each process is written to basic assumptions; for example, monthly CDRs will only have newly inserted rows and/or deleted rows, and no updated CDRs.

▶ **Business flow** Purpose of the processes in question from a pure business view.

▶ **DBA data flow** Disk space usage, partitioning details, and so forth from the view of the databases and underlying servers (also ensures DBA review).

▶ **Schedule flow** Diagram details showing execution timings and durations.

▶ **People flow** Details pertaining to process owners.

▶ **Dependencies** Details pertaining to execution dependencies, table dependencies, timing dependencies, and so forth, which includes whatever is lacking from the other diagrams.

Operational Data Store (ODS)

An *operational data sto*re (ODS) is a near-real-time operational system consisting of its own repository. Both Figures 10-8 and 10-9 include the ODS in the central data layer as part of the data warehouse system. In actuality, it is its own system as it stands alone outside the boundaries of a data warehouse. However, the ODS is highly aligned with a data warehouse in that the data acquisition layer would feed the ODS rather than the data warehouse, of course only for the data in the ODS. The data acquisition layer would perform all the cleansing and transformation as it would for the data warehouse but would feed the ODS from the source systems and be used itself as the feed to the data repository directly. Since the data has gone through the cleansing and transformation routines, the effort in loading the data warehouse repository from the ODS is minimal other than Type II (full history) processing.

The ODS typically only holds near-real-time data. This means no history, although there can be some history in the form of summary or profile tables. ODS came about for CRM applications for corporate help desks where customers would call up for support and support staff could access a central customer information database, which would contain up-to-date customer information with some status type information such as order status, recent transaction summaries, and so forth.

ODS is mentioned in this ETL chapter, as it becomes tightly coupled with the data warehouse ETL processes.

Source Systems

A data warehouse system is fed by source systems. This is where 99 percent of all reporting data originates. The whole point of a data warehouse system is to obtain data from the source systems and hold it over extended periods of time. Identifying these source systems along with its owner or subject matter expert is an absolute must for any data warehouse. Once the required data is identified for use in the data warehouse, the source system must also be identified. The target-to-source mapping documents, shown in Figures 10-6 and 10-7, are used to map between the two to get a feel for source data and its location. From this effort, any missing data can be identified in a Gap Analysis report. Once data modeling is underway, a detailed source-to-target mapping follows, as shown in Figure 10-4.

No Source

In some instances the data is not available in any source system and must be created within the boundaries of the data warehouse system. Examples are the Date and Time dimensions and many ISO-based tables, such as country or currency names.

The repository can be populated with a date table, which can in turn populate the date dimension, and the same idea applies to the time table and dimension. The repository can hold a denormalized version of the date table, which is fundamentally based on a calendar day. The table can be normalized to Calendar Year, Calendar Quarter, Calendar Month, Calendar Week, and Calendar Day tables (same for Fiscal dates), or it can be denormalized into one central table holding different granularities based on the "type" differentiator, as discussed in Chapter 8. Dimension tables can follow both of these rules depending on your familiarity with using the date dimension.

Typically the normalized repository holds a transactional event, which in turn has the date and time at an occurrence level. Once the data is in a data mart, the date dimension is realized based on the granularity required. Therefore, date dimensions can include each of the year, quarter, month, week, day granularities, with the day granularity holding all the previous as well.

The time dimension is typically not included in the date dimension but created via ETL as a distinct table. At the minute level there are 1440 rows and at the seconds level there would be 86400 rows, which is still not that much. Typically, a fact table would be sparsely populated at both levels.

Multiple Sources

In many scenarios, data may originate from a number of source systems. This means each source system must use its own identifying key to uniquely identify the occurrence; this is accomplished by using the source system's own natural key for the specific data item. This means that when data from these sources is inputted to the data warehouse, an identifying and merging effort must be undertaken. A row identifying Bob from the marketing source system and a row identifying Bob from the finance source system may be referring to the same person; therefore, a process must execute to identify if they are indeed the same person. If it is determined that they are, a merging effort must ensue to load once and yet keep each source system's natural identifying key.

Alternate Sources (SIFs)

In many instances, source systems are unknown to the data warehouse and will not be identified at any point during the project. In these cases, if you cannot identify the sources, then create input files to identify what the data warehouse requires. These are classic software package strategies, which allow the freedom to design based on requirements without having to profile the data or investigate the source system. Basically, if no one can tell you what is in the source systems, then you tell them what you need!

These are called *input layouts* or *structure input files* (SIFs). Figure 10-10 shows a sample of what a SIF layout might look like. Basically it identifies all the fields required for input to the data warehouse by the business along with an "Action" field to identify whether the row is an addition, update, or expired, all of which will help with the delta processing that follows.

The only difficulty with SIF files that must be managed is how they inter-relate. How does the customer input file associate to the address input file? The answer is in a third input file called "customer address input file" whereby the rules of association are detailed.

Input File	Column Name	Type	Description	Example	Valid Values	Usage	Notes	Rules and Comments
Customer			**Input file used to identify Customer Data**					
	Action	Char(1)	Defines the action that for this record	A	A = Add U = Update E = Expire	Used to determine the action to take for this record.	For initial load, this flag = Add For incremental load, see rules	• If Add, this is new in source system (delta processing done !!) • If Update, something has changed for this row in source system (determine Delta) • If Expire, row is no longer in source system (delta processing done !!)
	Customer Id	Varchar(64)	A value that uniquely identifies a Customer	83750501-AA	text	Source system key	Required - Uppercase compare if not present - fail the record	• Always compare in uppercase. • Must be present as it is the only true source system identifier available
	First name	Varchar(40)	Customer first name	John	text	As defined in source	Optional if not present - ignore	
	Middle name	Varchar(40)	Customer middle name	Franklin	text	As defined in source	Optional if not present - ignore	
	Last name	Varchar(40)	Customer last name	Smith	text	As defined in source	Optional if not present - ignore	
	Marital Status	Char(1)	Customers marital status	M	S = Single M = Married D = Divorced W = Widow E = Separated U = Unknown	As defined in source	Optional if not present - ignore	• Any other values will cause a warning notification

Figure 10-10 *Input file layout*

Unstructured Data

In many organizations, legacy and/or manual systems have what is called *unstructured data*. This is data without proper decomposition and formatting. For example, a structured address has distinct fields for street number and name, city, state/province, and postal code. An unstructured address may have all these fields in one extended column. In such cases the business must decide whether structuring the data is a requirement or not. If the business sees no value in structuring this type of data, it is recommended not to spend efforts in doing so as there will be no value to the current business. Store this data in the repository in a column as a whole. If later projects or requirements wish to have this data structured, then a data modeling exercise can take place and a population effort can structure the existing data into this secondary structured address area.

The key question then becomes: Is the unstructured data actually required in an analytical environment? Typically, the answer is "no."

Data Profiling

As mentioned earlier, data profiling is the task of getting to know the details of individual data items. This step is a must for every data warehouse system. Once a data source is identified, be it a database, flat file, or Excel-based, the ETL architect will execute routines and queries to determine all possible information about the data, which includes the most common aspects, which are data type (integer, text...), data format (char(40), number (14,2)...), and universe of values.

The latter is essentially performing a distinct on the data item to determine the full list of all possible values. From this list, along with the master documented list of what the item is suppose to hold (if it exists), a data quality review is performed.

In many ETL architectures, it is the list of all possible values of each data component that is highly managed in the ETL processes. If a source system row appears with a column having a value not on the master valid value list for that column for that table, then a decision must be made as to how it will be handled. Will the entire row be rejected from input to the data warehouse? Will the column be set to a default value or accepted with a notification message logged with a high priority? Did something change in the source system that was not communicated to the data warehouse ETL architect or data architect? Such events require immediate action to assess whether the warning is major or minor and what action to take either way.

Source system data profiling documentation can be done using the source-to-target mapping or in a single source system document. Each source system should have at minimum a source system data profile document explaining the tables and columns along with source system data owner with contact information.

Data Capture

The data capture is the data acquisition layer within the data population phase of a data warehouse system. This layer deals with obtaining the data from the source systems. Data can be pulled from the source system, which means that the data warehouse ETL team creates routines that access the source system and extracts whatever data is required. This strategy is risky as it intrudes on the source system and could interfere with the source system operations in one manner or another. Best practice is to create the extraction routines and have the source system operations execute the routines as they see fit within the agreed-to time period. This means minimal intrusion into the source systems by a third party.

These days there are a number of vendor tools in the marketplace that have many built-in features allowing for the control and management of source system extracts and receiving input files from source systems. The features include restart or retransmit capabilities, multiple same-source file transmissions, and so forth. Essentially they all deal with the same issues such as multiple large files, switch files, and failsafe strategy, as discussed in the following sections.

Multiple Large Files

In many cases for large organizations the feeds can be quite large files. In these cases it may be best to have the source system produce multiple files during the course of the day. These can be sent to the data warehouse file systems and processed in the data warehouse staging environment. If a large file is sent every 4 hours rather than one huge file every 24 hours, then the ETL routines can run six times per day, splitting the effort over the 24-hour period.

Switch Files

To stop programs or jobs from executing out of order, or from executing immediately upon the arrival of an input data file, or immediately after another program, which is time dependent, a switch file strategy could be used.

Simply put, a daemon job is run, which basically checks for the presence of a particular file, based on that file's name. When the file is present, the daemon job invokes the real program, which begins processing. The daemon job sleeps and every

5 minutes (or whatever time is deemed necessary) awakes and checks for the presence of the dummy (switch) file. If the file is not present, the daemon job does nothing and goes back to sleep. Five minutes later, it awakens and again checks for the presence of the dummy file. If the file exists, the daemon job initiates the real program, which begins processing. This method allows a level of control over the execution of the real program. A key point to this method is that once the daemon job does find the dummy file, before it initiates the real program, it deletes the dummy file and ends itself. In some instances, the strategy may be to not kill the daemon job but to continue checking for another dummy file so it can re-initiate another real program—as in processing batches of input data as it arrives. This latter point requires planning and coordination based on circumstances.

This strategy could also be used to initiate an ETL process but only after the input data has been FTP'd to the server. It functions as follows:

▶ A program runs to FTP a data set from one server to another. The first step in this program is to execute a daemon job that sleeps for 5 minutes and awakens to check for the presence of a dummy (switch) file, as mentioned earlier.

▶ The dummy file is sent from this FTP program as the last step after it transfers the input file.

▶ Then when the daemon awakens to find the dummy file, it deletes the dummy file and starts the execution of the input file ETL program.

This strategy would allow the ETL processing program to begin immediately after the input file has been transferred. If there are many input files being transferred and one processing program per input file, this means that the ETL program can begin immediately after the input file arrives.

An added control to this could be to add another small job to the daemon job whereby it checks a table, which records the number of ETL jobs running. For example, if there is a limit of five ETL jobs running and the daemon reads the table to find that five jobs are registered, meaning five jobs are running, the daemon goes back to sleep for another 5 minutes. This controls the number of ETL jobs running to ensure that the server and CPUs are not overburdened. Of course, the ETL job would have to register itself to the control table and deregister itself upon completion, again a sophisticated process that requires coordination and control.

Failsafe Strategy

If there is an issue of the same program executing twice or more, thus creating real problems in the ETL strategy because the same customer may be added twice to the database, a failsafe strategy could be used to stop the multiple executions.

There are many possible methods to ensure that the program does not execute more than desired. Several are

▶ Register the program name, date, and time of execution in a table. When the program runs, it checks this table to see if it previously ran on the same day, assuming it should only run once per day.

▶ A secondary method could be to register the first and last row in the input file. When the program executes, it will check the date and time of the last execution as well as the first and last row of data. If all are identical, the program halts.

These simple methods will ensure that the data is not added more than once to the database for the given date and same input file. Simply tune this strategy as needed depending on your individual circumstances.

Transformation and Staging

The transformation and staging areas have been combined in this section as they are very tightly coupled. The transformation of the captured data can be performed on flat files or within a staging database, and as such they are combined in the same topic discussion. Figure 10-11 shows these two areas as independent to ensure that the concepts are distinct; however, they can be discussed as one.

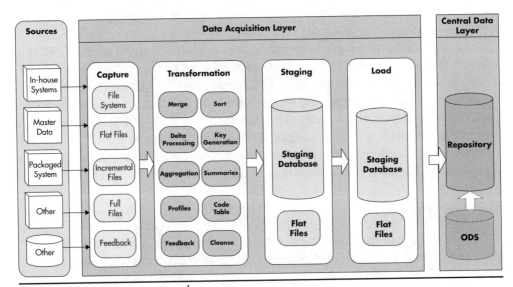

Figure 10-11   *Data acquisition layer*

In many cases, captured data can sit around waiting for dependent events to occur before being processed. Best practice is to perform whatever processing up front as soon as possible, to ensure that any issues become apparent earlier rather than later in the transformation pipeline.

As part of the initial steps in the transformation processes, cleansing is usually performed to ensure as high a level of data quality as possible. Any number of transformation steps can then occur with the goal of preparing the data as much as possible before loading into the repository or historical staging area.

Preparation

The cleansing aspect of the data preparation is, as the name implies, to clean the dirty data. Data is considered dirty simply because one aspect or another has a fundamental error. The following list details several of the most common types of dirty data scenarios:

- Fundamental aspects:

  - **Duplicate data**   A customer may show up a number of times due to misspelled names. The duplication is discovered when sorting on the source system unique identifier or natural key.

- Descriptive aspects:

  - **Missing data**   Fields that are required have no data values.

  - **Improper field usage**   For example, as mentioned earlier, the gender field may contain a mixture of gender and marital status.

  - **Invalid values within the field**   Such as a telephone number that contains non-numeric characters.

  - **Inconsistent values**   Both M for male and Male for male.

- Associative aspects:

  - **Inconsistency between fields**   For example, postal code and address do not match up.

Many years ago when data warehousing started, we analyzed the addresses of insurance claimants for one particular customer. It became apparent that four individuals were using a combination of four addresses for a good number of claims. When sorting on State, a Florida zip code would show up for a Texas address and vice versa. After considerable manual investigation and cleansing, it became apparent that there were some deliberate inconsistencies between data fields. An internal investigation later determined that many claims were fraudulent and legal proceedings were initiated—all because of "dirty" data and a proper cleansing focus.

In another instance, as mentioned in Chapter 1, an auto insurance company was having much difficulty in analyzing their customer policies and claims simply because there was poor input guidance, which leads to inconsistent data values. A FORD vehicle could be entered as FORD, FROD, ORD, FRAD, and FRID, and so on. Data cleansing corrected many of the issues and allowed the business to analyze their policies and claims based on proper data values. Before this effort the business knew about the data issues and simply gave up on trying to analyze them based on certain fundamental auto insurance details. After the fix, the data was much more usable and contributed to many new analytical insights.

Other transformation areas include delta processing, merging of data from multiple source system, and sorting.

Sorting

Sorting is done for a number of reasons. If it is done manually, the primary purpose is to visually recognize any discrepancies, as mentioned in the fraudulent claim example in the preceding section. However, most data warehouses capture large amounts of data and automate all ETL processes, as manual efforts would not be possible. Sorting is primarily used to load the data in a certain order, such as effective date and occurrence date, and is a staple of ETL processing.

Merging

Merging is simply combining data. This can be to merge input files to process one large file rather than a number of smaller files, or can be to include lookup code descriptions into a file. Merging is another fundamental step in data transformation. Merging within the DBMS system is done via SQL. It is recommended to understand the basics of how to merge data using SQL statements, as Figure 10-12 explains.

Figure 10-12 represents common database join terms as viewed from a Venn diagram perspective. It also shows results from each type of join using the Venn diagram and a simple list of data values.

Delta Processing

As mentioned several times in the book, delta processing is performed to determine whether an input row has changed from the previous capture. If the source system provides timestamps, then anything with a timestamp greater than the last capture date/time combination means that something changed and should be processed within the data warehouse. If the source systems do not have timestamps, best practice is to have them implement timestamps per table. This may be difficult and time-consuming to perform. Many legacy system owners will be against such efforts,

Universe	
Person	**Address**
Andy	123 Front
Bill	555 Main
Cindy	no address
Dexter	888 King
no person	999 Skid

Inner Join = All Persons with Addresses	
Andy	123 Front
Bill	555 Main
Dexter	888 King
Left Outer Join	
Andy	123 Front
Bill	555 Main
Cindy	no address
Dexter	888 King
Right Outer Join	
123 Front	Andy
555 Main	Bill
888 King	Dexter
999 Skid	no person
Outer Cartesian Product Join	
Andy	123 Front
Bill	555 Main
Cindy	no address
Dexter	888 King
no person	999 Skid

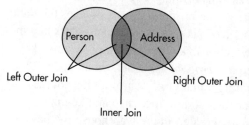

Note: Outer Cartesian Product Join is the combination of all data from all tables.

Figure 10-12   *Merge using fundamental SQL joins*

but if it is determined that delta processing is too costly, then a mini-project to include functional timestamps may be valuable to the organization. Note to project managers: it is best to seek out new funding for such an effort rather than take from your existing project budget.

If no timestamps are provided, the data warehouse system must determine whether the row changed since the last capture. If it did, the specific field must be pinpointed and processing must determine the impact to the data warehouse.

Surrogate Keys

In a data warehouse there are usually multiple source applications from which data will be gathered. A primary objective of the data warehouse is to consolidate information. This means taking data from two or more legacy applications and merging it into one centralized version. For example, if two source applications both hold the same person and identify this person differently, how should this be handled in the data warehouse, which has a goal of only holding one central version of the truth? The answer is to use a unique meaningless primary key called a *surrogate key*.

For instance, a customer is in a billing application and a product subscription application. In the first application, the person is recognized from a driver's license number; in the second application, the primary key is some identifier such as A3956. The issue then becomes whether the person can be identified time after time as the same person in each of these legacy applications. The answer for this example is yes, based on the keys just mentioned. Note that in many instances, there is no primary identifier in the source system, and a combination of fields must be used to uniquely identify the instance.

In the data warehouse, only one primary key is required, but which should you use? If a source system key is used, it means that the data warehouse is bound to that source system and the manner in which it assigns primary keys. If the source application for some reason decides to change the primary key, this leaves the data warehouse in a difficult spot. The best thing to do is to make a meaningless key in the warehouse and always map this data warehouse key to the source systems key. This type of key in the warehouse is called a *surrogate key*. Each time data is captured from each source system, it is simply a matter of mapping that source system key to the data warehouse surrogate key. Again, the surrogate key is a meaningless key. The surrogate key is usually created in the warehouse by the underlying database sequential number generator. If a new person is added, the surrogate key is the next available number. For example, if the highest sequential number for the customer key in the data warehouse is 123456, a new customer addition to the warehouse would have number 123457; the order is not really the issue, as is its uniqueness.

The technical method of creating and managing multiple source keys into a single data warehouse surrogate key is by maintaining a mapping table in the staging environment as shown in Figure 10-13.

The idea is to maintain each source system key and the data warehouse key and mapping to have the ETL routine compare against this staging table per source system input. This routine can just as easily be done outside a DBMS in flat files and have a sorting tool such as Syncsort or CoSort prepare a combined output file with proper data warehouse key values.

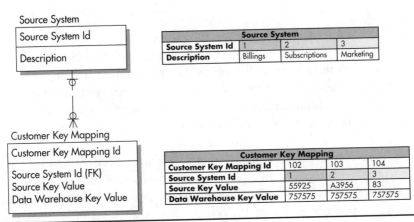

Source System

Source System Id
Description

Source System			
Source System Id	1	2	3
Description	Billings	Subscriptions	Marketing

Customer Key Mapping

Customer Key Mapping Id
Source System Id (FK) Source Key Value Data Warehouse Key Value

Customer Key Mapping			
Customer Key Mapping Id	102	103	104
Source System Id	1	2	3
Source Key Value	55925	A3956	83
Data Warehouse Key Value	757575	757575	757575

Figure 10-13   *Source to DW unique key mapping*

When the ETL routine for surrogate key mapping runs and you know which application source is being run, simply check the source type table and use the code for that source application in the processing.

In special cases where the key mapping ETL routine may be run concurrently for multiple source applications and for efficiency in processing, a secondary key mapping strategy could be used if table locking is a factor. Each application could have its own distinct key mapping table—so there would be one table per source. And a second process would later execute to merge the keys into the master key mapping table. Two main reasons for this approach are

▶ There are many records that must be mapped from each source system concurrently. This means less contention on the master key mapping table.

▶ If the source applications have compound keys; this means that if the billing system is not using just, for example, a driver's license to identify a person but a number of fields such as driver's license and birth date. Creating a key mapping table for this scenario means that the extra mapping processing is only affecting this one table and process. Later, however, the unique data warehouse key in this specific application key mapping table will have to be matched to the master key mapping table. This means overall additional processing, but the entire flow would now be streamlined.

In the first loading of the warehouse, with the bulk of the data being mapped, it may be more efficient to run through the master key mapping table to obtain the surrogate keys and then gather all mappings for each specific source application and create a specific application key mapping table. In future executions, the key mapping routine would use the smaller table (application key mapping table) and then map to the master key mapping table. Any new customers could then be identified and added to the master key mapping table. The same routine would then be used where the master surrogate key would replace the application key mapping for the new customers only. The point is that there would be many fewer new customers on a regular basis, and this means that the added functionality of maintaining the individual application key mapping tables would not be that much overhead compared to the initial load. The added bonus is that key mapping could run concurrently for multiple source applications and one would not lock out the other. If all were using the same master key mapping table, there would most likely be database resource contention, meaning that applications could possibly time out waiting for resources. This individual application key mapping method would allow for key mapping to run concurrently and map the existing customers quite easily. While extra processing is required for new customers per source application, if new customers are less frequent than the bulk of the existing customers, the overall process may be more efficient.

This secondary application key mapping strategy is an alternative approach that must be completely thought out for its viability and efficiency for each usage and should only be used for very heavy processing environments.

Referential Integrity

Referential integrity (RI) means that the value in a column of one table, B, must have an associated value from another table, A. In other words, the value in Table B column must refer to a value from Table A. The Table B column value is then automatically enforced by the DBMS to Table A by means of a foreign key.

In a data warehouse environment, the ETL in the data acquisition layer is processing and managing each column for each table and therefore should be managing the integrity of the data. This means that if the child table is supposed to have a value from a parent table, this will be ensured within the ETL. As such, there is really no need in the database to automatically enforce the integrity.

Also unlike a transaction processing system, in a data warehouse, data may lag behind other data that it is dependent on. Remember the earlier example of a customer being offered a 10 percent discount in a retail store for all purchases made that day if subscribing to and using that store's credit card on the spot? In that example, the sales transactions would normally trickle down to the data warehouse before the customer information arrives. If referential integrity were enforced in the database, the sales transactions would be rejected because the customer data was lacking. Having no DBMS-enforced RI would allow for the sales transactions to reside in the data warehouse and therefore allow aggregations upon the sales data as it arrives, which may be quite important to a dynamic sales and/or inventory analysis.

Aggregating, Profiling, and Summarizing

The data population and the data distribution area are both concerned with creating aggregate or summary data. A data warehouse repository is concerned with holding data at the atomic level. And business users are also concerned with analyzing the atomic data, but if the analysis requirements are known and consistent, data can be pre-aggregated, thus reducing the amount of rows in the resulting tables. This means faster results for database queries. While these generic aggregations and summarizations are typically done for data marts, the repository is a good place to hold many of them.

Profile tables are another type of table that can be of great value to business analysis. Rather than having to gather all data for each customer, a customer profile table can be used to generalize customers into group categories. This again allows for quicker processing in the analysis efforts but does require a good understanding of the business requirements.

Code Tables

Code tables are fundamental to a data warehouse system. Rather than have freeform text repeated time and again, centralizing the codes and standardizing the code values and descriptions allows for a high level of data quality. Each code table, as with any data warehouse table, should contain a surrogate key. The reason is that the table might be created from a number of source systems, or the value description combination may change, which means changing all the associated uses within the data warehouse system.

For example, suppose the source system has M and F for male and female respectively. A second source system uses 0 and 1 for male and female respectively. To merge these, a single value description combination must be determined. The value could be used as the key throughout a normalized or dimensional data model, but if the value description combination were to change at any point, the data warehouse would again be in a difficult spot. The best practice is to create surrogate keys for all code tables. That said, in some advanced instances it may be beneficial to use the natural key as the primary identifier, but this must be managed and documented to minimize associated risks.

Loading

Figure 10-11 shows loading as the final step in the data acquisition layer. In this scenario, the loading refers to the loading of the data warehouse repository. There are three types of loading in the acquisition layer:

▶ **Initial**   Refers to the first-time load.

▶ **Refresh**   Refers to dropping or deleting existing data and completing reloading the data in question.

▶ **Update**   Refers to the incremental load of new data to the data warehouse.

In theory a data warehouse is always added to; however, in reality existing data can be modified, which is known as Type I processing. Since loading can take place in phases, some data may be added at a later point, which technically would be the partial modification of an existing row.

Loading can also refer to the loading from the EDW repository to the data marts as seen earlier in this chapter. In this scenario the loading is tailored to the individual data mart designs, which can be 3NF, star or snowflaked.

History vs. No History

The design and definition of the individual tables in the data repository dictate whether history will or will not be loaded. Initially documented by Ralph Kimball, the Type I, II, and III categories can also be applied to a normalized data model, such as that of a data warehouse repository.

- ▶ **Type I**   Refers to maintaining no history.
- ▶ **Type II**   Refers to ensuring that history is fully kept.
- ▶ **Type III**   Refers to maintaining only the current and first or previous versions.

As discussed in Chapter 8, history can be kept at the fundamental, descriptive, and associative levels. In a normalized data model, history is thought of at the individual column level. If a person's marital status changes and full history is required, then several methods can be used:

- ▶ Create a new table just for that one column and associate it to its main table. This could result in a large number of additional tables. The middle example in Figure 8-26 in Chapter 8 shows such a scenario.
- ▶ Merge all these independent tables into one central table, as in Figure 8-27 of Chapter 8.
- ▶ History between fundamental tables is done via associative tables, as in Figure 8-23 of Chapter 8.

Insert/Update/Upsert/Delete

Data is added, updated, or deleted from the repository. Inserting is done for new data, and updating is to modify existing data. Upsert is a command pertaining to both the insert and update; if a row exists, then it is updated, or else the row is newly inserted. Deleting is a planned task based on business requirements. In many instances, specific data is first archived, then possibly summarized, and then removed from the database.

Population Information

Every repository table should have its associated population information for technical purposes as shown in Figure 10-14. ETL routines should append a population information identifier to every table to track when the table's row was populated, the ETL program that populated it, from which source system the row was sourced if the entire row can be traced back to one source system, and a "drop flag." In many instances the

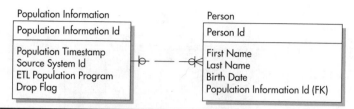

Figure 10-14   *Population Information table*

loading programs can take many hours. If something goes wrong, rather than dropping all the incorrect data rows, which may take a considerable amount of time, the Population Information table's drop flag can be set, indicating that any row using the particular Population Information Id can be dropped at a later time. This allows the correction of the ETL routine and the resubmission of the loading routine.

Load Scheduling

The loading of the repository must be coordinated with the input data availability and when the data distribution programs schedule. Be aware that if the repository loading is done between noon and 2:00 P.M. and the data marts pull from the repository at 1:00 P.M., there may be incomplete data issues. Ensure that the data distribution and data population phases are synchronized. Also ensure that the data acquisition capture schedule is synchronized with the source system operations and maintenance schedules.

Staging for EDW vs. Staging for Bus Architecture

The staging for EDW and the staging for the bus architecture are similar and different. Both simply contain data in preparation for loading to the main data warehouse areas. The EDW repository is the main central historical holding database in the central repository architecture, while the staging area for the bus architecture is used in preparation for conformed dimensions and fact tables.

Figure 10-11 shows the architecture for a central repository, and Figure 10-15 shows the data flow for a bus architecture. Figure 10-15 replaces the central repository layer with a staging layer. This staging area is primarily structured to hold all dimensions to which the data marts can replicate in whole or in part based on requirements. Typically, all measures are in data mart fact tables, surviving the staging layer only long enough for preparation purposes, if any.

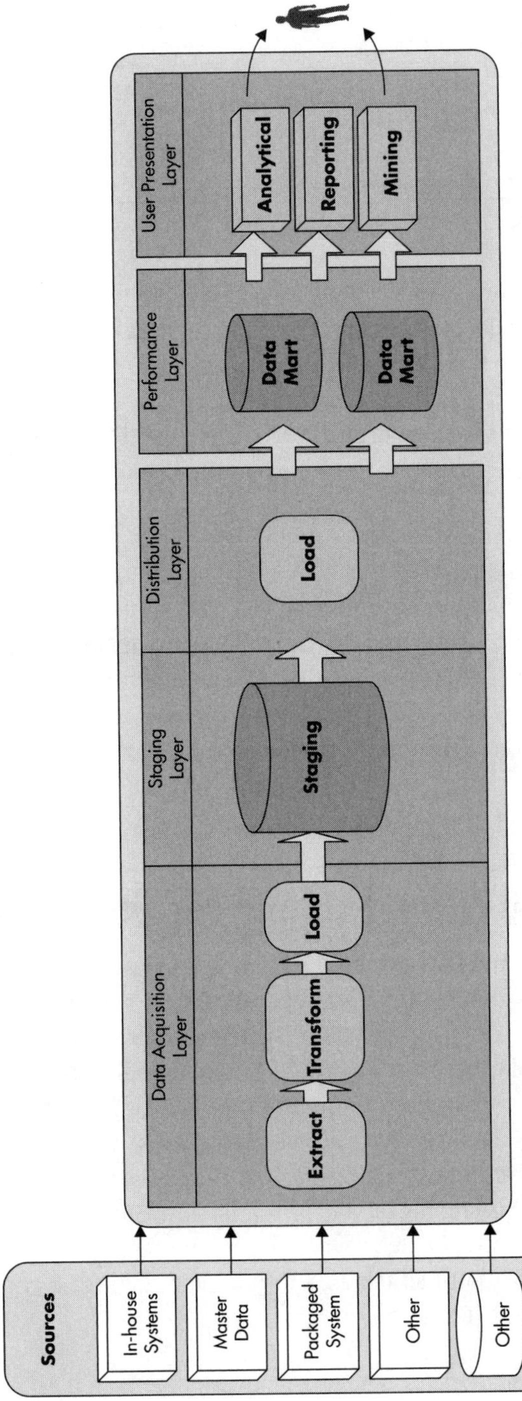

Figure 10-15 *Bus architecture*

Data Distribution

The function of the data distribution layer is specifically to take data from the holding area, central repository or bus architecture staging area, and distribute it to the individual data marts in the performance layer of the data warehouse architecture. This layer has its own steps, as seen in Figure 10-16, which include selection, transformation, and distribution.

The selection process consists of extracting from the holding area; the transformation is dependent on the differences and uses between the holding area and data mart; and the distribution is the actual loading into the data marts.

3NF to Star

If the data mart parallels a subset of the holding area, then the distribution layer is simply to extract from the holding area and load the data mart. The focus is then on ensuring that history is handled appropriately and ensuring the fullness of the data mart design usage. If the repository is in the third normal form and the data mart is a star design, then a translation effort will be needed between the designs.

Figure 10-17 gives an overview of a 3NF-to-star translation. First there must be a physical separation between the two models. If you're using Erwin, for example, it's best to create two distinct designs in two distinct files and use a mapping document to relate the two.

In a dimensional design version of the Person, the dimension could be denormalized to include both the home and work addresses, while the normalized data model would hold these in distinct tables called Person and Address with a Person/Address association table, as seen in Figure 10-18. Therefore the data distribution layer must select from the normalized repository, transform to the

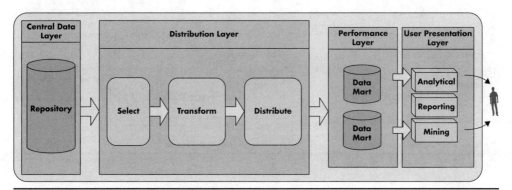

Figure 10-16   *Data distribution details*

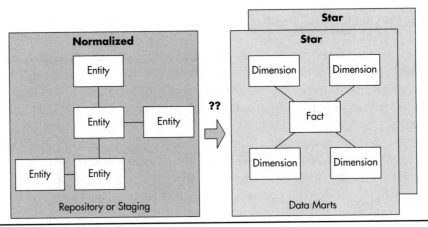

Figure 10-17 *Repository to data mart*

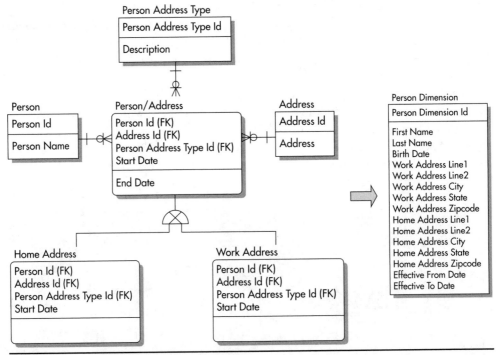

Figure 10-18 *3NF to dimension*

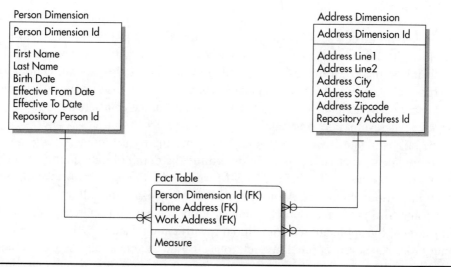

Figure 10-19 *Dimension usage*

dimensional data mart format, and distribute/load the data mart with the most current information.

It must be understood that the primary key values between the two designs will differ. In the normalized data design, when a change happens, it may be captured in the Person/Address associative table or in a code table, and therefore the Person Id will not change. However, in the Person Dimension design, when a historical change occurs there will be a new row instance. From a mapping perspective, the normalized repository Person table may have row 2195, which would map to Person Dimension rows; for example, 5980, 5981, 5982 and so forth. In this case the dimension could be designed with a Repository Person Id to refer back to the repository from within the data mart. This would be for technical mapping purposes.

Another dimensional design option is to keep the dimension fundamentals distinct, as shown in Figure 10-19. Here the Person and Address are both involved in a fact table used in whatever fashion dictates.

Data Quality

Data quality is part of a larger data governance effort with ownership, change control, and documentation but has been included in brief in this chapter, as the ETL portion of a data warehouse is where the data quality is realized.

The data-cleansing aspect of the data acquisition, as mentioned earlier, is the major step in determining the quality of the data at the physical level. At this level the data quality originates from the source systems, and if any issues arise, the source system should be corrected as soon as possible. This requires management to champion the effort, as source system owners may not be willing to change the data even if it is in their best interest for a number of political and/or operational reasons. Enterprise change control becomes a factor when data quality is discovered outside of the operational system itself and is a must to ensure that the data actually gets corrected wherever it may originate.

Several years ago I was involved in analyzing the requirements of a large telecommunications firm in Asia. To determine the depth of data quality issues in the business processes, I purchased a SIM card under the name of Mickey Mouse, a popular cartoon character. Although federal law insisted that all individuals purchasing SIM cards show proper identification, I managed to purchase the card by just filling in the application form without identification. Needless to say, the data quality routines never reported my fictitious customer name as an issue, even though the quality of the customer base was compromised. This event initiated a new intense data governance effort with the organization to ensure that resellers were indeed following proper customer application procedures and regulations. I'm not sure if this persisted after my departure, but within the year a terrorist bomb exploded in the capital and it was determined that it was detonated by a cell phone registered to a fictitious person (not Mickey Mouse). I'm not sure if the SIM card for that event was from this same organization or not; hopefully not!

It is here in the ETL processes that data is analyzed, filtered, cleansed, and transformed into the data warehouse requirements. Data quality, especially at the enterprise level, is in the coordination of all these steps of the data from all of its many possible sources throughout the enterprise. If the enterprise spans several countries, the efforts become more difficult but also more important from an enterprise data asset perspective. Ensuring the quality of the data into the data warehouse will support the overall system. After all analysis, designs, builds, and deployment, if the data warehouse and business intelligence system is perceived as having poor data quality, its usage will deteriorate as business users distance themselves to find alternate solutions.

Have you ever craved something and after a long wait or journey you finally obtain it, only to find it's just not what you expected? Perhaps the food just didn't taste as good as you remembered it, or the car just didn't go as fast as you thought it would. The same concept applies with a data warehouse; initially, hopes will be high with grand expectations of usage, but if the data quality is poor, the business will drop funding in a heartbeat.

ETL Tools

Certain points must always be taken into consideration when architecting the data warehouse from an ETL perspective. For instance, which ETL tools should be used, and what is the breadth of the tools' abilities? The ETL tools should be able to generate test data based on table design. This helps tremendously with the development process to show the architects, owners, and business people actual data values and how they would be handled within the data warehouse processes.

The tools must have certain fundamental aspects such as: scheduling capabilities, monitoring of jobs via logs and in real time, auto-restart abilities, notification abilities via connecting to email servers, parallel processing, and so forth. Every organization should evaluate the tools available at the onset of the first data warehouse project. You don't need to spend three to four months on the topic, but do perform research on the tools with an understanding of what your in-house resources have used in the past. Give extra rating points to the tool if your staff have used it in the past and feel comfortable with it or if you already have the tool on-site.

CHAPTER
11

Project Planning and Methodology

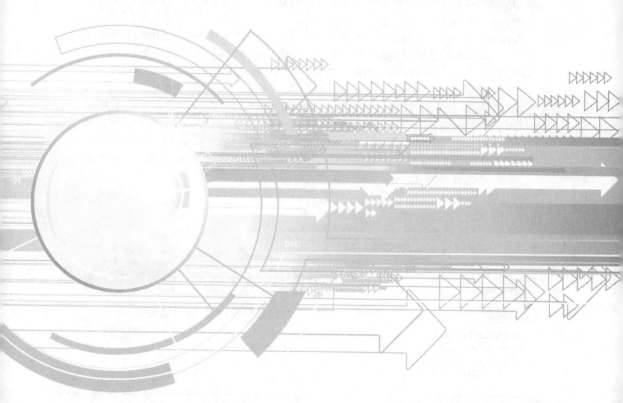

There are many books and methodologies on how to manage data warehouse and business intelligence projects, so the fine details will be left to those. This chapter's focus is on an overview of a DW/BI project with insights into fundamental issues and a look at steps within a particular approach methodology.

Since data is an asset to the organization, it is management's due diligence to ensure that the corporate asset is properly maintained. This means that the data has value to the organization and in many cases is fundamental to the operations of the organization. With poorly maintained or incorrect data, business decisions based on this information or knowledge, which are both data in context, will most likely be incorrect and misguide management, causing the organization to drift from its strategic course. Therefore it is vital that data is properly managed with a high degree of quality, confidence, and availability.

If your business is the delivery of flowers, the flowers themselves as well as the fleet of delivery trucks are the company assets, and if either is not maintained, your business will be at risk. Banks, insurance, telecommunications, retail, healthcare, travel, government, and nearly every sort of business has data at the heart of their operations, and if that data asset is not maintained, the business is at risk. The current reality is that it is impossible to run any sort of complex business without a solid and organized data asset.

A data warehouse system is usually the first attempt at managing the corporate data asset, since these sorts of systems consider vast amounts and differing types of data from across the organization. The first step in creating or enhancing a DW/BI system is in understanding its final goal and the breadth of data within the organization required to attain the goal. Figure 11-1 shows a flow diagram with data on one end and the resulting business improvement goal on the opposite. In a DW/BI system, the DW sets the foundation to support business intelligence and BI is the portal to support the business decision process. The business improvement aspect may be at the strategic, tactical, or operational level, each having an impact on the other with business intelligence tailored for any or each.

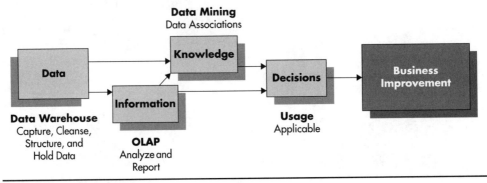

Figure 11-1 *BI evolution*

Project management's task, in this context, is therefore to manage the project of creating or enhancing a DW/BI system as a solution for the business in efforts to analyze and mine the enterprise data asset in order to guide the business decision-making process in an effort to improve the business in one or more focused areas.

Every project, including a DW/BI project, is concerned with overseeing resources, costs, timelines, and scope to ensure risk mitigation and the quality of the solution. The difference with a DW/BI project is that it is much more dynamic than other IT projects. The dynamic aspect refers to unforeseen data quality issues that can change the direction of a project and overzealous business users wanting to extend the boundaries of the project with as many deliverables as possible at reduced delivery timelines. Beware of scope creep and try to stick to fundamentals, especially on the first iteration. You should document any scope creep, including even the smallest of items, and tag each instance with resource requirements, integration duration estimates, and estimated costs. These little changes and/or additions will eventually add up, possibly causing considerable delays, and could become a major hindrance for the project phase and possibly the entire solution.

In many instances these two issues, data quality and scope creep, along with poor management support, leave the project team to fend for themselves by making business data decisions without proper business SME support for guidance. Being staffed with improper resource leads is another project failure catalyst as it directly relates to insufficient experience or business know-how when faced with making these business data decisions and therefore parallels the same criticality level.

Hence a DW/BI project, which may contain a number of associated programs, requires advanced knowledge of project management with enough experience and DW/BI insights to confront these types of major risk issues. This type of project should be led by a seasoned project manager with hands-on experience. Without data warehouse knowledge, the project manager will be at the mercy of the technical leads, meaning that direction may lag efforts. The project manager in these scenarios usually ends up being a timekeeper and a stickler for following a project plan without really knowing what the line items pertain to or their interdependence, which adds to potential failure no matter how many good intentions. Experience typically trumps theory; however, that said, I have known several project managers with little DW/BI experience who have led successful projects simply because they were savvy enough to partner with experienced solution, data warehouse, and ETL architects who possessed advanced communication and knowledge transfer skills. These types of DW/BI individuals work toward building business and technical solutions while enhancing resource skills at the same time; these people are called *mentors*.

DW/BI projects involve the management of many dynamic changes affecting resources, timelines, and costs, and they also give rise to a number of unforeseen risks along the way. Care must be taken in planning, hence a methodology should be in place and adhered to, ensuring phased deliverables for a number of mini-successes for the business and IT alike, drastically increasing the likelihood of an overall successful solution supporting the business decision-making process and therefore likely tangible business improvements.

Fundamentals

The first and foremost aspect of project planning for a DW/BI project is, as with any other IT project, to ensure that the requirements are identified, understood, and documented. There must be an understanding of why numbers are being gathered and not just an effort to gather specific numbers. From Chapter 2, DW/BI should be part of the business, contributing to the business proactively with IT as an extension of the business unit. The second step is to create a strategy to deliver the solution, which includes how to approach specific major issues and how to design, build, and deploy the solution, all based on expected usage given the environment and set boundaries.

There is usually a disconnect between what the business wants and in how IT interprets the requirements. The reason is usually twofold: IT does not fully understand what the business wants to accomplish, and IT looks at the fundamental details, which can be interpreted in a number of ways depending on the business purpose. If business guidance is not available at any point along the project timeline, deviations will occur.

To alleviate these issues, best practice is to ensure ongoing communication starting with documentation and the creation of a mock solution to validate expectations.

For instance, if an OLAP environment (nice communicative graphs or pie charts and drill-down/up capabilities) is required, create a demo report with some drill-down scenarios along with fundamental data. Pillar diagrams, as seen in Chapter 2, Figures 2-11 and 2-12, can also be useful in understanding the initial data fundamentals at a high but working level. The main point to always keep in mind is that the business leads the DW/BI project by setting the requirements and usage. IT then supports the efforts by obtaining an understanding of the underlying data, designing a solution, and realizing the design guided by the business users and their requirements. Ensuring communications between the two is paramount. Creating a mock solution can solidify understanding and set expectations.

Success will be based on people, not technology. Ensuring management support, proper resources, and ongoing communications will help with the management of expectations. Technology will help with the development, but it is the people, and how they manage their roles and the technology, who are critical to the overall success.

For all projects, there must be a basic understanding of what a data warehouse system is and the difference between the BI and DW components:

▶ **Business Intelligence**   Empowering business decision makers with trusted data in a value-driven context, which is usable and delivered in a timely manner.

▶ **Data Warehouse**   A system for collecting, organizing, holding, and sharing historical data. It consists of "used" data, as the data comes from operational systems that capture and use the data within the context of that system's purpose. Of course, other systems or sources are also possible, but in a DW project the term "operational systems" is widely used. There is usually more than one source system for a data warehouse. Data warehouses are typically thought of as enterprise-wide, but in many instances can be focused on a particular line of business such as finance or marketing.

A data warehouse system is typically characterized by and for the business with the following points:

▶ Single version of the truth

▶ Clean, trusted, and accurate data

▶ Accessible

▶ Facilitates consistent reporting

▶ Business integrity

It must be understood that a DW/BI project has a number of specific risks more pronounced than those in regular IT projects. Each must be handled carefully to ensure a successful delivery.

Risk: Phased Development

Since data is at the enterprise level and centralized typically in one accessible area, the business sees great value and typically would like to dive in as quickly as possible. With so much data, however, the effort in identifying, describing, modeling, performing all the data population steps, and so on would be much too broad and time-consuming for a big bang approach. There must be a focused delivery for both top-down and bottom-up approaches to set boundaries and overall expectations.

A phased approach also reduces scope creep as added requirements can be mixed into different phases and/or projects.

Risk: Data Quality

The primary area of focus and effort in a data warehouse revolves around the data itself. And because data is at the enterprise level, meaning that it comes from a number of operational or other systems, there are usually many data quality issues and risks which become more pronounced when merged and centralized by design (definitions and structures) and later physically (actual data values). Due to this scenario, projects must deal with unforeseen issues, such as what to do with unclean data, invalid data, incorrect data, discrepancies between source systems, and so forth. In many instances, management severely underestimates the data quality issues or believes that data issues can be fixed on the spot as the project progresses. Do not give in to the misconception that years of data issues can be resolved overnight under the umbrella of a data warehouse project. A data warehouse project does not own the source system data, but will usually detect data quality issues within them and will bring these to management for correction. A side project is usually created for the source systems to correct their pre-existing data issues.

If the data is not of sufficient quality, then the information becomes unreliable, the acquired knowledge is skewed, and the business decisions become unpredictable, leading the business into a state of not trusting their data. Under such scenarios many DW/BI projects have been cancelled or shelved to allow for data cleansing efforts and/or strategic re-evaluation. On the other hand, if excess effort is spent on ensuring a high standard of data quality that is unnecessary for the business solution at hand, the end result will be cost overruns, delays in delivery, and the lowering of trust between the business users and the project, especially of the project leads.

Risk: Resources

Another major risk is in not having the proper resources. If a required end report of the DW/BI project is dropped on the project manager's lap, it can be dismantled into data components, but without guidance, these data items are usually not fully understood. To alleviate this risk, in-house senior business analysts who are familiar with how the organization operates are critical. Bringing in external resources who are not familiar with the corporate culture or business operations, no matter what their line of business insights and experiences, cannot help to the extent of an in-house business SME, which is a must on every DW/BI project.

As mentioned earlier, the project manager is another role that must be properly fitted. A project manager should have an in-depth understanding of what a data warehouse and business intelligence solution is and what it takes to develop it. There is no need to be a data architect or solution architect expert, but the roles and the major issues should be well understood.

All lead roles should be well versed in DW/BI efforts in their own silos and in how they inter-relate to the overall solution. Several years ago, a very large data warehouse project having over 100 skilled resources would shift resources to different roles every six months so that everyone could get a chance to perform other roles. The problem was that database administrators would take on business analysis, ETL programmers would take on data modeling, data modelers would take on database administration, and so forth—all without having any previous experience in the new roles. This led to confusion with not one person being able to describe or understand the overall data flow. The ETL lead, data architecture lead, database administrator lead, BI lead, and solution lead must all remain in their roles for the duration of the project and should be well versed, with a handful of previous projects under their belts.

When it comes to the business subject matter expert, the person should understand how the business operates, what fundamental data is required, and why the data is required. If the business SME can name specific data files, you have the wrong person as the SME since this knowledge is usually too technical for a true business-side SME. The business SME's core competency should be business processes insights, identification of source systems at a high level, and the ability to discuss overall business issues. The source system SME on the IT side will identify files, timings, and operational details.

Risk: Cost

Cost overruns are typical in a DW/BI project but by no means accepted, hence management of costs is critical, as with any project.

Scope in a DW/BI project is in many instances unclear at the onset and therefore cost overruns are expected. It is always remarkable to see a project begin with hopes of creating a solid solution without knowing what is required; it's kind of like grocery shopping for a friend without knowing their tastes. Without a solid scope the project should not proceed past the strategy and high-level planning phase into the development cycle. It would be much better to spend more effort up front to ensure that the creation of the solution for the business is absolutely understood. There will be many issues with data and design for effective usage within the course of the project, so no need to compound this with added risks of not knowing what type of data warehouse system is being built or why.

Change Management

Change management for any project is a must, but even more so for a DW/BI project since data is "used" or secondhand, as it comes from other application systems. Plus a data warehouse project is dynamic, with changes potentially happening weekly.

Change resolves to extended timelines, additional resources, and therefore added costs.

To manage such changes throughout the course of the project, a change management effort must be implemented at the start of the project. This should be a transparent and structured process that is understood both within the project team and by the key stakeholders. Within this process are listed the details of the issue, the change to the existing plan, the expected impact of that change to the project in regard to time and resources, along with sign-offs to the same by the project manager and the business lead. Track all scope changes, deviations, and data quality changes to ensure that management later understands why the project budget doubled, tripled, or worse.

Best Practices

A DW/BI project must be managed in a phased approach rather than a big bang approach in order to control expectations and ensure levels of success. Build with focus and deliver as solutions are created to ensure that expectations are fully met and accepted. The downside of this proposal is that the business users will ask for changes and additions that will affect later phase timelines and costs. Again, be sure of a proper change management process and understand that reassessments will be required more than once on deliverables, timeliness, resource allocations, and costs.

The project manager must always remember the purpose of the project, what the business is trying to resolve or create, and keep focus, no matter what the deviations of the efforts are. Keep the vision and move toward the primary goal of the project. If the goals change, document and reassess past efforts with new direction and take appropriate action with changes to project plans, timelines, resources, and so forth. The primary task for a DW/BI project manager is communications with the team, with business users, and with project sponsors while managing the plan, monitoring, and controlling the efforts and environment in a structured manner.

Mistakes

Common mistakes seen over and over that take away from DW/BI project effectiveness are detailed in the following list. These errors resurface on nearly every project and must be managed.

▶ Not spending enough effort on defining the solution. I am constantly amazed at the number of data warehouse projects that have not solidified their deliverables. So many projects are set off-course with IT wondering what documents, designs, and diagrams should be delivered to the business users. Projects should have clear and concise deliverables. BI projects should have defined data marts up front showing expectations. Do not assume that the data warehouse project will define the business requirements as it progresses.

▶ Communication is essential. Projects that do not communicate to the team or the business users are positioning themselves for failure. Set weekly meetings with the business sponsors and users to show progress, issues, delays, and so forth. If no business users exist, consider the overall effort an education and prepare for failure.

▶ Hiring only external people or too many external people to fill business and technical roles. Use in-house business people who know how the organization operates, and use in-house technical people who know how the data is used. Hiring specialists is great to get a running start, but using internal resources that know and understand how the organization operates has tremendous value.

▶ Taking on junior resources in a data warehouse project. A DW/BI effort is an advanced project that requires seasoned resources. Junior resources should be trained on operational systems that are fairly stable. The dynamic aspects of a data warehouse system require insights in how to incorporate change in an efficient and effective manner. And in many instances, the project resources are left to interpret the business data due to the lack of business SME guidance; hence senior technical resources would be more appropriate in a DW/BI effort.

▶ Define all data items. Many projects move forward without setting definitions for each entity and attribute. Once the solution is determined, every data item created, gathered, or captured must be documented to ensure a complete understanding of its fundamental purpose. Data quality starts with identifying and defining all data elements.

▶ Not encouraging openness within the project team. With most resources being quite experienced, the team resources will most likely have loads of experience and can offer different perspectives within their silos and toward the overall architecture and project. Encourage an open forum to share ideas. Once a week, have the team gather to discuss any issues and solutions that have come up during the most recent time period.

Project Plan Methodology

Every project should follow some sort of guidelines; a DW/BI project is no exception. The following section presents a project development methodology, as seen in Figure 11-2, containing the following fundamental steps:

▶ Identifying and analyzing the business requirements

▶ Creating a strategy and roadmap

▶ Putting together a solution outline based on a phased approach of delivery

Figure 11-2 *Project methodology steps*

▶ Designing, building, and deploying the solution

▶ The final usage by the business user

Figure 11-3 shows the methodology within one box but separates the business requirements, strategy, and usage from the actual data warehouse build project. The reason for this is to show that the business requirements and strategy can stand alone outside the development process. The Business DW and BI Solution is the ongoing business usage environment being added to as phases are delivered from independent delivery cycles. The concept is that efforts have been spent discovering the business requirements and strategizing an overall plan with the solution outline being phased into single builds to deliver islands of success within the overall strategy. Think of each phase as a major milestone in the overall strategic solution and direction.

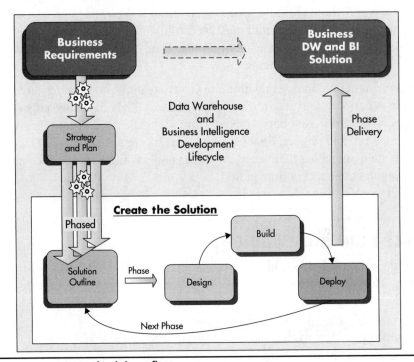

Figure 11-3 *Project methodology flow*

The actual development process, where the proverbial construction workers with hard hats set foot on the grounds, is the design, build, and deployment steps. These steps are the areas referred to in Chapter 4 in the section titled "How Long Will It Take, Revisited." While the section in Chapter 4 had specific durations per roles for the development cycle for calculation purposes, the actual resources could perform independent and parallel tasks throughout the duration of the project.

There should be several project plans: one for the business requirements and strategy steps and another for the solution development, which should contain all the phases for the overall solution.

Business Requirements

The business requirements step in the DW/BI development lifecycle methodology, Figure 11-3, is to initiate the overall project from a business perspective. This step is concerned with the discovery of needs, wants, and wish-list items with a view toward the benefit to and for the business.

This step is concerned with discovery and added value to the business. In theory, the business units will understand the gaps in their value chains and have an eye toward a data warehouse and business intelligence solution specifically to manage their data into informational pockets and knowledge bases to support their business decision making to improve the business. At this level, an in-depth effort may have been done by the business to identify focused areas of concern, or such efforts may be explored as part of the business requirements stage.

Typical analysis and insights at this point include the following:

▶ Review of the business process

▶ Identification of the business gap(s)

▶ Potential benefit to the business

▶ Users of the solution

▶ Anticipated solution effects in regards to the decision processes

Relevant questions to ask include the following:

▶ Will the solution support a strategic direction?

▶ Is the solution a foundation stepping-stone or a tangible end result?

▶ What is the time to market (timeline)?

▶ What budget is possible or available?

Discussions at this stage are led by the business sponsor, not by IT. This is a business requirements step that requires the actual business owners to relay their insights, vision, and issues. IT's role is to understand the high-level needs and value proposition to the business. The key is to have the business users themselves detail their vision. Hopefully, at this point, a high-level BI solution has been successfully pitched to upper management, who are championing the efforts.

Strategy and Plan

This step involves the analysis of the requirements with the goal of creating a solution strategy with a plan of action. If the business requirement step did not produce some sort of roadmap, this step can. In short, this step translates the business requirements into an IT perspective.

The strategy will include and define the major fundamental components to an overall DW/BI solution. Initial efforts will include an analysis of the current organization, which typically includes:

- ► Current infrastructure
- ► Current technologies: software, tools, data models, DBMS, and so on
- ► Current data architecture, technical architectures, and so on
- ► Source system inventory
  - ► Source system logistics
  - ► Source system owners and go-to persons (business and IT)
  - ► Source for fundamental data items (customer, product, transactions...)
  - ► History insights per source system
  - ► Update frequency
  - ► Volumes
  - ► Data quality confidence levels
- ► Current resources and skill levels
- ► Current processes of IT and the business
- ► Organization insights: local and foreign
- ► Organization activity; other significant efforts and projects happening throughout the organization that may impact the DW/BI efforts

The goal is to assess the landscape and identify operational issues and gaps that must be taken into consideration as factors in a viable plan toward the business requirements solution. Efforts will be guided by the business focus areas realized from the business requirements step. Further efforts during the forthcoming development stage will validate the discoveries from this step and usually add to it as insights are gained. As the investigative aspect progresses, expect extensions to the requirements as lower-level details are uncovered.

Following the gathering phase, an assessment is derived and a solution overview is developed. The overview can include the following points:

- ▶ High-level data flow architecture detailed with the technical architecture
- ▶ Required resources and roles
- ▶ Documented business sponsors, owners, and users
- ▶ Recommendations on software purchases according to the data flow architecture: ETL tools, data models, databases, BI tools
- ▶ Overall data architecture recommendation
- ▶ Technical architecture recommendation
- ▶ Resource usage recommendation
- ▶ Phased approach recommendation for the initial and continuing phases
    - ▶ Details on phases
- ▶ Documented areas of concern; risks
- ▶ Risk resolution recommendations

The goal is to understand the business requirements by focus area, identify a realistic strategy to deliver a recommended solution, and deliver a project plan detailing an approach to be refined as the solution outline progresses. In many cases a mock solution is created at this stage to give a flavor as to the final deliverable for the business users. This can be in the simple form of Excel reports with drill-down capabilities (if this type of solution is appropriate). The business users can then get a feel for what to expect and participate in the overall high-level solution design. In other instances, the strategy may recommend a proof-of-concept project as the first development phase.

All recommendations and designs should be communicated and confirmed with the business sponsor and users for feedback, which would then be incorporated moving forward. Important: There should be no movement toward the next solution outline step without proper business approval. Many projects continue into a work-at-risk scenario, hoping that the strategy, project plan, and solution are approved while efforts are under way in the development phase. This can rapidly lead to a stop work order as strategies and direction are altered, leaving resources at a standstill and quickly deployed to other projects.

For BI solutions, it is always good to produce a prototype data mart, reports, and documentation showing the business what the resulting solution is leaning towards. The result is usually a simple Excel file and documents, with no active systems developed yet. This gives insights into data, volume, usage, and source systems, and it drives expectations for business and IT. The more closely the solution is designed up front, the higher is the likelihood of a tangible solution being achieved and therefore success. Added issues such as metadata, repository design, roles, infrastructure requirements, and so forth may come to light, reducing the unknowns up front. The only major potential risk is continuing the prototype into a solution without the proper back-end design infrastructure. In many cases the business and information architectures decide to forgo the proper design aspects, which tend to haunt efforts after several development phases. The design infrastructure is practical to ensure that the data vocabulary and fundamental and associative aspects of the data are understood at a conformed enterprise level.

This step is led by the solution architect and project manager in partnership with the business sponsor and end users.

Solution Outline

The solution outline step is to specify the details of the development process. It defines the phased project scope with a detailed project plan. The project manager is in full swing removing political roadblocks and acquiring and managing resources while the solution architect is in full design mode. Both project manager and solution architect are refining details in the project plan including roles, resources, timelines, technical insights, and costs, all while communicating to the business users, who are validating as efforts move forward.

Continued assessments of the business, technical, and source environments are in progress, as much as possible, as more insights are gained. The solution is constantly being refined and confirmed. A working prototype might be produced in this step depending on the complexity and planned result.

In short, the full technical infrastructure should be known at this point, a set solution is in full view, and a plan of attack is developed to the point that development efforts can begin—the workers with the hard hats can now enter the work area.

Design

The design step is the first step in the actual development stage. The initial task is to put thoughts down on paper. The actual blueprints are now being created at a detailed level. The business analyst is in full swing with the business users to understand the fine details of the business processes within focus and documenting detailed business requirements. The data architect is designing the logical data models, with the ETL lead profiling the source data as the data architect points the direction.

As the fundamental, descriptive, associative, and temporal aspects of the data are being uncovered and understood, a mapping effort is under way to show where the data is from and where in the data model each aspect should reside. These mapping specifications are the ETL program specs used to develop the ETL routines to populate the repository and data marts. Of course, the data structures are being developed and the data flow strategy is refined to its most atomic level and to its data mart levels. Initial efforts are with the logical business data model and flow into the logical application repository and logical data mart designs. The BI architect should be in full swing as well designing specific solutions, while the business analyst documents the detail solution requirements.

Build

The build step is a "work boots and hard hat area only." The first task is to physicalize the logical designs, taking into account data volumetrics and anticipated usage. This involves the data architect or DBA coming up with the physical data models and the DBA creating DDL and database tables. Included are the partitioning and indexing strategies. The DBA should be in full swing, reviewing ETL database queries to the source systems, if any, and reviewing and optimizing database load routines for the repository. For data mart distribution, the DBA will be very active in reviewing the SQL routines, usually the main routines as there may be too many for a complete review in the usually tight timelines.

ETL jobs should be written and tested with initial test data to populate the database and for the BI architect to test the resulting deliverables. The BI efforts are to write and finalize the actual reports and OLAP routines. The data architect and BI architect are refining and finalizing the data mart designs, which should usually be one-to-one with the physical designs, and the DBA should be implementing them once completed.

The design and build steps are very iterative as they are tightly coupled. They do not necessarily form a firm waterfall-style development approach, as some efforts of development may function in parallel, such as the BI architect designing BI structures to support OLAP requirements with the data architect lagging to ensure conformity to data models a day or two later.

At this point, production data is being used to ensure all functions as planned and designed. All should be ready for a production implementation at the end of the build step.

Deploy

The deployment step is the final step in the development cycle. By now a solution has been planned, designed, and built. Much development testing has been done, and it is now time to polish the car and take it out for a test drive with the customer.

Acceptance testing is being done, users are being trained, the production environment is set up, and a full cut-over is taking place with operations taking ownership. Change control is set up with the data warehouse and business intelligence system now fully integrated within production control and the enterprise operations.

Use

At this point the development is completed and a solution is ready for and being used for the specific business focus area. At first there is much buzz from the business community as business gaps are filled with information and knowledge is being absorbed in business decision-making processes. The value proposition is being realized and the value chain is enhanced with business improvement. For replacement systems, the usage will continue in parallel for a number of months while outputs are being compared to legacy reporting to ensure minimal reporting deviations.

Let's Build

This part discusses best practices for the
design and construction of a data warehouse.

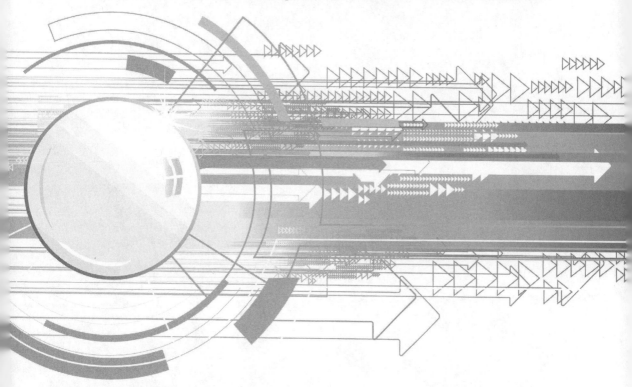

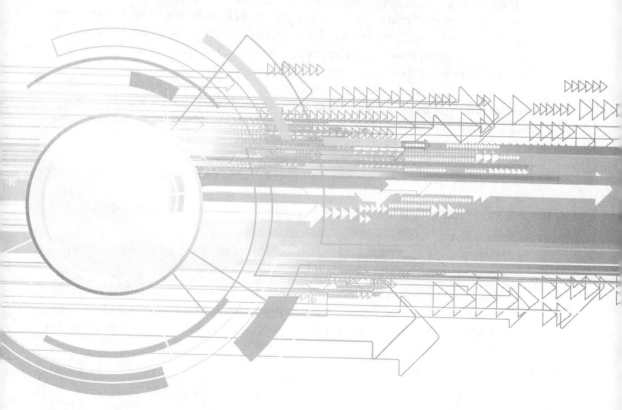

T his chapter looks at data warehousing and business intelligence from the different popular approaches currently being used:

▶ **Top-Down**   Enterprise data with and without a business usage perspective

▶ **Bottom-Up**   Pure end-user usage perspective

▶ **Hybrid**   Using both of the preceding two perspectives within the same development project

This chapter also gives insights on several popular concerns within a data warehouse system development. The chapter ends with a very brief discussion on enterprise information architecture, which is the next evolutionary step after (or with) a data warehouse system within an organization.

A data warehouse system development project is a big event that requires much attention. Without the proper know-how, these sorts of projects often fail. To ensure a successful deliverable, much preparation must be done by experienced DW/BI professionals.

The first step is to determine the purpose of the data warehouse system. Figure 12-1 shows a decision tree from requirements to the type of system usage and its supporting data environment. The figure helps break down and identify the data warehouse components required from a usage perspective rather than thinking of a data warehouse as one massive effort for one massive single result.

The second step is to understand that innovative thinking, efficient development, and risk minimization planning are keys to a successful delivery for a large system such as a data warehouse. Typically, with more experienced resources, the higher the degree of innovative thinking, and more effective planning occurs, resulting in a highly focused IT solution for a specific business issue.

Figure 12-2 shows the value proposition calculation consisting of

▶ **Innovation**   The leveraging of leading-edge solutions into new and successful approaches to current issues

▶ **Efficiency**   Reflects the ability to perform common sets of actions in faster time and/or lower costs resulting in the same or better result

▶ **Risk Reduction**   The process of identifying unknowns that could damage the progress and success of the project with a set of pre-emptive actions to reduce the chance that they occur, or if they do occur, to reduce the damage and time lost

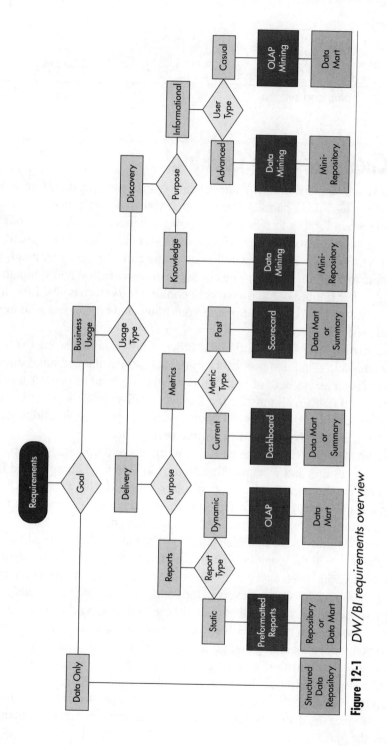

Figure 12-1 *DW/BI requirements overview*

Figure 12-2   *Value and success*

The Chef: Let's Get Cooking!

Let us take a somewhat colorful and structured approach to a hands-on DW/BI project using a cooking parallel. Imagine that you went to a grocery store and were stumbling around trying to figure out what ingredients to purchase to cook for your special event. Suddenly you bump into a world-famous chef. Well, actually it was the chef who bumped into you with his shopping cart and hurt your hand, leaving you unable to cook for the day. The chef was so embarrassed and sympathetic, especially after finding out that you were cooking for your parents' fiftieth wedding anniversary, that he decided to come to your home and cook a fantastic meal, which you graciously accepted.

Upon arriving at your home, the first order of business for the chef is to determine what you have in mind and how everything is currently planned out. Following this discussion is an assessment of your kitchen (which is kind of messy), available ingredients (of course, all must be top freshest quality), and the abilities, availability, and willingness of your helpers. Of course, your budgetary restrictions are inquired into as well, as this gives the entire effort a reality check.

The next step is to review the guest list to understand how many people will be attending the dinner and whether there are any known food allergies and likes or dislikes of specific ingredients. If any discrepancies exist between what is planned and what is available, the chef offers to help with the acquisition of any missing ingredients and possibly bring in extra help if required.

The chef will also have to understand how the meal will be served and seating arrangements: Will the event be a sit-down meal with specific items on their plates, or a standing event such as a buffet where people can take as they need, or perhaps a carving station where someone serves the food based on specific needs and wants? Will guests be in one spot or all over the house: indoors, outdoors, or a combination? We must also plan on being flexible in case there are any last-minute attendees. And with so many people coming and going, the chef wants to understand if there are typically any gate crashers in your neighborhood and the impact this typically has on planned activities. From all these insights and after an understanding of the menu and serving schedule, the chef and you can begin preparations toward the planned event: planning the dishes and the actual cooking, serving, and enjoyment of the meal by the guests.

If time permits, hopefully the chef can prepare samples for your tasting and review beforehand just so you fully comprehend what will be served. Plus, this removes the risk of a bad surprise when it would be too late to change things and after your budget has been spent. Of course, you plan on supervising everything to ensure that what leaves the kitchen actually meets with your expectations of quality (nothing burnt) and that any special meals are served to the proper guests. As an added bonus, you just found out your generous uncle will also be joining the celebrations and will contribute handsomely toward the event, which is greatly needed, but he does expect that his special diabetes concerns will be met.

In the corporate world, the anniversary dinner scenario has all the classic data warehouse and business intelligence project hurdles:

► Limited timeframe

► Limited resources

► Set budget

► Vision but unfocused project plan

► Unclear goals

► Limited access to source data

► Last-minute additions

► Security concerns

► Data quality concerns

► Data governance concerns

And the list goes on.

The chef follows a specific methodology in creating and preparing meals for large events, which also parallels our data warehouse project plan methodology, as seen in Chapter 11:

► Identify goals and requirements.

► Analyze and then create a strategy and a plan.

   ► Perform a technical analysis.

   ► Perform a gap analysis.

   ► Assess the business usage.

   ► Identify the corporate culture/environment.

   ► Evaluate a solution based on cost and budget.

> ▶ Outline a practical solution.
>
>> ▶ If possible, create a proof of concept (taste test).

To ensure that the event will be a success and all guests will have a meal to their satisfaction, certain fundamental aspects must be met, which again parallels data warehouse system best practices:

▶ Ingredients must be of a consistent quality; all food must be edible and fresh.

>> ▶ Data quality

▶ People must want to eat.

>> ▶ Business interest

▶ Someone must be willing to own the cooking of the meal.

>> ▶ Business sponsor

▶ You must have adequate and knowledgeable resources to cook the meal.

>> ▶ Proper resources

▶ The kitchen must be capable of sustaining the cooking efforts.

>> ▶ Stable and usable environment (technical architecture)

▶ The project must be within budget.

>> ▶ Cost contained

▶ The project must be managed and coordinated.

>> ▶ Proper management

>> ▶ Risk mitigation

Along with these fundamentals there needs to be a high-level plan of action on how to proceed; ensuring that ingredients are available, timely as required, and highlighted as used throughout the cooking process. Plus, with so many guests and given the number of meals to create, there must be some sort of preparation flow in the kitchen to ensure effectiveness and coordination. In other words, there must be some sort of roadmap, including a project plan and data flow architecture, to guide the design and development efforts.

Before the actual cooking begins, the chef would like to sit down and discuss the meals, the delivery schedule, the preparation flow, and then convert this plan into action and finally into a real deliverable. The chef says everything is rather simple as long as some basic points are followed:

▶ Determine exactly what the goal is.

▶ Figure out the high-level details up front.

▶ Make a strategy and plan for the build and delivery.

▶ Design the details (menu, dishes, environment…).

▶ Using the plan and design, build (cook).

▶ Once built, deploy (serve the meal).

▶ Once the meal is deployed, the guests can use the product (eat).

▶ Success!

Of course, being the expert and having much experience with such large events, the chef offers views on whether components should be created from scratch or purchased based on a number of insights: whether the kitchen help needs help, whether timelines dictate direction, advanced preparation requirements (repository), and required deliverables (data marts). His guidance is as follows:

▶ For big events, get expert help if none is available in-house.

▶ Ensure that everyone uses the same terminology.

   ▶ Shallot or spring onion?

▶ Keep it simple.

   ▶ Especially during the planning and design phases.

▶ Think of the big picture, but cook with a focus.

   ▶ Plan big, but implement in small controlled phases.

▶ Do what is right.

   ▶ Cutting corners leads to problems.

▶ Minimize risks.

   ▶ Investigate, ask questions, and plan, plan, plan.

Let us now have a look at different types of approaches and see what would be involved in each.

Top-Down (Enterprise Repository)

Projects with a top-down architecture, as shown in Figure 12-3, are typically focused on data within the organization first and reporting or analysis later. The primary reason for a pure top-down effort from a design perspective is to set an enterprise data vocabulary up front. From a data flow perspective, it is to focus on a centralized acquisition and holding of enterprise data in a structured manner.

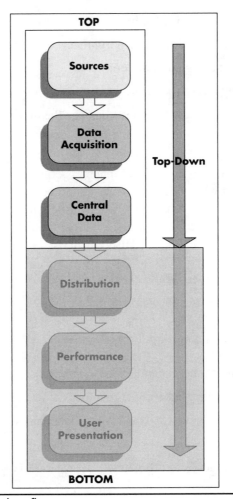

Figure 12-3 *Top-down data flow*

Typically the top-down methodology is strategic to the organization and driven by an IT initiative. Organizations considering this strategy are usually concerned with their data, which is considered a corporate-wide asset. Such organizations also consider risk management in relation to their data, which involves a keen eye on data quality and data governance before the data is used by the business areas.

To parallel the previous chef scenario, a top-down context perspective would be if many food items were purchased without really knowing what the final dishes would be, the number of guests, or how the meals were to be served. The plan in this context would be to gather, prepare, and cook all the food first and deal with who wants what and when later. This idea may work for a captive crowd of hungry guests over other scenarios as there is a perception of the type of foods people generally enjoy at social events. The venue would be more of a buffet rather than a sit-down dinner. Many may enjoy the chicken but few would enjoy the super-spicy casserole. Unfortunately, it may have taken 25 percent of your time and budget to create the super-spicy casserole—time, effort, and budget that could have been spent in more rewarding areas if only you had insight before starting. Alternatively, the chef may only have time to plan the event's meal, resulting in a list of all ingredients required and how to prepare them in a very efficient manner.

Many top-down efforts lean toward the academic side or science of data modeling, starting with a conformed data vocabulary and taxonomies of data. Projects with a top-down initiative usually plan on the delivery of an enterprise data warehouse repository design. The effort is more toward understanding and defining the data items and their sources, and being able to organize the data based on a common vocabulary into enterprise structures typically used in a data warehouse environment.

Some projects move toward realizing a physical central repository, while others, after the design is realized, move toward a focused business analysis area and physicalize only dependent data requirements. Others, depending on budgets, resources, and time-to-market considerations, move toward realizing focused data marts conformed to the central business data model design, which is an output of a top-down perspective. In these cases the strategic expectation is that an enterprise repository will be created at a later date, usually after a first data warehouse deliverable has proven to be accepted and an overall success with the business user community and upper management.

Vocabulary

A key focus for top-down scenarios is on centralizing data terminology within the organization to ensure that everyone is discussing and referring to the same data. There are two aspects to vocabulary: business terminology and data terminology. Business terminology refers to items such as "demographics," which can contain any number of underlying data components. Or it can refer to very specific terms such as "gender" or more generic terms such as "product," which is used interchangeably as business and data terminology.

Business terminology is difficult to change within an organization as the business people have been using it for years and would resist changing their language simply because IT deems it more effective. A problem arises when one person calls something by the same name as another person but the meanings are different, as is the case for many business measures or key performance indicators (KPIs). For example, the number of claims can be quite different for finance than for adjudicators since the context may not be the same.

For all business terms, definitions must be set and documented in a central area where any business person can access them as needed. Communication is essential and is the primary focus when referring to an enterprise vocabulary.

Data terminology is the decomposition of the business terminology into finer levels of detail called the *atomic level*. "Demographics" can be any number of data components based on its usage: person, address, income, gender, state/province, or whatever. It is the role of IT to decompose the business terms into data terms and to ensure a proper mapping between the two to communicate to the business how these inter-relate. It is these data terms that are modeled, as these are the fundamental components to the business.

Popular subjects in the discussion of a common enterprise vocabulary are

▶ Taxonomy, which is the classification and structuring of business terms and/or data components, for example, a vehicle subtype is car and/or truck and/or motorcycle and/or boat, and so forth

▶ Ontology, which is categories within context and can include a number of taxonomies

The author prefers using the simple term "vocabulary." When discussing how the data is organized, preference is toward the three aspects of data: fundamental, descriptive, and associative, with all these related in a supertype/subtype classification structure.

Centralized Data Model

The centralized aspect of the data begins with the logical design of the business data. In simple terms, the effort is to organize the data in one central data model showing all the aspects of the data. The physicalization of the data comes later. The first effort is in designing the structures showing each data item and how each relates to itself and other data items. The difficulty is in creating a data model flexible enough to allow the integration of the next data source without having to redesign the model each time. Due to this flexibility, many decide to either start with the most extensive data model within the organization, which is usually the primary source for the initial data items, or they decide to purchase an industry-specific data model and extend it as needed. Both require effort, the latter most likely requiring less effort since a data warehouse design is already created.

An industry data model tends to be quite large as it takes into account many facets of the industry that your organization may or may not require, or perhaps may not consider in its first development efforts. Either way, these models are large and can be quite abstract, meaning generalized. Such large data models have specific modeling techniques and structures, allowing nice flexible designs for future additions. On the negative side, these large data models tend to be difficult to understand. New users tend to require a bit of hand-holding up front. On the flip side of the coin, industry data models that are easy to understand are usually very specific, which means they can be quite static or difficult to extend. So there is a trade-off between the types of industry models, their coverage, and their communicative simplicity.

Data models are designed to communicate data requirements. A centralized enterprise repository data model should be designed for flexibility and extendibility. These types of data models are used to design large normalized database designs with the purpose of acquiring and holding data across an enterprise, not for extracting data. Extraction data models in the context of a data warehouse are data mart designs. A centralized enterprise repository data model is data-driven, not business usage–driven.

Data Architecture

Figure 12-4 presents a focus on the top-down aspect of the data flow in an enterprise data warehouse. The architecture is concerned with data sources, acquiring, transforming, staging, and loading the data into the repository. Of course, as just mentioned earlier, this all starts off with the design aspect before any physical aspects can be realized.

The first step toward a tangible solution is to identify the data. Data is typically from a number of sources, prioritized based on a business value chain. In the insurance industry, for example, this could be claim processing. Therefore all systems relating to claim processing would be the first focus. There must be some sort of boundaries in a top-down scenario, or else efforts would be scattered all over the data subjects throughout the enterprise. Many prefer a focus on the fundamental pillars of the organization such as customers and products, closely followed by specific focus areas such as policy administration and claim processing following typical business process flows.

Chapter 10 has already introduced the steps within the data acquisition layer with a goal of communicating the intricate aspects of the ETL stage and consideration in its architecture. While all methodologies—top-down, bottom-up, and a hybrid approach—require many of the same efforts, the top-down scenario must slice efforts into focused silos to ensure productivity.

In general, the myth behind a top-down initiative is that if data within the primary focus of the organization is acquired and loaded with a keen focus on vocabulary and data quality, business intelligence requirements and usage will magically appear. There is a perception that the business users are on the sidelines eagerly awaiting a repository full of perfect data, and once the repository is available, its usage will be imminent. The reality is that a top-down perspective without focused business usage tends to be a design effort rather than a build effort, which would be difficult to justify from an ROI perspective. Creating a culture of top-down enterprise data modeling within a central data architecture group is excellent, however, and allows a bottom-up business effort to conform to an enterprise data design.

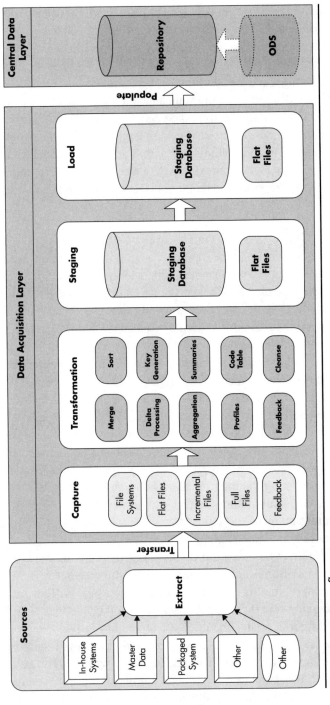

Figure 12-4 *Data flow steps*

The best usage of a top-down effort this author has witnessed was in identifying the key business value chains, focusing on the fundamental data pillars first, followed by the value chain events second. This means a strategy and planned approach with the identification of sources followed by the design.

Sources

In the grand scheme of data architecture and design, data sources are usually identified for specific data subjects. For instance, claim data could be from two operational systems and also contain policyholder information. The two sources are X and Y. This is usually discovered as part of the strategy and planning phase. Figure 12-5 shows a simple document designed as a first glimpse at a source system. It also forms part of the target-to-source mapping document, as seen in Chapter 10, Figure 10-7. Notice the extension with Business Owner and IT Owner information.

If possible, and highly advisable, it's a good idea to discuss each source system with the business SME. The discussion should be toward understanding the data concepts within the source system and in how they inter-relate at a high level. A good method of capturing this information is via a pillar diagram, as shown in Figure 12-6.

Data Model

This area consists of the complete data model for the enterprise, data warehouse repository, and possibly the staging area, which is also shared with the acquisition phase. The data model in the design phase deals with the logical enterprise data model (EDM), also known as the logical business data model, and the logical data warehouse application data model (EDW), which is a data warehouse repository. There must be a decision on whether the EDW is fashioned based on the Inmon 3NF design, which spins at the attribute level, or the mixture of 3NF and history at the entity-level design. *Spinning* refers to the maintaining of history. In theory, the logical enterprise data model does not include any reference to history since it is concerned with the atomic data items and how they inter-relate. However, the logical data warehouse application data model does consider history, which may be recorded at the attribute or entity level, as explained in Chapter 8.

Source System						
Source System Name	File Name	Table Name	Column Name	Description	Business Owner	IT Owner
Claims processing	X			claims - primary claim information source system	Jack Buffet	Jack Buffet
Legacy claim system	Y			claims - secondary claim processing system	Susy Back	Rolan Flash
Legacy claim system	Y			policyholder info	Susy Back	John Harrison

Figure 12-5   *Source system document*

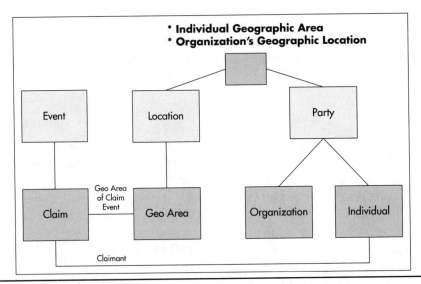

Figure 12-6 *Pillar diagram*

It is recommended to purchase an industry enterprise data model, which can save many person-years of design and redesign effort. Focus can then be on scoping and extending the designs.

Figure 12-7 shows a generic source-to-repository mapping document, which must be created to identify the source and its data items and how they map to the repository's data items. The mapping area becomes the start of the ETL specifications. The mapping area can be as detailed as necessary depending on the complexity and understanding of the physical source system captured data file or DBMS tables. Note that a target-to-source mapping document is usually created first to identify where repository data concepts originate; for instance, the Claim entity is sourced from the claim processing system X. Later, when creating the detailed data model, the source-to-target mapping document is used. Depending on data acquisition layer steps, as seen in Figure 12-4, the

Source	Mapping	ATOMIC Repository					
Define as need be.		Entity Name	Attribute Name	Data Type	Nulls	Value	Description

Figure 12-7 *Source-to-repository mapping document*

source-to-target mapping document may refer to the intermediate captured source data files rather than the actual source system.

Database

In many top-down projects, the efforts end with a realized logical enterprise data model, which is used to guide all future data architecture efforts, where each project would map its data models to this enterprise data model. In other projects, efforts end at the logical data warehouse application data model, ready for a later focused physicalization effort. However, if the project continues, the next step is to convert the logical data warehouse application data model to a physical data warehouse data model.

While a logical data model takes into account the variety of data items, the physicalization takes into account parameters such as volumetrics, partitioning, indexing, and other such DBMS issues. The physical data model can be one-to-one with the logical data model but is usually optimized for efficiency of capturing and holding the data. Of course, the physical data model must exist before the ETL portion begins but can be altered as the ETL unravels any new details that may affect the ETL programming.

The DBA will work closely with the data architect and the ETL architect in creating the physical database structures.

Acquisition

The acquisition phase includes all the ETL components including data capture, transformation steps, staging, and loading. This area takes a considerable amount of time as each source system data component is managed. This includes delta processing if any, all sorting, merging, standardizing, and so forth. For the ETL programmers to understand the required task at hand, the data architect would guide the high-level efforts with the source-to-target mapping document.

Before arriving at this phase of the project, the ETL architect is typically called upon in the strategy and planning phase to perform a high-level data profiling of the identified sources. This gives the data architect a good view of the actual data values, which would validate or alter expectations. The data modeling phase would then perform a forensic analysis of the source data, using the data profiling results to model the enterprise data within the data repository.

The ETL phase evolves into a high priority almost from the moment efforts begin. Once designs are completed, the actual build is watched closely with anticipation. ETL is an iterative effort with all deliveries being anxiously awaited. It is rare to find a project populating a data warehouse repository without the business wanting to use it, and therefore, in many cases, there can be an analysis or data-mining side project guiding the data warehouse load stream.

Solution Overview

Figure 12-8 shows the top-down architecture with both the logical and physical data models along with the final data flow from source to target, which is the enterprise data warehouse repository.

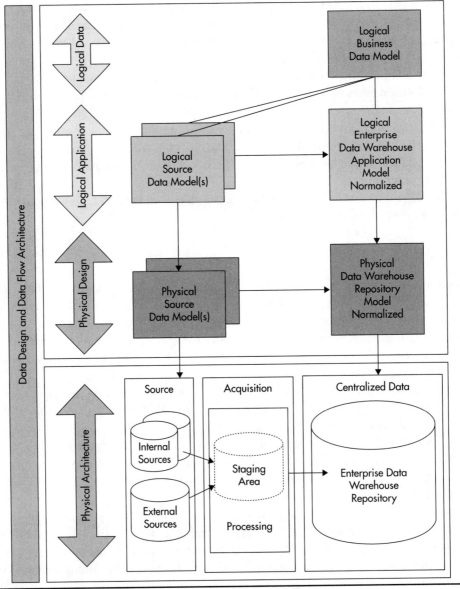

Figure 12-8 *Top-down data architecture and data flow*

Top-down efforts are very interested in setting an enterprise data vocabulary and a standardized methodology in data modeling and data architecture. Along with these, many begin a data quality and data governance effort. The difficulty for many is in changing the corporate culture into accepting a governance policy and in its implementation.

The author finds that the best practice is to think of this big picture but have a business focus to show how these efforts can be implemented and used throughout the business and IT community. More information will be presented on this when we describe the hybrid approach.

Bottom-Up (OLAP Reporting)

Projects taking a bottom-up approach are looking to create a business usage solution. The final result tends to be a reporting or an OLAP analytical solution; see Figure 12-1. These projects are business-initiated for one reason or another and require the help of IT for planning, design, build, and governance.

Do not confuse business-initiated with business participation. Hopefully, the business is participating in the overall project from start to end, but in reality for many projects, the business may simply initiate the project, similar to ordering a meal. In these sorts of projects the business expects IT to create the solution with minimal guidance. These are the projects that take enormous budgets and seem to flounder in one phase or another. The project manager constantly has to reaffirm the overall strategy and refocus efforts when one aspect overrides another. Think of a project based on regulatory reporting requirements. The effort is a cost with no profit potential to the organization and is a general pain for most organizations, which would never produce such reports if it were not enforced upon them. These projects, in many cases, are perfect for a data warehouse initiative, but no business person wants to spend the time mentoring the effort. For these, seek executive support and an assigned business SME contact.

Figure 12-9 shows a top-down data flow with a bottom-up focus. Efforts begin with the user presentation, or in other words, the reports or analytical solution requirements. In these projects, business analysis efforts will identify and analyze focused business areas with a view on an exact deliverable. The more focused and precise the requirements up front, the higher the probability of success simply because the end result is known and the project can work toward a specific deliverable.

To parallel the initial chef scenario, a bottom-up context perspective would be to first determine what every guest prefers for their meal. The idea would be to find the common ingredients and organize around these items. This would be a very specific

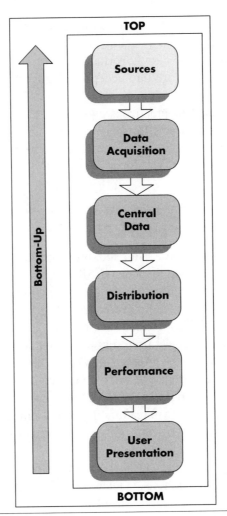

Figure 12-9 *Bottom-up approach*

and tailored cooking event, allowing the chef to fully understand each and every deliverable. Rather than a buffet, the venue would be a sit-down dinner with each guest receiving what he or she ordered. Of course, it would be up to you and the chef to refine the guests' wants and wish list into something more manageable so that delivery can be efficient and focused. The concept is that there would be less wasted time and budget preparing items nobody wants or repackaging, so to speak, the fundamental cooked items into more desirable items. Here the spotlight is on producing exactly what is required.

End Result

In most cases the business has a fairly good vision of what they require, such as "customer relationship management," "financial reporting," "regulatory reports," "sales analysis," "inventory analysis," and so on. These types of projects typically involve environments with existing business reports that are inflexible, difficult to create, possibly based on unconformed data models, of poor data quality, and the list goes on. The point is that the business has specific requirements, usually with a sense of delivery priority.

Step 1 for a bottom-up project is to determine the business requirements, which are usually specific business reports but with added requirements such as drill-down capabilities. One particular customer decided on a bottom-up strategy and prioritized over 120,000 static business reports. Fortunately, these were easily converted to a handful of dynamic data marts, which gave amazing freedom, flexibility, and simplicity to the business decision-making process and drastically changed the way the users performed their business. The business had more insights into their data and therefore once in context, in whichever manner they decided, had more information at their fingertips.

Figure 12-10, taken from Chapter 4, shows how an existing report is decomposed into data items categorized as dimensions or measures. To differentiate, dimensions are fairly static while the measures change over the sampled time periods.

The data items are then gathered into a dimension/measure and report cross-reference matrix, as in Figure 12-11. The best approach is to group reports into some sort of

Daily Net Product Sales - Northern Region

Day Week 44	Net Sales 2008	Net Sales 2007	Variance 08 vs 07	Customers 2008	Variance 08 vs 07
Monday	€ 22,485,104	€ 21,359,944	5.0%	345,987	3.0%
Tuesday	€ 14,303,432	€ 15,303,432	-7.0%	356,743	-1.0%
Wednesday	€ 17,506,111	€ 14,506,111	17.1%	233,111	11.0%
Thursday	€ 18,099,000	€ 17,099,000	5.5%	387,111	4.0%
Friday	€ 19,876,323	€ 19,456,123	2.1%	298,000	20.0%
Saturday	€ 25,999,345	€ 24,999,345	3.8%	401,222	1.0%
Sunday	€ 12,456,111	€ 11,456,111	8.0%	212,000	5.6%
WEEK	**€ 130,725,426**	**€ 124,180,066**	**5.0%**	**2,234,174**	**4.6%**

Dimensions

	Time Period	Year, Week, Day
	Region	North
	Product	Goods not services
	Store	All northern stores

Measures

	Net Sales	Derived from Point-of-Sales transactions
	Net Sales Variance	Derived (Net Sales 2008 - Net Sales 2007) / Net Sales 2008 * 100
	Num of Customers	Given from source
	Num of Customer Variance	Given from source

Figure 12-10   *Sample report decomposition*

Dimensions and Measures / Reports	Dimensions	Scenario	Year	Quarter	Month	Week	Day	Store - Name	Store - Number	Region	Division	LOB	Brand	Product Type	Product - Name	Product - SKU	Product - Size	Product - Fin Hierarchy	Product Color	Measures	POS Gross Sales Amount	POS Return Amount	Number of POS Transaction	COGS	Profit Margin
(count)		0	0	0	1	3	1	0	1	3	3	1	0	2	2	2	0	0	0		1	1	1	1	1
Weekly Sales						×			×	×	×	×									×	×	×	×	×
Weekly Shipment					×	×				×	×			×	×	×									
SKU Performance						×	×			×	×			×	×	×									

Figure 12-11 *Sample dimension vs. report cross-reference matrix*

business focus. Then as all reports in each focus area are analyzed, similar data items tend to repeat and are easily standardized in name and definition. The overall effect is that as more focus areas are decomposed, the overall data similarities emerge, otherwise known as conformed dimensions and measures.

As mentioned earlier, take care with conformed measures. Measures can have the same name, but their usage or context can vary greatly. A number of claims can be used in many contexts and at different granularities; it's best to extend the measure name to communicate its proper meaning.

The dimensions and measures can then be arranged in a star schema fashion, as in Figure 12-12, which is very communicative of the underlying data and allows the business simple access to their data. Dimension names are standardized to business terms, making the usage much simpler for the business to understand.

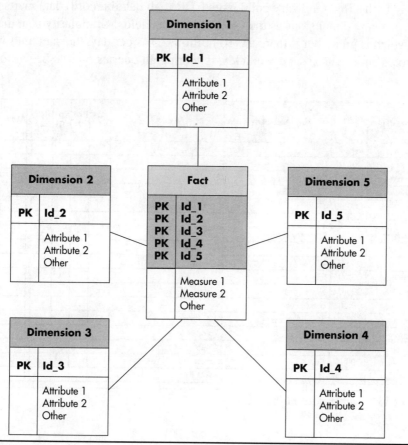

Figure 12-12   *Star schema design*

The next step is to add columns to the dimensions, which can be done via a second cross-reference matrix. Figure 12-13 shows a breakdown by dimension and its attributes with an association to usage within business reports and data marts. Reports and data marts were combined in this document simply to show traceability. Another view of these parameters could be with a third cross-reference matrix of reports to data marts.

The idea here is to be very communicative of the data items to the business users. Showing the business the data model design will set expectations and keep both IT and the business users on the same page.

The real power of the dimensional model is the dimension hierarchies, as shown in Figure 12-14. These hierarchies allow the business to drill up or down into measure granularities. Of course, the build challenge is to create these star schema data marts at a measure granularity that allows for the drill-down and drill-up capabilities while controlling the underlying data volumes. Many designs are too generalized, meaning that the amount of data is just too much to inquire upon to achieve a proper response time.

Many in the Telco industry build large CDR (call detail record) data marts with almost as many dimensions as the CDR record has fields. Granularity is at the CDR level, which is great, but if there are 10 million CDRs per day, the data mart will grow to an enormous size very quickly, rendering all queries on it to be so slow that

Dimension	Dim Seq	Dimensional Attribute	Values	Rpt 1	Rpt 2	Rpt 3	Rpt 4	Data Mart A	Data Mart B
Country	D01.00		List of ISO country codes					x	x
Country	D01.01	Country Id						x	x
Country	D01.02	Country Name	USA		x		x	x	x
Country	D01.03	Country Code	2		x				x
Currency	D02.00		List of ISO currency codes						x
Currency	D02.01	Currency Id							x
Currency	D02.02	Currency Name	GBP / US / EURO..			x			x
Currency	D02.03	Currency code	ISO based						
Customer	D03.00		Individuals					x	x
Customer	D03.01	Customer Id							x
Customer	D03.02	First Name		x					x
Customer	D03.03	Last Name		x					x
Customer	D03.04	Street Address	123 Front						
Customer	D03.05	City	Toronto			x			x
Customer	D03.06	Province	Ontario			x			x
Customer	D03.07	Country	Canada			x		x	x
Customer	D03.08	Postal Code	M1M2H2						

Figure 12-13   *Dimension attribute list*

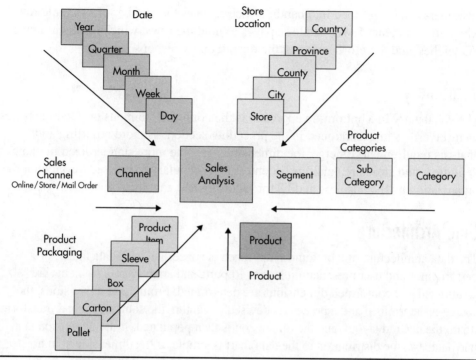

Figure 12-14   *Dimension hierarchies*

no business user will use the solution. The key is to understand what the business wants to do and then design at an appropriate granularity, allowing response times to be quick. Of course, there is a trade-off between design and ETL loads. Creating more data mart environments means more ETL routines to populate these data marts.

The keys to a star schema design and the delivery of a successful data mart solution are communication of the data components and for the data mart to be usable to the business as and when the business requires. Much analysis of business usage is required to architect a solution that will allow for usage. The solution may be an aggregate level for first inquiries followed by more detailed granularity of measures for further analysis if required. A goal may be to answer 80 percent of user queries rather quickly based on a small number of data mart designs and the more detailed 20 percent of user queries with other data mart designs, with the expectation that these will take considerably more execution time, resulting in a longer response time. There are many design options that can help reduce response time, such as using customer profile dimensions rather than a customer dimension. In this case, customers can be grouped into bands, which reduces the number of fact table rows, which in turn means fewer database pages to hold the rows, which results in fewer I/O fetches, and therefore lowering the overall query response time.

Vocabulary

The vocabulary in a bottom-up approach is the conformed dimensions and measures themselves. As just mentioned in the preceding section, as more reporting and analysis requirements emerge, the dimensions become more standardized in name, definition, and structure, and this becomes the vocabulary to be used throughout the organization by the business and IT for reporting and analytical purposes.

Data Architecture

The data architecture of a bottom-up approach is concerned with data marts, or performance and user presentation layers. Reports and analysis requirements are scrutinized and conformed dimensions are determined. From these dimensions, the source is determined and a process is devised to capture the source data and transform it into the desired layout, and the dimension is then populated. If the dimension is in one database, the distribution to the data mart is simple; if the dimension is in a number of data marts, the distribution is repetitive and time-consuming.

Measure data is captured from the sources as well, or can be derived from source data, as is the case for calculated or aggregated measures. The data mart fact table is then populated with the appropriate granularity once the dimensions are finalized.

Figure 12-15 shows a conformed dimension bottom-up data warehouse approach. The same arguments apply to capturing data from the source systems as with the top-down methodology, but in the bottom-up approach the acquisition layer is more focused on specific dimensions and measures rather than the normalized data items themselves. For instance, the top-down historical repository views the person, address, and their associations in a normalized fashion, while in a bottom-up staging environment the person and address would be combined into one occurrence of person, allowing for history at the row level, rather than at the attribute or association level, which is a denormalized design. This is not to say that an enterprise data repository cannot be created in a quasi-normalized/denormalized design whereby history is kept on versions of entities rather than via associations.

In both cases, top-down and bottom-up, the ETL routines must determine whether what has been acquired is different than what is in the database (or vice versa). Once the delta is determined, the ETL processes must figure out how to properly load the database given the type of design in use.

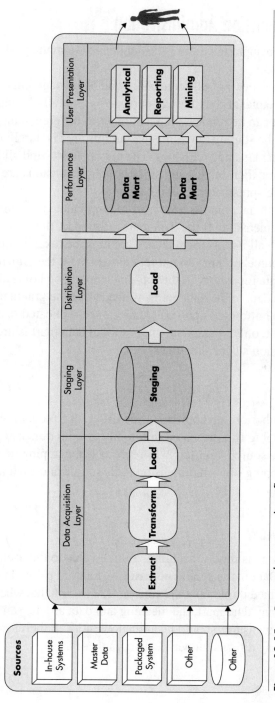

Figure 12-15 *Bus architecture data flow*

Conformed Dimension Administration

In a pure bottom-up approach there is no single area to manage all dimensions and their historical data.

From a design perspective, all dimensions can be managed in one data model along with all fact tables. From a usage perspective, not all dimensions will be in the same data mart but can be replicated in a number of different data marts. The logical place would be in the staging environment, but this area is purely to prepare data for loading into dimensions and fact tables. The only place to find all historical data is within the data marts themselves, and since not all dimensions are in all data marts, the data is therefore spread across all data marts.

What happens if a data mart is no longer required and is the only environment to hold a particular dimension? If the data mart is dropped, the dimension will be dropped along with all its historical data. Care must be taken in these cases, especially if the source systems do not retain history for the dimension in question.

A centralized data repository in the top-down approach holds all data over time and distributes the data to the data marts as needed, at the granularity and time slices required. In a pure bottom-up approach, data can be replicated to a number of data marts or can be held only in one data mart—if that data mart is dropped, it means the loss of that dimension's data altogether.

Sources

Data sourcing in a bottom-up approach is no different from a top-down approach. However, the mapping is represented differently as both dimensions and measures map directly to the source. Figure 12-16 represents a mapping document layout that allows for the mapping of each dimension to its source and each measure to its source as well.

Solution Overview

Business intelligence is timely, accurate, of high value to the user, and usable by the business person. Data marts should be business-focused using dimensions that are reusable or conformed throughout the enterprise, ensuring that when these dimensions are being used in any data mart, the meaning and data are the same each time. The granularity of the measures should be at the lowest level, therefore allowing any type of analysis from any dimension perspective, in theory.

Initial Source	Mapping	Dimension					
Define as need be.		Dimension Name	Attribute Name	Data Type	Nulls	Value	Description

Initial Source	Mapping	Measure					
Define as need be.		Measure Name	Granularity	Data Type	Nulls	Value	Description

Figure 12-16   *Data mart mapping document*

In cases where there is too much data for a data mart, which would negatively influence the responsiveness of its usage, data marts with aggregated or different levels of granularity can be created. In other words, summarized-level data marts can be created specifically to ensure acceptable response times. For example, if a data mart with all CDRs, in a telecommunication organization, is too large, then perhaps a data mart with summarized number and duration of calls by time period can be created. Of course, this all depends on the business usage and its focus. There must be a thorough understanding of the business requirements and usage to enable a tailored data mart environment.

One particular customer left all data mart designs to the data warehouse team with no business guidance. Management said that IT should understand the business and be able to supply a usable environment to enhance the business responsiveness. Well, with such little guidance, generalized data marts were created, and they quickly grew in size as each day passed. To be sure that any analysis could be performed, the granularity was at the lowest level possible. It was not too long before the business began complaining about response time. New data marts were soon under way, guided by the business with specific focus areas based on the business usage.

Figure 12-17 shows a bottom-up conformed data mart data flow and data architecture. As mentioned earlier, data is acquired from source systems, transformed, and loaded into the required data marts. If a dimension is repeated in a number of distinct data marts, there will be redundancy.

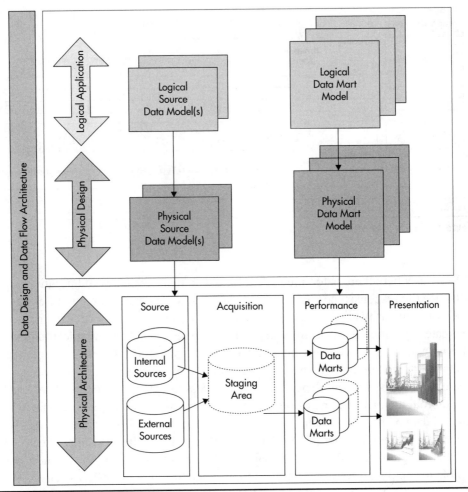

Figure 12-17 *Data mart architecture and data flow*

Hybrid (Normalized Design and OLAP)

The question now is: what is the best approach, and where is a good starting point to create a data warehouse system, as per Figure 12-18? Should a pure bottom-up business perspective be used, or should an enterprise vocabulary and data design initiate efforts? The answer is that it depends on what the organization is trying to create and whether the business is involved in the process. Obviously if there is only an interest in designing a central data repository, then a pure top-down approach is best. But very few projects look only at data without a context of its usage. In the

Where to Start ?

Two typical project approach methods:

Start from Reporting Requirements	Start from Data Requirements
Bottom-Up	**Top-Down**
Reporting requirements are understood and defined.	Reporting requirements are not yet defined.
May be based on existing data marts and/or on local reporting standards.	Scope data requirements from source systems.

Figure 12-18   *Where to start?*

cases where a business usage focus is required, which would be most projects, a bottom-up approach is best but with the top-down data guidance.

The hybrid approach is this author's recommended approach for a full enterprise data warehouse and business intelligence architecture. The hybrid approach takes the best from both methods. For business usage, the bottom-up conformed dimension design is excellent for understanding the deliverable, and for data as a corporate asset, the top-down enterprise vocabulary and enterprise business data model is perfect for understanding the data at its atomic level.

At minimum the hybrid approach offers a dimensional design conformed to a logical enterprise data model. This means a normalized enterprise data design, thus ensuring that all data is fully understood and can support any business application including a data warehouse and business intelligence application.

Going back to the chef scenario, a hybrid approach means planning the meals based on the guests' wants in a controlled manner with the guidance of the food items available. This means that available food is planned and prepared in a manner flexible enough for a more advanced usage rather than a simple prepare-and-eat scenario. In a hybrid approach there may be multiple events going on, mostly all based on the same fundamental food items, and servings might be at different times. Knowing what the guests want allows for planning and delivery. Planning the food at the fundamental level allows for the flexibility of combining items in different ways suitable for different uses. Think of the bottom-up approach as going to a restaurant and ordering what you desire. The top-down approach would be going to a grocery store and obtaining what you need. The hybrid approach would be the chef determining what the guests want and how to prepare it, then going to the grocery store to purchase what is required for the guest needs. If the chef is preparing many different meals on a regular basis, the chef may purchase items in bulk and hold them in stock for future cooking events.

First Efforts

Having a data repository for a data warehouse in a normalized design offers tremendous flexibility. However, many overestimate the initial efforts and believe that a realized repository must be created. As long as an enterprise data model design exists, the data is understood. And as such, efficiencies can be obtained by bypassing the physical data repository build step in the first efforts and going from data source directly to data marts guided by the business data model and data warehouse repository logical designs. If the initial project is to create data marts and no added value would be realized by a data stopover in a database repository, then direct from source to data mart is acceptable as long as the data is designed and governed within an enterprise and data warehouse repository data model. This strategy reduces the time to market and allows the business to realize their analytical environments to enhance their business decision-making process. This is an advanced hybrid scenario and does require planning and coordination.

Of course, the next phase may have to realize the data warehouse repository and there will be additional overhead in integrating it within the first phase ETL processes. ETL routines will have to be re-created to load the repository, and new ETL routines will be required to pull from the repository and load the data marts. Opportunity costs must be evaluated to determine which avenue grants the most reward now and later.

A normalized logical enterprise data model is an understanding of the fundamental business data, its descriptive aspects as well as its associative relationships. With such an insight, any sort of downstream application data model can be created in any normalized or denormalized design style. The normalized design gives great insights into the data, which a dimensional data model cannot fully appreciate, especially if designed purely from business reports that do not show the whole business data picture. On the other hand, while a normalized repository design is good for capturing and holding data, it is much less efficient for retrieving data, which is why a denormalized dimensional data model is used in data marts. With a focus on specific business usage, a subset of the larger enterprise data repository can be extracted and organized in a dimensional design, which is much more optimized for retrieval and therefore conducive to business usage. Choose the purpose of the data warehouse components and design accordingly.

Data Models

An issue with using a hybrid approach is in having two different data model designs, as shown in Figure 12-19. As discussed in Chapter 10 in the "3NF to Star" section,

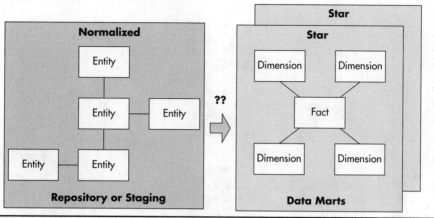

Figure 12-19   *Data model designs*

having two data model designs means having to create ETL to distribute from the repository to the data marts but to convert from the repository normalized design to the data mart denormalized star design.

Of course, having a full historical repository means that the data mart subsets can take all or partial historical data, allowing for the flexibility of volumetrics in the performance and presentation layers to be guided by the business usage.

To use a hybrid approach, the best method is to purchase a pre-created data warehouse model for your specific line of business. Once the design and methodology is understood, it serves well as a guide and foundation to build on and allows the hybrid approach to take root.

Once the focused business data requirements are understood, an effort is required to map these to the prebuilt enterprise data model rather than having to create or add to an in-house enterprise data model. This means there is a huge risk minimization since the data model is already created and redesign will be minimal on subsequent project efforts. This allows for more flexibility in managing the enterprise data asset.

Data Architecture

Figure 12-20 shows a complete hybrid approach to a data warehouse and business intelligence system with logical and physical designs and data flow perspectives. With this architecture, the corporate data asset is managed primarily with the logical business data model. The data warehouse application, which has both a logical repository normalized data model and many logical data mart models that can be denormalized or

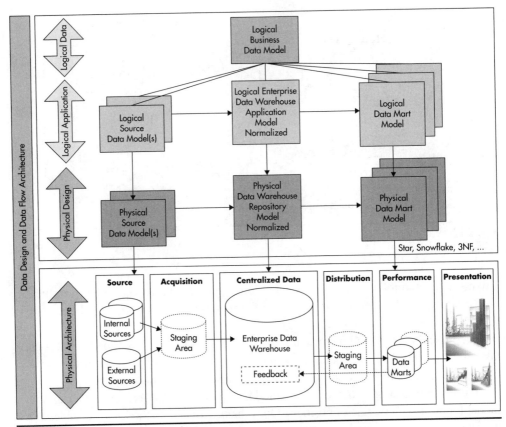

Figure 12-20 *Hybrid data architecture*

normalized depending on its usage, is conformed to the enterprise business data model. This allows the data warehouse models to have whatever historical or normalized designs are desired, which offers great flexibility of usage and design.

It is recommended to not limit the data architecture from a data modeling perspective. To maintain a fully flexible environment, allow the data mart designs to remain open and guided by its desired usage. In other words, do not set hard rules that all data marts must be denormalized and in star designs. In certain instances, snowflake and fully normalized designs may be beneficial to the business usage context.

As mentioned earlier, if the initial effort is to get up and running as quickly as possible to show tangible results for the business, several projects have been quite successful with the bottom-up data flow approach but conformed to the central logical business data model. The trick is to conform the data marts to the logical enterprise data warehouse repository model, which is not realized and is already conformed to the enterprise business data model itself. Figure 12-21 shows all

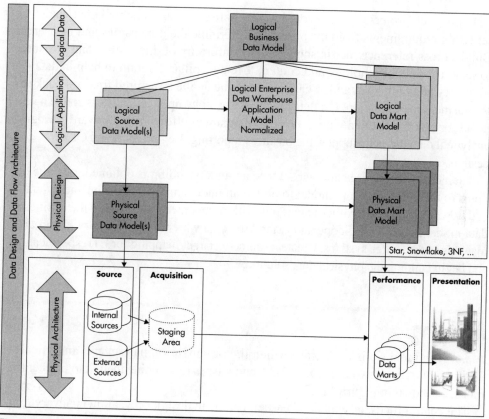

Figure 12-21   *Conformed to design*

conforming to the high-level logical business data model and to the data warehouse repository but without the physical data warehouse repository being built. Of course, as mentioned earlier, there will be an ETL effort in the next phase in realizing the repository. The reason for eventually building the physical data warehouse repository is to hold data in a normalized fashion and to hold data over time, since not all data marts may necessarily require full history in this phase of the data warehouse system lifecycle. Having all data normalized in the repository means that any subset can be realized in later phases as desired.

Solution Overview

The hybrid methodology of data warehouse system development allows full flexibility in data modeling based on business requirements and the underlying corporate data. The hybrid approach grants a full focus on business requirements at the onset with the governance at the atomic enterprise data level as a guide.

Begin such projects as you would with a bottom-up approach: Gather analytical/reporting requirements from the business. Determine the dimensions and measures. Build a cross-reference matrix showing the conformity of dimensions and measure to set consistent terminology and content. Create a pillar diagram to help in data discovery at a high level and to easily communicate the structured findings back to the business for validation. If a data model exists, draw upon the anchors and leaf-level nodes, or else create them within the pillar diagram as efforts move forward. Design analytical data marts to support the business reporting. Begin report and OLAP designs.

Then determine source and gaps. Once an understanding is obtained, map the data items to the enterprise data model to obtain an understanding of the business data and how it associates to other data items within the enterprise. Extend the business data model as required. Scope and extend the data warehouse repository model and map this to the source systems. Create a source-to-target mapping for ETL specifications and begin building the physical data solution.

Merging

A *merging* scenario is essentially when the organization has several analytical environments, as shown in Figure 12-22, and wishes to combine them into one central focus, as shown in Figure 12-23.

The central focus, as explained earlier, can be in design only, allowing everything to conform to the same terminology and structures or as a realized physical environment where all data is captured in a central repository.

In this type of project many events may be happening at the same time; perhaps a re-platforming effort, new business analytical tooling, new application systems, and so forth. In many scenarios the organization has many departmental data marts, all of which were developed independently. Now the effort is in conforming all the data marts to use the same dimensions rather than a version of the same concept.

Typically, a central data model, otherwise known as an enterprise data model, is used to act as the glue that makes all the data marts stick together. In essence, the organization is using the data marts for their analytical reporting needs and therefore a bottom-up approach was used. Now there needs to be a top-down effort to conform all the data items. The end result is that all data marts will be derived from the same source repository, which itself will be populated from defined source systems.

All data would be governed by the same body, allowing all departments and organizations to benefit from the same data items, definitions, structures, quality,

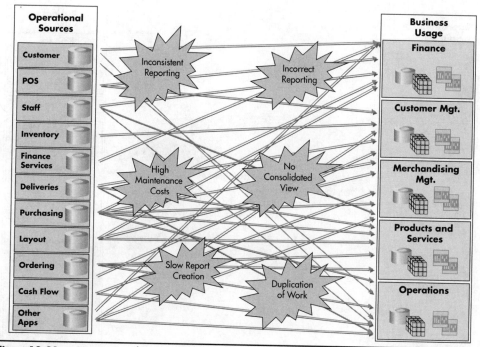

Figure 12-22   *Disparate data analytical environments*

and data values. This effectively transforms the organization's data architecture from a silo vision to a shared central and single-version-of-the-truth data strategy. The corporation is now thinking in data terms and considers data as a valuable asset to the organization as a whole. Along with this type of effort is an information model strategy whereby all data must be administered, controlled, and governed.

Benefits from a merging effort include the ability to easily integrate new source systems, replace existing source system applications, and audit at the departmental level with data flow traceable back to the central repository and onwards to its source system. Governance is now possible where before, the effort was difficult to impossible.

Plan of Action

These types of efforts typically involve a number of parallel projects: installing or upgrading software, changing applications over from one operating system platform to another, discovering departmental data mart purpose and usage, and the list goes on.

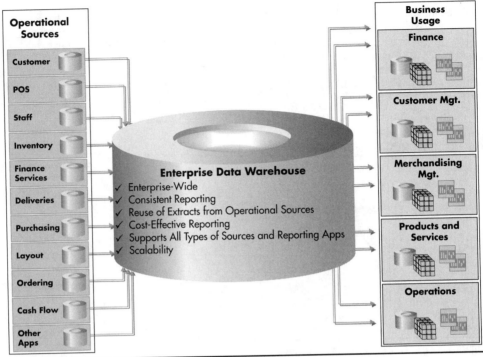

Figure 12-23 *Conformed data environments to central architecture*

From an analytical perspective, the business has been using the existing data marts as part of their decision-making process and as such typically wants to continue business as usual. In other words, this is a heart transplant operation and the patient must remain alive throughout the entire process. Business continuity is paramount for existing analytical environment.

The best initial approach in these situations is to first identify the existing data marts, which may or may not be true data marts but in many cases are simply data environments used as input to a complicated process of aggregations and distributed downstream to the next person, who in turn may perform their own calculation for their own purpose. In these cases, a business process discovery phase is in order to fully understand the relationship between the business requirements and the data. As mentioned in the early chapters of this book, this effort can discover a labyrinth of complications and data paths.

Once the data marts are identified, a bottom-up approach is taken to understand the dimensions and measures being used. This is also an attempt to conform the dimensions across the departments to create some sort of consistency. The next step is to discover what exactly the data requirements are by questioning each of these environments. Conforming everything to a central data model very much helps in understanding not only what data is required but volumetrics, sources, and ownership. From here the hybrid approach takes form, where both ends of the architecture design are being focused on. Both the data and business usage are being evaluated.

For business continuity reasons, in many cases the existing data marts must remain in the first phase since reporting is directly based on them. In these cases, the data mart population is changed from current source to the data repository sources, thus moving the governance from each data mart to a central environment, which is much more cost-effective and manageable. Plus this allows for a single operational system extract rather than multiple efforts. Of course, all the usual project guidelines would be followed with both old and new systems running in parallel for a defined time period to ensure that the business can indeed continue operating without much deviation.

No Input: Structured Input Files

As discussed in Part II of this book, there are many instances where no data is available for profiling and no data sources exist from which to load into the data repository or to load into the data marts after the design phase. These are usually when the source applications are in a state of flux and/or in cases of software development where customers who purchase the software will load their own data from any number of unforeseen physical environments.

These projects, however, still require testing and as such must create their own input. One method to accomplish this is with the use of structured input files, as shown in Figure 12-24. This strategy allows the data modeling and ETL teams to define data requirements themselves. If the enterprise data warehouse repository is developed, then the simplest method is to design input files for each table, remembering dependent associations.

Software vendors do an excellent job of developing input files that define the data required and the structure of the data, all based on the documented definitions and examples. This allows the users to know exactly what data is required for the packaged application.

Structured input files can also be used when the reporting or user presentation layer of the architecture is developed independently from the other areas of the data warehouse, as shown in Figure 12-25. If a software vendor offers a reporting solution out of the box, so to speak, it could connect to any data warehouse application via the predefined interface, which is the structured input files. This would allow a very flexible purchased environment regardless of the underlying data source.

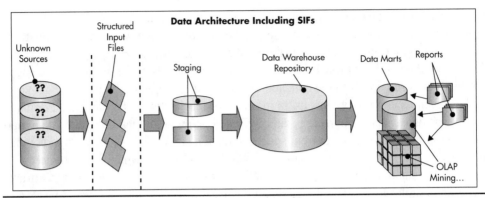

Figure 12-24 *Data architecture with structured input files*

This concept can also be used when the business intelligence reporting team is developing the business reports based on specific data structure designs, which they put together specifically to support their development. In effect, the BI modelers created their own designs, which must now be integrated into the data architecture of the data warehouse system. Consider these BI data model designs as the structured input requirements for the reporting solution. For instance, the BI team may have defined the term Person based on business analysis and user input. The data warehouse repository may be holding data for a table called Individual. This then becomes a source-to-target mapping exercise to connect both ends. Of course, data governance would go a long way in these scenarios to ease the development on both ends if a business terminology glued both ends together before efforts began, but this is rarely possible.

In short, if the source systems are not available or data layouts do not exist, define your own based on the application being developed.

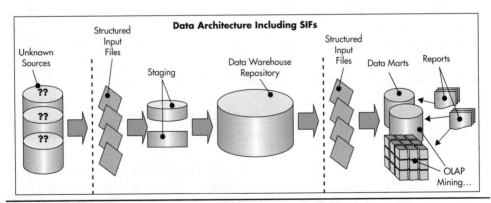

Figure 12-25 *Structured input files on both ends*

Integrating Phase 2

The first phase of a data warehouse system is the most consuming phase. Business requirements are being discovered and refined; the data warehouse system is being architected; data models are being created, integrated, and deployed while the data quality is being assessed and rectified. The entire data warehouse architecture is being developed and realized as requirements, and their underlying data components are being understood and modeled. The learning curve is usually very high, the time period always seems too short, and business as well as upper management expectations are heavy burdens on the project manager and solution architect. Once the first phase is completed and hopefully successful to both IT and the business, Phase 2 begins.

Phase 2 typically consists of adding in all the components a good project manager managed to purposely exclude from Phase 1. From a project manager's perspective, agreement on the smallest effort and deliverable as possible in the first phase is the best scenario. This reduces risks and increases the potential for success for both IT and the business. The focus for the first phase should be on an exact deliverable, but unfortunately, in most cases, the business pushes for large numbers of deliverables as they want value for their investment. True value is not in a one-time deliverable but in the setup and ongoing usage of the data warehouse and business intelligence system. This requires much effort and strategy. It's always best to deliver a unified solid foundation first and lead the following build phases knowing that the path has been cleared and secured.

Additional phases usually involve the inclusion of more business reporting and therefore more data marts, different sources, and of course an ongoing data quality and governance effort. As with the first round, a phased approach is always best. Assess the requirements, think of the big picture, but create a project plan to produce in a phased and controlled delivery a bit at a time. Do not get swept away by scope creep.

In most cases, post–Phase 1 data warehouse system efforts usually are focused on business requirements, which follow the bottom-up methodology. Data mart creation for all following phases should follow a simple four-step process given some sort of focused business perspective:

▶ Assess the main business processes to understand how the requested analytical solution can help the business decision-making process.

▶ Determine the grain of the analysis required not only for the time period (day, week, month, quarter, year) but also for the key data pillars in the business process (product, customer…).

▶ Identify the required business dimensions and their underlying data components.

▶ Identify the key measures which the business requires to make those business decisions.

These general steps can be used to help with every new analytical requirement. Following this investigative effort, the hybrid approach can be used to document the data marts, identify new sources, and identify and structure the underlying data components more thoroughly.

Change Management

A major aspect of further data warehouse and business intelligence development is in the ongoing maintenance and support of the data warehouse system itself. Because a data warehouse system is downstream from operational or whatever source systems, any changes to these source systems can have a dramatic impact on the data warehouse system. If a column is removed from a table in the source system that the data warehouse requires, all ETL processes using the column need to be updated and any analytics on this information will no longer function, causing report generation to fail.

Without proper change management, and depending on the severity of the issue, production support may be calling the data warehouse system support person in the middle of the night wondering what to do because the loading routines are failing. The data warehouse support team must be aware of all changes that are dependent upon upstream applications before they happen. Enterprise change control meetings give a heads-up to dependent applications, allowing them the time to analyze their environments to assess whether or not the change will affect their operations. If the change requires incorporation efforts, the source system must hold off pushing the change through to production status until the data warehouse can handle the impact.

The Bigger Picture:
Enterprise Information Architecture (EIA)

Building a data warehouse system is a large undertaking, especially the initial efforts. Because a data warehouse considers a large amount of data throughout the organization, it deals with many more source systems than any other application project. As such, organizations are realizing the value of data within the organization and are now viewing their data as a tangible corporate asset. Going a step further, leaders are seeing the value of the information held in siloed pockets within the organization and are looking at ways to manage the enterprise information which is, of course, the enterprise data, which goes beyond the boundaries of an enterprise data warehouse system.

The big picture then becomes a look at all systems within the organization supplying information to the business and a look at how this information, think data, flows through the organization from source to usage. This brings in the idea of organizations being information-based rather than siloed data holders.

The vision now becomes more than just a data warehouse and analytics, but the organization of all systems under one roof and a structured approach to the data from an IT and business perspective. Business uses specific terminology within each area of the company, which may have conflicting meanings. Therefore efforts are to standardize on business terminology by definitions and usage and to decompose this into its underlying data components. These data items can then be defined, organized, and governed as a corporate asset. This then becomes known as the enterprise information model under the enterprise information architecture of the organization. This sounds like the reason why data warehouses were developed, to create trusted business analytics, but this goes a step further and throughout all applications within the organization.

The EIA contains more areas and elements than are presented here, but it's safe to say that the concept is to raise consciousness of the symbiotic relationship between the business and information technology and how they are intertwined. It involves a deep understanding of how to map the business terminology and data components in such a manner as to ensure a flexible and open architecture. And it also involves identifying and managing the information systems within the overall corporation.

The end result is more awareness and insight into the many structured and unstructured data components and areas within the organization, giving emphasis on data quality and usage with the downstream effect of reliable and trusted information throughout the enterprise. The effect is not only a historical reporting environment but an enterprise positioned to anticipate events and trends based on their information systems and to respond appropriately and in a timely manner, therefore increasing customer satisfaction and time to market, increasing market share, enhancing employee experience, and facilitating financial growth while sustaining financial stability. The final result: a smarter company.

CHAPTER
13

Data Governance

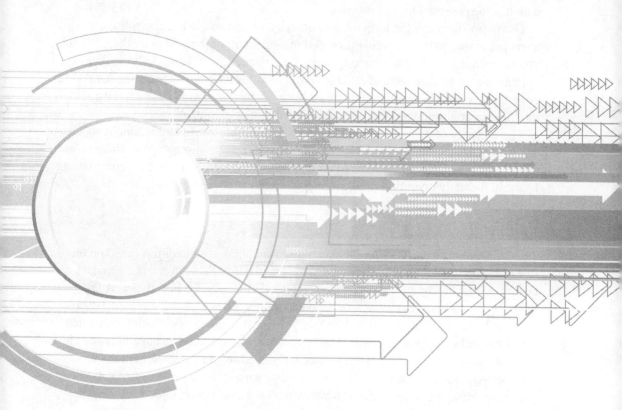

The discussion of data governance in this book is not simply as a component of a data warehouse system or a set of governing rules for the corporate data, but as a practicality. The topic has been included in Part III, "Let's Build," to emphasize its direct usage in the building and usage of a data warehouse and within the overall organization.

Not all aspects of data governance are mentioned, as this chapter highlights the most common elements from a data warehouse perspective.

What Is Data Governance?

Since data is a corporate asset, it must be managed with the same respect as any financial asset. Data is vital to every organization's operation and continuing prosperity. Without proper management, the entire organization may be at risk. Data governance is therefore a risk management and mitigation strategy and should be pushed to the forefront of business consciousness. Part of the risk should not only be defined as lost time and costs associated with support but to the more important risk, which is the potential loss of revenue.

Data governance is the term used to describe the efforts, activities, roles, and areas pertaining to the administration and management of the corporate data. When you're building a data warehouse system, the governance of the underlying data is critical to ensure a trusted and reliable foundation for its usage. Therefore, data governance must be considered on equal terms as the data warehouse and business intelligence solution within the strategic vision of the organization.

The majority of data governance within the corporate world at this time is mostly an awareness of its requirement. Many organizations are ramping up in this area, but the current perception still seems to be that data governance should be a contributing factor in the daily operations and a strategic direction for the organization.

Definition

The definition of data governance within a data warehouse system differs based on the role of the person defining it. An ETL architect may define data governance as a data quality effort whereby the data is defined and has definitive value boundaries. A DBA might define data governance as specific database structures with predetermined data types and formats, while the BI architect may define data governance with security and privacy aspects. The project manager and solution architect would be quite interested in controlling the dynamic aspects of the data, and therefore change control in source systems would be important. Business users may be expecting consistency of key performance metrics, reporting, and stewardship for a single point of contact. And the data architecture group would be interested in all these aspects while balancing them with overall metadata and master data management details.

Each of these factors contributes to data governance, and each lends to the overall definition of data governance. Data governance is the governing of data. Governance involves the management of the data's availability, which includes data quality, security, usage, change control, and ownership. Data pertains to the individual data items at the atomic level as well as the data in specific contexts, which translates to information and knowledge. Therefore, the topic extends to information governance, which emphasizes usage and privacy aspects along with the chain of responsibility and authority for these data components.

Communication is also an important aspect of data and information governance. First, users must be aware of the data's existence, followed by its source, derivations, and sensitivity. The metadata of the data items must be communicated for a full understanding of the business aspect of the data and for technical purposes, to understand the data flow processing. If data is to empower the business users in the business decision-making process, the users must be fully aware of the nature of the data and whether it can be trusted. If fault is found with the data, there must be a way to trace its origins and process footsteps. Consider a scenario of tainted baby food in the retail markets of your community. If one infant consumed the product and became severely ill, the media would pull out all the stops to determine exactly which product is at fault, where it is sold, who made it, what ingredients were involved, where these were obtained, and so forth. An end-to-end data flow would be determined to analyze where the issue originates in order to control the dangerous aspects of the item. Efforts would obviously include a media communication alert campaign, recall of the product itself, and most likely a government inquiry. Communication delivers empowerment to the users in understanding the circumstances and in facilitating appropriate action. Note that communication which is only from the data management group to the users is really called "broadcasting." Feedback and involvement of the users in a conversational manner is best and is critical in making efforts successful in the longer term.

From a pure system process perspective, data governance establishes a system of measurement to standardize and regulate data values, context, usage, ownership, and so forth to enable the business consumers.

Reasons for Data Governance

From a business point of view, controlling and ensuring the data asset should be a critical ongoing effort for any organization.

The media has time and time again reported credit card processing center breaches with thousands of card and card owner details being stolen. Recent media broadcasts have reported government system breaches with war plans and undercover agents being compromised. These days, credit and financial information, medical files, and corporate information are being stolen more often. The next major war may be won or lost based on electronic discoveries and hacking. Regulatory efforts such as Basel II, Sarbanes-Oxley, and Solvency II are all efforts in governing the data assets within the financial sector. If information is power, data is its currency.

Data governance deals with

- ▶ Safeguarding corporate information from within and outside the organization
- ▶ Setting guidelines for usage
- ▶ Determining stewardship
- ▶ Providing audit traceability
- ▶ Improving data quality
- ▶ Ensuring trusted, accurate, and timely enterprise information
- ▶ Encouraging usage and innovation within the business community
- ▶ Facilitating corporate growth
- ▶ Mitigating risk

Organizational Structure

To govern the finances within a corporation, there is the Chief Financial Officer (CFO); to govern technology, there is a Chief Technology Officer (CTO); and to govern the operations, there is a Chief Operating Officer (COO). Data governance falls under the Chief Information Officer (CIO) umbrella if one exists. Essentially, governance begins with executive leadership to ensure guidance and bring the importance of the effort to the forefront of the organization's consciousness. Leadership is accomplished by an executive data committee led by several top-level corporate officers. The purpose is to lead and supervise governance throughout the organization by ensuring alignment with developed policies, regulatory requirements, and an in-house data governance program. The executive data committee consists of the executive sponsor along with business and IT representation.

Figure 13-1 shows an executive data committee overlooking a data governance office (DGO) structure consisting of a chair and representatives from each line of business. The chair serves as the single point of contact for both lines of business and committee members as well as the coordinator of events and communication between the two. The line-of-business representatives ensure proper data stewardship and full communication within their business silos and between the business and IT. They also develop policies and enforce the associated activities, ensuring proper governance throughout the organization.

Typically the committee meets twice a year, while the data governance office meets monthly, especially if a data warehouse project is planned or underway.

In many cases the corporate information architect will lead the DGO meetings, reporting data quality discoveries and resolutions along with security issues and breaches. Data auditors usually also attend to ensure that proper resolution procedures are followed. Any unresolved issues are escalated to the executive data committee. The line-of-business stewards each ensure that their own silos follow data governance policies, including all data quality and security activities, as well as ensuring the documentation of all data issues, especially in the operational aspects of their systems.

A key responsibility of the executive committee is to define governance programs, guidelines, and detail issues for the DGO with a priority on communicating these items and tasks in a manner easily understood by the DGO and data stewards, to facilitate rapid responses. Remember: a good idea without action is simply a good idea!

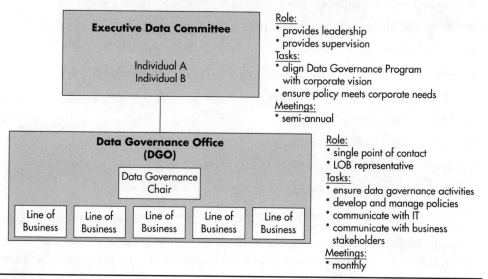

Figure 13-1   *Data governance structure*

Drivers and Initiatives

The current data governance driver other than the obvious regulatory councils and security objectives is data warehouse and business intelligence efforts.

With data warehouse systems being built to centralize data across the enterprise with a vision of obtaining one version of the truth, a major element has become the data governance aspect. Earlier efforts led to the realization that corporate data quality was an issue that had to be managed to ensure a trusted business intelligence environment. Along with the data quality realization came the effort of having to correct source systems, which can become quite political. Source system owners would see no value in correcting or converting data since the requests were not from their primary users. As such, executive support is required to work the solution into a priority for lines of business, thus ensuring conformity of information throughout the enterprise.

From these data warehouse and business intelligence efforts emerged typical data management questions:

- ▶ Who owns the data?
- ▶ Who is accountable for the information?
- ▶ Who stewards each operational system?
- ▶ How should data be managed across the enterprise?
- ▶ How will changes be authorized and managed throughout the enterprise?
- ▶ Should data management policies be created, and if so, by whom?
- ▶ Who will enforce the governing policies?
- ▶ What/which technology should be used to manage the data?
- ▶ What role do IT and business each have in regards to managing the data?
- ▶ Who authorizes changes and usage?
- ▶ How is data quality managed?
- ▶ What metrics are used to measure data quality and governance?
- ▶ How is data governance monitored and enforced?
- ▶ What security aspects should be in place?

These and other similar questions have elevated the awareness of data governance within the business and in many cases initiated data management policies within the corporate world championed by the executive branch of the organization. It became apparent that data was a fundamental asset to the organization and care must be taken in its ongoing management. Not only would data quality and security guidelines be required, but a higher level of involvement, including the alignment of people, technology, and processes to manage the corporate data asset across the enterprise, would also be required. No longer would data be considered a regional asset. The entire organization would have to act as one driving force in the management of data.

Employees across the enterprise would now be accountable and responsible for managing the data within set policies and guidelines. Applications would no longer be the sole users or owners of data. Applications would now be considered vessels in acquiring, processing, and presenting data with the underlying data larger than the application from which it originates. Technology could now integrate the vast data items into a central perspective of information designed and managed as common fundamental and derived business data.

Data Governance: Major Points

Data governance has many aspects, with key points based on the role of the person being asked. From a business perspective, the main points are security, sensitivity, data quality, ownership, and change control.

Security and Sensitivity

Arguably, security is the top priority within data governance. If data is a corporate asset, then it must be safeguarded against theft, corruption, catastrophe, and unauthorized prying eyes. The majority of us lock our vehicles when not in use, so why would your data be any different? How would you feel if after a long day at the office, you went to your vehicle to drive home and found a stranger sitting in the vehicle? Would this shock you, annoy you, scare you? What if you repeatedly found that person sitting in your vehicle every evening? The same concern and emphasis should be applied to your data.

In many organizations the development team is not allowed to view the actual production data, while in other organizations, human resource details are easily visible to anyone in IT with database access. In many instances, it is common practice to copy highly secured production data to test environments to test newly developed programs. Any person with access to the development environment, which usually has minimal security restrictions, can then view potentially sensitive data.

Safeguarding the corporate asset is paramount, especially for organizations that could not function without the data. Organizations spend mounds of resources ensuring that their data is correct. Auditors review and re-review billing accounts, payments, and ledgers with a goal of ensuring that the data is proper and correct. If errors pop up, they are adjusted, and if discrepancies are discovered, they are investigated. Safeguarding the data, the quality of the data, and the usage of the data is a continuous effort within an organization.

Security forms the foundation of data governance, and data governance is the cornerstone to data and information management. Specific areas of interest for security within data governance include

- ▶ The identification of the data itself
- ▶ Sensitivity level of the data item
- ▶ Method of storage for the data
- ▶ Access authorization of the data:
  - ▶ Directly
  - ▶ By using an application of some sort

There are many areas of security to manage and monitor, all with the underlying purpose of safeguarding the data to ensure that the business is going on as usual without delays. All of these areas form part of the data governance policies, spelling out the security aspects in detail and enforced first by the data stewards and then supervised by the data governance office and executive data committee.

Best practice in a DW/BI effort is to set a task within the project plan to review data sensitivity. When analyzing the requirements, the business analyst should be reviewing the sensitivity levels of the data with the business users and reviewing results with the data stewards. Data architecture should be aware of the sensitivity levels when designing the data structures, and the BI architect must be aware of any access restrictions and authorization levels in place.

Data Quality

Data quality is an absolute within a data warehouse and business intelligence effort. It also forms the foundation of data governance. Individual data items are realized within the business analysis and data modeling phases with characteristics noted, with the obvious goal of determining what the data is and how it relates to other data items. One aspect of understanding the fundamental and descriptive aspects of a data item is to understand its values. As already mentioned several times in this book, a person's gender may be analyzed and set to either "male," "female," or possibly "unknown" under certain circumstances. However, the value "married" would certainly not be a proper value for gender. Hence, identifying the universal set of values is usually a foundation to proper data quality. If values other than those expected make their way into the data warehouse system, the quality of the data lessens and its reliability worsens.

Setting a distinct definition conformed throughout the enterprise is the first step in setting a data quality base. From this vocabulary, structures, and designated data values can be established.

Since data in a data warehouse system can be from a number of distinct source systems, its merging into a central structure under a conformed definition and rules can be tricky and is the essence of a data warehouse. If values from either system do not conform to expectations, then the ETL rules dictate how to proceed. Data quality is also within the context of its usage; if customer data does not exist, is a related transaction valid? Rules and policies must be created to guide the development efforts and to understand the essence of data within the DW/BI system.

Best practice is to first identify the data item, describe it, document it with values and examples, and identify its source and usages. If a data flow perspective is required, show its path along with the processing rules and dependencies, including all timings. For codes, all values and descriptions should be documented. For text fields, in many instances manual errors can occur in the source inputs and not much can be done for these. However, if the text is descriptive, then standardization may be possible.

On several occasions, projects were quickly creeping up on their milestone timelines and managers quickly decided to forgo any data quality efforts to meet these milestone deadlines. In all instances, once the system was delivered, the business users found that the quality of the data was low due to the many data value errors, and they quickly found the system unreliable. Usage of the DW/BI system dropped quickly and funding ended for future development additions. This resulted in the data warehouse effort being considered unsuccessful. Data quality is an absolute for a data warehouse and business intelligence system; bypassing the quality issue guarantees failure.

Ownership

For data quality or security to exist, the data must be owned by a specific individual. In efforts to determine data quality and data sensitivity levels, the analyst and/or architect must consult someone to set the levels and values; that someone is either explicitly or implicitly the data owner. Hopefully that person is an officially designated data steward responsible for the content, sourcing, usage, security, and lifecycle of the data.

Data stewardship is not an IT responsibility. Data belongs to the business and IT simply manages it; therefore, the business owns the data and IT is its custodian. IT enforces governance policies upon the data and prudently manages the data, but it is the business that sets the data policies guided by IT.

Every data warehouse project should perform a data profiling step on the in-scope data. This involves a forensic analysis of the data items from their source systems to identify the data structures and values. Added to this are the definitions; if no definitions exist, then one should be created. All should be documented and validated with the data steward; if no steward exists, the person who can validate the data becomes the steward. If no one can validate the data, the issue is raised to the executive sponsor of the project, who must then appoint a steward.

Data stewards must always attend the monthly Data Governance Office meetings.

Change Control

Data stewards must always be aware of any impacts and dependencies to and of their data, proposed changes to their data, and where it is being used. To be aware of changes that would impact the data or dependent systems, the organization should have weekly change control meetings to communicate what is being developed, the impacts, and exactly which data is affected. It is only through proper change control that these issues can be documented and timelined to ensure that no downstream applications are affected. Since a data warehouse application system deals with "used data" from operational systems, any changes to these operational systems may drastically affect the data warehouse ETL routines.

The worst-case scenario is a call at 2:00 A.M. from operations explaining how the transaction data loads would not run because of some data misalignment. Later, efforts would discover that the source system had changed and no one notified the data warehouse ETL owner, possibly resulting in the data warehouse not being loaded for several days until ETL programs could be changed. This means that anyone relying on dashboards, scorecards, reports, or OLAP analysis environments would be left waiting for everything to be fixed, which could affect the business decision process, similar to being stranded at an airport due to unforeseen delays when rushing to an important meeting—very disruptive.

Change control is the one controlling area within data governance that has the most impact on a data warehouse. Source system stewards, application stewards, and data stewards should all meet once a week to discuss planned changes. If any unforeseen scenarios exist, the changes may have to wait until downstream dependencies and data structures can be altered to accommodate the changes.

Data Governance Readiness

There are many benefits to an enterprise data governance program and many challenges in creating one. There is a balance between being too strict, which impacts advancements, and too loose, which invites security breaches. Depending on where the organization currently sits in a comprehensive data governance plan, efforts may vary.

From a data warehouse and business intelligence perspective, there are several data governance readiness points to assess:

▶ **Leadership**   A data governor is the single point of contact to lead and supervise the continuous data governance policy enforcements throughout the enterprise. Without such a leader, the lower echelons are free to do as they wish, which may affect the enterprise, in many cases adversely. Executive sponsorship is critical to ensure that policies are created and followed.

▶ **Data stewards**   Do data stewards exist? Who are they? Where is this documented? For which data are they responsible? Without data stewards, who would you contact to discuss specific data issues?

▶ **Know your data environments**   Being able to identify data sources and data usage within the organization is an aspect of knowing your data. Of course, someone within the organization knows where pockets of data reside, but is there any one-stop resource that tracks data within the organization? Usually data architecture is the first place to look, along with BI architecture, from a data warehouse perspective. Knowing your data environments gives insights into which systems would be impacted if specific data were to change.

▶ **Rules**   Are any rules or policies currently in place? Again, from a data warehouse perspective, there should be a document identifying data quality rules: data items, values, formats, data types, and so on. This document should also identify how and where the data is being used, which BI tools have access, which users have access or permission, and so forth.

▶ **Change control**   Is there a weekly change control meeting within your organization? Is the data warehouse represented? Do not wait until development ends to join or create a weekly change control meeting. Be aware of other projects and efforts within the organization that may impact the DW/BI project.

▶ **Value**   Understanding the value of your data is an overall data governance readiness task, which helps in associating a severity or risk level with the data. Data risk management involves reducing the probability of negative effects on the business due to a misfortune in relation to the corporate data asset.

▶ **Monitoring**   To continually ensure proper data governance within a data warehouse system, there must be some sort of monitoring to assess whether or not boundaries have been compromised. For security, this involves user access permissions; for data quality, this may be ETL reporting routines; and for change control, this may be weekly meeting attendance. Whatever the form, there must be some way to monitor compliance and dependencies to ensure that the data asset is aligned within set rules and policies.

CHAPTER 1

Post-Project Review

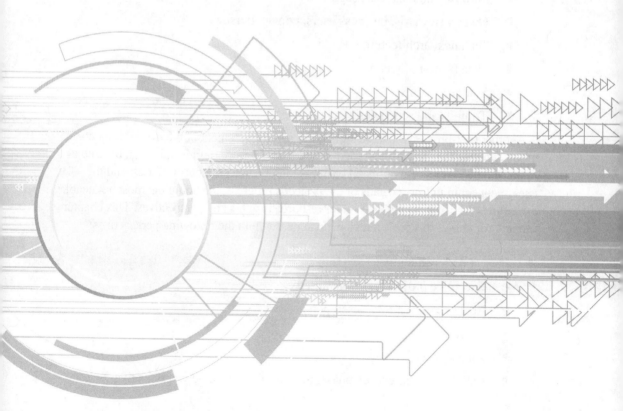

T his chapter presents a postmortem perspective on a data warehouse and business intelligence development effort. DW/BI projects may fail and end abruptly, or they can be in whole or in part successful with continued phases advancing the overall incorporation of enterprise data and usage. This chapter covers all of these scenarios.

Synopsis

Development efforts of a data warehouse and business intelligence solution may end, but the system lives on and must be maintained, like any other application system, with ongoing efforts toward ensuring its daily operations. A data warehouse system must have certain basic documentation as it moves from development, user testing and acceptance, and into production. The following are several key points that should be documented:

- ► Delivered solution document
    - ► Purpose and business usage
    - ► Owner, stewards, business users, contact persons
    - ► Technical architecture
    - ► Data flow architecture
    - ► Source systems
    - ► Timings and schedules

Another post-project task to be carried out is the assessment of the overall project efforts, whether the project succeeded or not. These postmortem insights can be used as input for future data warehouse and business intelligence projects or phases, and the assessment communicates details of the project's progress, including the most noticeable and influencing issues along with major resource insights and perspectives. This chapter primarily discusses this project review document within the following perspectives:

- ► Project review document
    - ► Executive project review summary
    - ► Reviews from a role-based perspective
    - ► Reviews from a individual's perspective
    - ► Anonymous reviews
    - ► End-of-project, end-of-phase, or end-of-effort review perspective

Yet another post-project document may be a brief write-up on the outstanding and future vision for the data warehouse solution. If the project failed to deliver a final solution, this document would include details about why the project failed and how to avoid or alleviate these issues the next time around. Documenting both the business and IT perspectives along with dependencies may greatly influence any future strategic approaches and development efforts.

- ▶ Outstanding and future vision document
  - ▶ Business perspective review
  - ▶ IT perspective review
  - ▶ Planned additions, if any
  - ▶ Dependencies
  - ▶ Enterprise integration—how would the IT and business teams mix in the future based on lessons learned from the current development efforts?

It is always a good idea to poll the hands-on resources to include their comments and reactions as well as upper management and business end users alike.

Project Review

Project review surveys are a great way of soliciting feedback. A project review survey should always be performed before resources are lost and memories fade. Consider the survey as an exit interview for each person associated with the project while events are still fresh in that person's mind.

A project review survey may also be used to solicit insights during extended projects, at the end of project phases, and of course, during the closing phase of a project or of a particular project effort. If a phase is particularly long, a project review survey can help extract opinions, issues, and individual views of the project before the ending period. For extended project phases, these insights can be discussed as a team at a special project review meeting, which may occur every two to three months or depending on the project manager's scheduled plan. Another usage may be when a new manager or architect joins an existing project; a project review survey can gather insights and personal views as to where the current environment, system, and efforts rest. A project review survey can also save a DW/BI review auditor many days of interviews and can form the foundation of an overall evaluation.

Under perfect circumstances people will give some sort of feedback, but if the project or effort was not successful or a person left under less than amicable circumstances, feedback may be overly focused in one or two areas. This feedback should be gathered and considered all the same.

A two-part project review survey with one being anonymous and the other being on the record, so to speak, allows for both unspoken and official feedback to be collected. Anonymous feedback allows personal opinions that might not otherwise be heard to be recognized. If possible, the project manager should discuss these anonymous feedback issues, if appropriate, in the project review meeting at a general level without a word-for-word rendition of the actual comment, which will hopefully bypass any finger-pointing or implicit identification of the author.

The point of a project review survey and analysis of the results is not to create a mini-project in itself; its goal is to solicit actionable feedback and determine the effort's current stance. It should not take weeks to develop and analyze; participation in the survey itself should take less than 30 minutes and response analysis should take approximately a day or two. Usually there is no budget to perform a project review, so the goal should be to introduce a survey just before the project ends to facilitate an executive summary report at the end of a project. Or the survey could be introduced any time during the project as time permits, to solicit feedback in order to facilitate team building and project scheduling and planning.

Surveys can be tailored toward executive management, business users, project management, technical hands-on resources, support staff, or others, such as source system owners. Or a survey can be generalized for all to add to as they see fit. After the survey results have been gathered and analyzed, a summary write-up should be created, specifically for the executive sponsor, which may or may not include all aspects of the survey. The following list is an example of an outline:

- ► **Executive Summary**
  - ► Project overview
  - ► End of project/effort summary
  - ► Comments and recommendations
- ► **Costs and Timelines**
  - ► Initial schedule and cost overview
  - ► Deviations and reasons
  - ► Comments and recommendations
- ► **Lessons Learned**
  - ► What worked well
  - ► What did not work well
  - ► Comments and recommendations

When you are creating the survey itself, the goal should be to obtain an overall impression of the project from all resources. Using a data flow perspective, as shown in Figure 14-1, can guide the survey questions and plot responses along the data architecture, which can be quite useful to pinpoint hotspots.

The survey itself can be directed to the roles and/or the individuals. The following list is an example of questions geared toward the roles within a project. Of course, not all roles and perspectives have been represented.

- ▶ **Business Users**
  - ▶ Is the data timely?
  - ▶ Is the data accurate?
  - ▶ Is the result usable?
  - ▶ Is the result valuable to the business?
  - ▶ Did IT adhere to the business requirements?

- ▶ **Business Analyst**
  - ▶ Did scope creep drastically alter the business requirements?
  - ▶ Was the analytical tool used capable of performing on each of the phases of the project?

- ▶ **Solution Architect**
  - ▶ Was the initial design adequate?
  - ▶ Were there major revisions?
  - ▶ Did scope creep drastically alter the architecture design?

- ▶ **Project Manager**
  - ▶ Did scope creep extend the project boundaries?
  - ▶ Was the initial timeline adequate?
  - ▶ Was the initial budget adequate?
  - ▶ Was there sufficient executive support?
  - ▶ Were there sufficient resources?
  - ▶ Were resources available according to planned activities?

- ▶ **Data Architect**
  - ▶ Were business SMEs adequately available?
  - ▶ Were many assumptions used or was there good guidance?

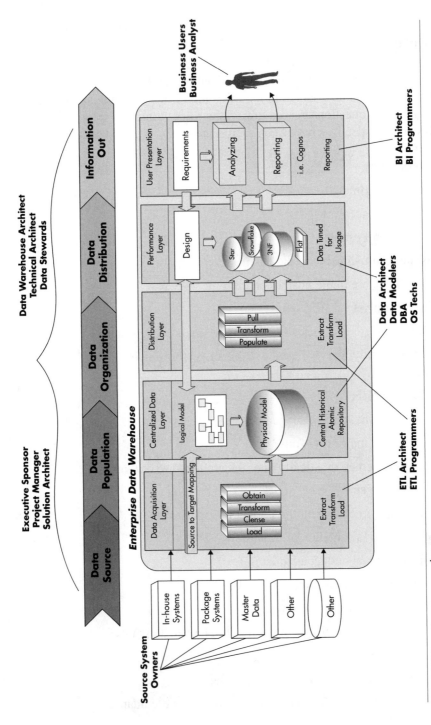

Figure 14-1 *Resource roles to survey*

- ► Was the data model too flexible, or too static?
- ► Was the data model too generic, or too specific?
- ► Were data stewards available and consulted?
- ► **BI Architect**
  - ► Were there any reporting/analytic solution issues?
  - ► Were there any software misconceptions that forced a new technical solution direction?
  - ► Were there any delays due to software issues? If so, how long were the delays?
  - ► Were there any data model synchronization issues?
  - ► Were there any end-user solution performance issues?
- ► **ETL Architect**
  - ► Were there unforeseen data quality issues that delayed efforts?
  - ► Were data quality issues resolved in a timely manner?
- ► **DBA**
  - ► Were there any database issues that delayed efforts?
  - ► Is the system being monitored adequately?
  - ► Was enough time allowed for tuning and optimization?

The survey may also be directed toward the individual's perspectives on the overall project, with them as the center of focus, to obtain emotional and professional viewpoints. The following list is an example of categories and questions in a person-focused survey:

- ► **Goals and Deliverables**
  - ► Were project goal(s) and deliverables clear up front?
  - ► Were project goal(s) and deliverables clearly understood for your role?
  - ► Does the result satisfy the initial goal(s)?
  - ► Were the overall timelines adequate?
- ► **Leadership**
  - ► How effective was the executive leadership?
  - ► How effective was the project management leadership?
  - ► How effective was the technical leadership?
  - ► How effective was the business SME?

- ► **Communication**
  - ► How was the overall communication between the project and your role?
  - ► Were milestones adequately communicated?
  - ► Are the project and the silos adequately documented?
- ► **People**
  - ► Was there a lack of proper resources?
  - ► Were there any interpersonal issues that hindered the project or your progress?
- ► **Your Role**
  - ► Were you 100 percent supportive of the project?
  - ► Were you 100 percent of the time allocated to the project?
  - ► Did you feel appreciated and recognized on the project?
  - ► Did you have enough time to perform your duties?
  - ► Did you have adequate time to document your efforts?
  - ► What would have helped you more in your efforts?
- ► **Technical**
  - ► How effective is the overall architecture? (technical, data, ETL, BI...)
  - ► Looking back, can you think of any process improvements?
- ► **Overall**
  - ► What were the roses and thorns of the project?
  - ► What lessons did you learn?

Next Phase

The next phase, project, or effort may require special insights from the past efforts. Document any specifics that may influence labors going forward. For example, the first-phase efforts were to create specific data marts for specific reporting purposes with all data conformed to a central business data model, which is to be implemented in Phase 2 efforts as the data warehouse repository. Areas affected going forward would be data modeling, ETL, and DBA.

Document all assumptions made in the current phase or efforts that led to the current state and that will help efforts or have dependencies in the next phase.

A data warehouse system can be quite complicated, as it looks at data from across the enterprise and as such requires much communication between the business and IT development efforts. Document all issues that form the foundation of the current efforts and all those which may help the next phase move forward.

Index